OARS ACROSS THE PACIFIC

John Fairfax & Sylvia Cook

Oars Across the Pacific

W · W · NORTON & COMPANY · INC ·

NEW YORK

Copyright © 1972 by John Farquharson Limited

FIRST AMERICAN EDITION 1973

Library of Congress Cataloging in Publication Data
Fairfax, John, 1937-
  Oars across the Pacific.
    1. Britannia II (Rowboat)   2. Pacific Ocean.
3. Rowing   I. Cook, Sylvia, joint author.
II. Title.
G530.F136 1973   910'.09'164   73-1705
ISBN 0-393-03175-6

PRINTED IN THE UNITED STATES OF AMERICA

1 2 3 4 5 6 7 8 9 0

To Our Parents

for their patient forbearance

Contents

A map showing the course across
the Pacific appears on pages 232-33

The plan of *Britannia II* on page 46
is reproduced by permission of Mr. Uffa Fox.

List of Illustrations

1. We Leave England

Never again! I am fed up with rowing!

Famous last words. Less than two years had gone since then, and there I was again, pulling on a pair of oars for all I was worth against a twenty knot wind, in the second — or was it the third? — attempt at clearing the San Francisco bay. This time I was not alone. Rower extraordinaire Sylvia Cook was on board the *Britannia II*, as girl friend, first mate, A.B., chef, cox, nurse, photographer, and hopefully, a few other things I would, no doubt, think up. She was at the tiller now, trying to aim *Britannia's* bows at the Golden Gate Bridge, getting the full force of wind and spray slap in the face and looking none too happy about it. It was hopeless, of course, a single man could not row a boat like *Britannia II* into the wind, even a light breeze, and we were struggling against half a gale.

We had been out an hour and gained, maybe, a third of a mile. Jolly good progress too, considering the conditions. Although we knew beforehand that the entire exercise would be a complete waste of time, we had to try because the newspaper that was covering our story, the *Sunday People*, had asked us to leave on a Friday, if at all possible. Since they had been very good to us, we felt morally obliged to put on a bit of a show.

For the other gentlemen of the press, about forty of them, crowding the decks of the cutter *Alert*, our 'mother' ship in San Francisco, we had nothing but sympathy. This would be the third time they had been routed out of bed to report our departure and we sincerely hoped that they would not lose their sense of humour.

It was bitterly cold and Sylvia, huddled astern without the benefit of exercise, soaked and shivering, was mumbling something or other. I could not hear what but the expression on her face was enough to guess. Mutiny at such an early stage was unlikely, but I thought it wiser to play safe and call it a day.

'Cheer up darling', I yelled, 'Enough is enough. All astarboard! We are going back.' With a beautiful turn to port, *Britannia* swung around, was nearly swamped, brushed alongside a boat from the Dolphin Rowing Club and, with the wind dead aft, surfed back towards Fisherman's Wharf, our point of departure. If the difference between port and starboard was lost to Sylvia, her logic was impeccable. When I pointed out that she had turned the wrong way and had we rammed the other boat, it would have been her fault, her reply was;

'Nonsense! You are always telling me that the captain is responsible for everything that happens on a ship. Besides you know I don't understand your silly nautical terms, so why not say right or left like everybody else does? *And* that was a masterpiece of judgment, since they had no business being so near us anyway!'

With the *Alert* back to her moorings and *Britannia II* alongside, I was soon involved in other arguments. 'Mr Fairfax, if you cannot even leave our Bay, how do you expect to reach Australia?' 'Could you please explain to us, Mr Fairfax, why you . . .? Will you request a tow? Are you giving up? When . . .?'

When, why, how, what . . . How did I ever manage to get myself mixed up in this again? When I had staggered to the beach in Florida, after six months of continuous battle with the Atlantic, I had sworn never to touch an oar again. 180 days of life as a galley slave, of sleeplessness, burned by the sun, drenched by the waves, dried by the wind, eating so much fish I almost grew scales, and always, always the mind bogging, brutalising nightmare of manning the oars, day and night, and row, row, row . . . hell's bells, how could I even *dream* of going through it all again?

Yet, dream I did and, as usual, I found that from dreams to actions, as far as I was concerned, was but one short step.

As with the Atlantic I decided to cross the Pacific at its

widest, from San Francisco to Australia. Acapulco, in Mexico, would have been a much better place to start, weatherwise, but San Francisco, aside from being my favourite city in the USA, held many sweet, romantic memories for me. Beautiful San Francisco, where, in 1960, as a starry eyed twenty-two year old, I had found myself, after a two week stay, utterly broke and destitute, thanks to the charms of the most tantalising Chinese call girl that ever lived. Ah, but what a fortnight! After a most unfortunate love affair I was on a world pilgrimage, hoping that time and distance would eventually heal my shattered heart. The Chinese girl failed to cure me of course, but she did try, ever so hard. I shall never forget the agonising sorrow in her little face, her sad smile when, the last of my two thousand dollars gone, she had bid me goodbye and good luck. Women! What would I do without them!

Sylvia now. From our very first meeting we liked each other and sensed that, one day, we would go places together. Don't ask me why. She wasn't my type and I wasn't hers, but there was *something* between us. I also told her not to get funny ideas since I was not marriage minded and all she could ever hope to get out of me was a lot of fun. Don't go falling in love with me either, I added, as that would definitely ruin everything.

Her reaction? 'Big headed twit, I'll teach you.'

She did too. I had five girl friends at the time and one by one they all fell over the side until Sylvia reigned supreme. From economic necessity on my part, we started living together, she helped me prepare the Atlantic venture, met me at the other side at the end of it, typed the book for me, and, in general, pampered me in such a way that I was absolutely delighted to let the years go by in her company.

Thus, when I came around to attempt the Pacific crossing, since I was determined to have a feminine crew, who else could I ask but her? She said yes right away and we were off.

At the beginning everything seemed to go without a hitch. As usual I had no money but, also as usual, I had complete confidence in my ability to cope. Uffa Fox promised to design the boat, which would be exactly the same as

Britannia I, only twelve feet longer. Clare Lallow, at Cowes, would build her for us. I figured that the whole project would cost about six or seven thousand pounds. Getting sponsors shouldn't have been too difficult but I was determined to finance the lot myself. That way I would remain my own boss and do things as I pleased.

Suddenly I had a brainwave. During my Atlantic journey I had been attacked by a ten foot shark while scraping *Britannia*'s bottom. Flattening myself against her hull — there had been no time to get out of the water — I had, by an accidental, fortunate stroke of luck, managed to rip its belly with my knife. The shark had swum away and I had climbed back on board. The incident, as far as I was concerned, once reported and logged, was closed.

However, long after I had landed in America, a Florida newspaper, the *Miami Herald*, published a short comment, saying, among other things, that according to some experts and sceptics — they were not named — it was impossible for a man to sink a knife underwater into a shark's belly, the skin of a shark being too tough for it. As the comment was directed at my own exploit, it amounted to calling me a liar. Naturally I did not take kindly to that and challenged them, or any other newspaper who thought along the same lines, to put up a shark of their own choice — except a Great White — anywhere, anytime, and I would fight it under the same conditions I had experienced at sea, for ten thousand pounds.

The *Miami Herald* were unwilling to put their money where their mouth was and nobody else seemed interested, so I let the whole episode lapse. My new idea was to have some photographer film the shark fight, and make a short documentary and, presto, I would have all the money I needed to finance the Pacific row.

The idea was brilliant and I did my bit, off the Bahamas, killing an eight foot two inches Hammerhead. I had the great satisfaction of towing it all the way back to Florida and dumping it on the doorstep of the *Miami Herald* so that they could check that the shark had not been drugged and had no wounds other than those caused by my knife. Aside from that I had photographic evidence, in film. Unfortunately the film was not good enough for a documentary but, by selling the story to the *Sunday People*, I paid my expenses and that was all.

Back in London I found a steadily increasing pile of bills, no money was forthcoming from anywhere and none would be until I finished the book I was writing about the Atlantic row. This book was long overdue by then and my publishers were beginning to lose interest. All I had written so far were four chapters, although, officially, I was retouching the last one. The *Sunday People* advanced some money, which I never saw as it went straight to Clare Lallow, the boat builder. Eventually I hit on another brilliant idea.

Fight another shark and convince somebody to give me ten thousand dollars to film another documentary. To cut a long story short, Great American Industries, an American firm that distributes a fully comprehensive range of diving equipment, was considering it and gave me a one way ticket to New York so that I could go and discuss the deal. Utterly broke, I borrowed £50 from Sylvia's dad and went to America to see them. Should I fail to convince the Americans of the worthiness of my cause, I would find myself stranded but, since I could not afford to fail, I didn't. They lent me the money on condition that if I didn't produce a decent documentary, I would have to return it.

Three weeks later I flew back to England, with ten pounds in my pocket and a couple of thousand feet of film that, in my opinion, was not even worth developing.

The boat I had chartered had broken down, the weather was foul, the sharks refused to co-operate, and during the last week a tiny nurse shark about four feet long had bitten me in the arm when my photographer was not around, so I didn't even get that on film.

After that I ran out of brilliant ideas and sat down to finish the book.

Britannia II was tearfully launched by my mother, visiting from Argentina, shortly after the book was finished. Aside from the distress of my own mother, Sylvia's mother, together with her brother, had refused to come, as a gesture of disapproval at the whole project, and Sylvia and myself were in the midst of our first major argument and were barely speaking. To make matters worse, the press continually asked us to row together, which we couldn't as our two styles are so completely 'diverse, so we swore at each other instead. Other than rowing together all that was required of us was that we smile.

On a day like that?

Still determined to finance the Pacific Row out of my own pocket and borrowing money from left, right and centre, I kept things going till the day of departure, when I left poor George Greenfield, our literary agent on whom I had graciously bestowed Power of Attorney, to unravel the incredible tangle of my affairs. After many a sad experience I respect few agents besides George. George is a star of unique splendour in a firmament of dead meteorites. The most unkind thing I ever heard anyone say about him is 'safe as the Bank of England'. It must have been quite a shock for him to suddenly find himself in the midst of my 'business' doings and undoings — the more so since I myself had long forgotten what they were. As he puts it, I seem to have a 'happy knack' of making a mess of the most simple, straightforward deals. The amazing thing about George is that he has not once lost his patience with me. That is, not yet.

Our departure from these shores was only made possible by the co-operation of two wonderful shipping lines. Holland America Line, who agreed to take *Britannia II* to San Francisco free of charge, and P. & O. Lines who offered Sylvia and me a free cruise on the *Chusan*. Thus a few days after seeing our little boat safely delivered into the capable hands of Captain Dobbimba and securely stowed on the deck of the *Kamperdyk*, we ourselves were boarding *Chusan* at Southampton. Since this was a social event, and one in which her family and not mine were involved, and since she is so much more sociable than I am, at this stage I will pass the narrative over to Sylvia.

John refers to our departure as a social event, but at the time it appeared in anything but that light. We arrived at

Southampton Docks in a howling gale at the most unsociable hour of 9 a.m., our big old Rover crammed full of luggage and equipment for the trip, and our ten enormous oars lashed on her sagging roof.

After a short friendly welcome, we were taken up to the bridge to meet the Mayor of Southampton, who had kindly come along to present us with the P. & O. flag that we were to carry across the Pacific in *Britannia II* and present to the Mayor of Sydney at the end of our crossing. The Mayor was absolutely charming and I had the utmost admiration for her turning out at such an unearthly hour in deep mid-winter. Following this little ceremony we were ushered down to the Junior Room where a press reception was in full swing. A quick glance round the beautiful savouries offered was enough to tell me I was going to enjoy this cruise very much indeed — the great tragedy was that the press never gave me time to sample this selection, but I was absolutely right about the food aboard *Chusan* — delicious!

Besides the press, my mother and father, a few close friends, and, to my surprise, my brother had come to see us off. My brother had been most reluctant to be associated in any way with our venture. He is quite conservative, although not overtly so, and in his opinion the whole project was suicidal, so I suppose it is excusable that he wanted to do nothing that might possibly be construed as encouraging the escapade. However, he had come now, so I gladly presumed all was well. The difficulty was that it wasn't till the last twenty minutes before all visitors had to disembark that I or John had any time to talk to our friends or family. And it wasn't till we were all together in my green and teak stateroom that my brave Mum showed her first sign of tears. They crept into sight as I took off the gold *Britannia* bracelet (formerly John's watch bracelet, which he had given me to wear for good luck whilst he was rowing the Atlantic), and by the time I had fastened it round her plump little wrist she was weeping buckets.*

* During my absence my mother, in defiance of hospital rules, had refused to remove the bracelet preceding a major operation.

That was the moment my father's lighter decided to retire from service and, quite unthinkingly, I told him to keep mine, immediately realizing too late that this was interpreted in the same manner as the bracelet. After that who said what, if anything, is lost to me. I just remember friends going, David Farr and Doug Eatwell of the *People*, Ian Sanderson, our chess combatant, Jacky Berry, my friend of twenty-eight years' standing, with her family, and George Greenfield with his wife Anne, all of whom reminded me of other friends who were not there, and finally there was just the family, and then they went too and we were on our own. Our journey had begun.

2. Preparations in America

As I lay sobbing on my bunk, my mind swamped by the picture of my poor mother's distraught tears mingled with the image of my father's determined severity, I wondered how ever I had managed to wind up in this incredible position. However had I convinced myself this was possible, this crazy scheme of rowing the Pacific, let alone that I could do it? How had I ever become involved in such an outlandish plot? Come to that, how had I ever got involved with a character like John Fairfax in the first place?

The *Times* Personal Column, on 7th June, 1967, had carried the following announcement:

> I, John Fairfax, will row the Atlantic singlehanded from East to West in a boat specially designed by Uffa Fox. If you wish to be associated in any way with this project, please telephone Brian Watkins* at ...... or write ......

and I had written.

After washing up a disastrous eighteen months of marriage nine months previously, I was still feeling rather unsettled and on the lookout for something which I would find fully absorbing and worthwhile. My hobby for some years had been rowing, the shell racing variety, and I had always been an armchair adventurer, so I thought John's idea was great and wrote immediately offering my part-time services in a secretarial or administrative capacity. To my surprise, two days later John telephoned me from his flatlet, a mere two

* John's friend and thentime agent.

hundred yards from the flat I was sharing with three other girls, and said he'd be round in half an hour.

Thrown into an instant panic, I was in a mess and the flat was in an even bigger one, I didn't know which to do first, decided on the flat, made a whistle-stop tour with the Ewbank, bunged four girls' rubbish out of sight under anything, and even had time to powder my nose before the doorbell rang.

I opened the door on a bronzed muscleman not much taller than myself, with sun-bleached brown hair flopping into his crinkly hazel eyes, who just oozed vitality and enthusiasm. He bounded across the vast empty wastes of our Cromwell Road lounge and installed himself in an upright chair by the dining table overlooking the street (the better to pursue his favourite hobby of bird-watching, I was soon thinking cynically), and an hour later bounded out again. Planting a quick kiss on my cheek he had disappeared with the words 'Now we are friends'.

Well! He had talked of everything under the sun, hardly mentioned the proposed trip at all, told the most outrageous stories and had kept asking me for glasses of water. I was as sure that no one could be that thirsty as I was that his tales must be taken with a pinch of salt. I was right about the water, that was to give him the pleasure of looking me up and down as I crossed and recrossed the vastness of our lounge. About the stories I was wrong, time, his mother, and several other people, have confirmed them over and over again, besides adding many more to the collection!

Two weeks passed before another word was heard from my strange visitor and I was beginning to think that perhaps I hadn't roused as much interest as I had hoped. Then, one day, sitting at my desk in the Old Masters Gallery which had provided my bread and butter over the past eight years, I heard my boss's young son telling me there was someone to see me. I immediately knew who it was and, from then on, we saw more and more of each other until John left to row the Atlantic eighteen months later.

During this time I had helped as much as I could and so I learned that more than half the success of an operation of this nature is due to careful and extensive planning and preparation. John set off and I was left to answer the cynics when no news was forthcoming. Although I never doubted that he would bob up safely in or around Florida, when he did, and I heard all he said and read all he wrote about it, it wasn't enough. I had been involved as much as anyone outside his boat could be, yet I was still in the dark. I could never understand unless I did it myself. Now I had left my job to meet John in Florida there was nothing to hold me down and my adventures didn't have to stop at page two hundred and fifty-three, or whatever. Never mind that I had not even been as much as camping, one had to start somewhere, and now I was free the sky was the limit.

For a long time before John's Atlantic crossing I had known that he had been considering a hat trick; rowing the Atlantic, rowing Cape Horn, and rowing the Pacific. I also knew that he had abandoned the idea of rowing Cape Horn, and that he had missed having a girl in his boat from the first day aboard *Britannia*. It didn't require any great brilliance, therefore, to deduce that he would probably invite me to join him when the time came (which it undoubtedly would — thanks to the human mind's remarkable knack of forgetting the bad and miserable, and thanks to John's stubborn determination) to row the Pacific.

I thought it over very thoroughly, considered all the known risks, evaluated them according to my own optimistic standards, and concluded that the odds were on success, and that even if the worst happened, by the time it did I would have had a far more eventful and interesting time than I had had up to now. When John actually got around to asking me, my reply was such a foregone conclusion in my own mind that he deserves every praise for failing to show the surprise he must have felt at such an unhesitating acceptance of his 'new idea'!

Of course I had reasons, other than simply that Johnny had asked me, for wanting to undergo the trip. I felt that my life had been far too easy so far, I had never endured any serious hardships or discomforts, nor even faced a real crisis. I wanted to find out my own reactions, would I be thrown into a panic at the critical moment of an emergency, or had I been deceiving myself throughout my life in assuming I would stay calm and capable no matter what? Was I really the outdoor type I fondly imagined myself to be, or was it that I had never been out of doors long enough to know? Would I enjoy watching fish and birds at the business of living, or would nature in the raw be more than I could take? Was I as unsociable as I imagined, or would I be craving for company after a few days? At my age, thirty, I decided it was time I found out.

A few months after my decision John went to America to film his shark-fighting venture and generously sent me on holiday in Italy with his mother. This was very nearly a disastrous mistake because weeks after we had all returned my maternal instinct started to stir. Italy had been full of the most beautiful bambinos and their memory was waking me up.

One day I told Johnny, 'Darling, I'm sorry but I'm not going on your Pacific trip. There have been too many delays already, there will be more, the trip will take longer than we anticipate and then we'll have to write a book on it. This will mean being tied up with you for another three or four years and I'm afraid I just can't afford the time. I'm thirty now, and I want my own children. This thing is going to make me thirty-four before I can even start looking for the prospective father, then a couple of years to get to know him and get married, then another couple before the baby arrives. That makes me thirty-eight before I've even started a family.' He reacted very calmly to this bombshell, said he quite understood and would advertise for another girl.

I felt a real heel and, although he never complained, it was perfectly obvious that I had well and truly landed poor Johnny up a gum tree. Even if he did find a suitable volunteer, it would be a pretty grim proposition for them both to step into a boat for a year with a total stranger. In the end, I thought I would be an utter fool to miss such an opportunity, and would never forgive myself when he landed in Australia with some other bird, so I decided to go after all. It was the right decision.

Now I was aboard a beautiful liner, crying my eyes out in my own luxurious cabin, whilst this strange man who had entered my life so unceremoniously four and a half years ago, and who had then warned me not to become involved with him, waited for me in some other part of the ship. Had he been right? Maybe I should have left him alone, but in his way he was a challenge too. What a cheek he had, telling me in the first few days how many hearts he had broken, how he could never live with a woman, how he needed variety and had five current girl friends — I'd show him!

Maybe I did, or maybe I didn't, it doesn't much matter because he showed me. He showed me how to live and how to appreciate life and nature and people, and this is beyond value and can never be lost. So what am I doing, lying down here crying? This is every girl's dream, a first class cruise on a first class liner. This is to be the most fabulous holiday, get up and enjoy it!

I wandered along *Chusan*'s spacious sycamore panelled corridors and stairs till I came to John's cabin (to appease P. & O.'s sense of propriety, on a different deck at the far end of the ship — I can't imagine how they expected us to manage on *Britannia II*!), and dragged him away from his book to escort me on an inspection tour of our new temporary home. She was beautiful.

We had already met several officers and now we found ourselves on nodding terms with many fellow passengers and it was becoming increasingly obvious that we were on the brink of having a whale of a time — our last holiday before going on twenty-four hour daily duty for at least ten months.

On February 16th, fourteen pounds heavier and several shades darker, I stepped ashore in San Francisco with a brown, well-rounded young man bearing little resemblance to the slim rather worried looking fellow who had escorted me aboard at Southampton twenty-seven days before. The holiday was over, we'd seen many exotic places (Panama, Acapulco and Madeira, to name but a few), we'd played more games and had more fun than for years, we'd eaten fantastically well, met many delightful people, and lazed till our hearts' content. Now it was finished and work and adversity had to be faced once more.

Our most urgent problem, that of accommodation, was solved even before our arrival by the Olympic Hotel kindly putting their Directors' suite at our disposal for a few days, and then very generously allowing this concession to stretch into a third week. A third week in San Francisco in itself was a disaster as our funds were so pathetically depleted by this time that every day ashore was a further severe strain on our resources, especially as we had hoped that our sojourn in the United States would be a couple of weeks at the most.

The reason for our delay was that we had left England without much essential equipment, and with no food. With insufficient money to pay for it all, we had tried to interest companies in supplying us free in exchange for the publicity they would undoubtedly receive once the journey was completed. Our main snag had been that most people considered our chances of success less than nil, and so reckoned that in associating with the project, any publicity they might receive would be bad rather than good. The courageous souls who did support us, we have lately discovered, usually did so entirely off their own backs and against the judgment of the other members of their companies, a brave few who dared to stick their necks out and for their sakes, if none others, we are glad we made it!

In fact, by assuming that the Americans were more publicity minded than the British and therefore more willing to be associated with our project, we had badly miscalculated. We soon realized that we were in really bad trouble before even setting foot in the boat. We had eighty pounds in our pocket, didn't know a soul other than our friend Ken Crutchlow in San Francisco, had an enormous list of requirements for our trip, including all our food, and didn't know where we would sleep the following week.

Our assets consisted of speaking the language (after a fashion!), and David Llewellyn, a confident and enthusiastic young agent working on our behalf in New York. How we survived until our eventual departure on 26th April is a constant source of wonder to me! On top of all this our thirty-five foot boat was due to arrive in a few days time and where on earth can one store a boat that size free of charge?

Fortunately for us, our one friend in San Francisco proved to be the right one. Ken Crutchlow has a happy knack of providing solutions to the most insoluble problems, usually with just one telephone call. In San Francisco Ken is a member of the Dolphin Club and, through Ken, the club agreed to house our boat during our stay.

Regrettably, this kind offer wasn't a great success as *Britannia II* was damaged in handling because the Club was not equipped for her bulk or weight (over half a ton unladen). However, it was no-one's fault but ours, for not checking their facilities before taking the boat there, and we made so many good friends through our introduction to the Club that it seemed small price to pay for such excellent company.

Early in March we left San Francisco for New York, where we were booked to appear on the David Frost and Dick Cavett Shows, as well as having several meetings arranged by David Llewellyn. New York is too tough a city for folk like us. The noise never stops, day and night the hooters blare constantly, hardly five minutes pass without the siren or wailer of an ambulance, fire-engine or police car, the rattling roar of the subway trains drums up at you through grills in the pavement, and canned music blares out of every other shop doorway.

Security men, or policemen — I still haven't learnt the difference — lurk in pairs both indoors and out, and everyone is in too much of a hurry, or too frightened, to be even passably civil. Besides all this, we have only one friend in the entire city, Peter Learmont, the English manager of the Royal Manhatten Hotel, where we are always made most welcome whenever circumstances necessitate our being there. This visit was even less enjoyable than most because, during our absence for an hour one morning, our suite was burgled and we returned to discover the briefcase containing all our papers, a Rolex watch, five Ronson lighters, a camera and one of John's suits, had been stolen. The papers were our greatest concern because amongst them were operating and assembling instructions for some of the vital equipment for our trip, including those for the water distilling apparatus which could mean the difference between death or survival.

Peter was most distressed and made sure that everything possible was done to recover the stolen property, the police were called and statements were made, every single room in the hotel was searched, in itself a major undertaking for a hotel with accommodation for two and a half thousand guests, and it was even arranged for us to make an appeal to the thief to return the papers anonymously, on television news.

This appeal was unsuccessful but rather amusing. The television company asked Johnny to make the appeal and, in my opinion, it is against a man's nature to appeal — especially to another man. John started talking softly and coolly but became increasingly angry as he spoke, which showed, so that by the end of his allotted time he was almost shaking his fist at the criminal.

He also caused gasps of horror all round the studio by, in the middle of his fury, coming out with 'for Christ's sake' on a live television programme. Altogether I had the feeling that if the poor crook did still possess his worthless bag of papers, and hadn't yet found the opportunity of dumping the lot in the river, and had considered their return at the start of the 'appeal', by the end of it, wild horses would not have induced him to make the remotest contact with anyone, however far removed, connected with the fierce John Fairfax.

This incident was a serious inconvenience to us, although not a shattering blow. We had to contact all those persons whose documents had been lost requesting duplicate papers, and it was difficult to remember exactly what had been there. We feared some serious oversight, but luckily none ever came to light, even though our two large business address books were included in the theft. The lesson learnt here, strangely enough, is that over ten kilos of essential indispensable papers can disappear completely and never be badly missed.

The following day we went to Washington for television's *Panorama*. We had been in the studio an hour or more, watching the other guests and waiting our turn, when a technician approached me and whispered, 'Leave the studio, immediately'. I asked why, since we were due on the set in half a minute, and was told, 'We've got problems'.

A girl ushered us downstairs to the reception area and gave the same answer to my question. Once there I noticed a nineteen-thirties news film on the monitor set, instead of the people on the stage upstairs, and after a few moments all those who had been up there were milling around us again, and I heard mutterings of a bomb. Everyone seemed pretty het up about it and the building was cleared just as the bomb squad arrived.

Considering the previous week a rival Washington television station had had a similar call and a bomb had indeed been discovered in their studio, and that this was shortly after the dreadful bomb that had blasted the Capitol, they had every justification for being scared, but for we innocents, fresh from sleepy England, the whole episode had an unreal quality and our main concern was in having spent a hundred precious dollars on our train fares for nought!

Altogether we must have spent about ten exhausting days chasing round New York before we returned to San Francisco, none the richer but with a loan from Oliver Swan of Paul R. Reynolds, Inc., (George's American ally) to tide us over till our departure, and assurances from David Llewellyn that great things were in the air and, most important, that we no longer need worry about food for the trip.

One of our new friends, Ivan Sharpe, met us at the airport and drove us to a small, cheap hotel. Ivan is an English free-lance journalist who had been assigned by the *Sunday People* to write our story. In spite of thinking us both crazy, as I'm sure he did, and although living in Sausalito, which is the other side of the Golden Gate Bridge from San Francisco, Ivan was a constant and invaluable help to us. It was Ivan who arranged the loan of a car from British Motors in San Francisco for our use, without which we would really have been marooned.

Ivan found us Anderson's excellent boatyard in Sausalito and persuaded them to start work immediately on *Britannia II*'s poor holed bottom and the building of a new stronger rudder. Lastly, Ivan found us the company which finally supplied us with the palatable food which formed the major part of our diet during the crossing, at a vast reduction. All this besides having his garage littered with mounds of boat equipment for weeks on end, acting chauffeur occasionally, and frequently lumbering John and myself on his long suffering wife, Ann, for unexpected meals. Poor Ivan, I bet he was glad when we finally pushed off!

One way in which Ivan was unable to help us was with our accommodation, now a really pressing problem because it was obvious we would be spending at least another two weeks in San Francisco. Although the hotel into which we had so hurriedly checked on our return from New York was cheap, for us it wasn't cheap enough so we had to find an alternative — and soon.

Once again, indirectly, it was Ken Crutchlow to the rescue. Ken had mentioned our plight to a fellow diner at a recent Dolphin Club function and she had valiantly offered to share her flat with us. Her name was Vivian Dahl, or 'our mother in America' and she opened her doors in wide welcome. We stayed with her very happily, hopefully without upsetting her routine too drastically, until a couple of nights before our departure.

During our daytimes we were driving around trying our best to interest various companies in our merchandise, i.e. publicity, in exchange for their more tangible assets, goods. The usual pattern was one day with a classified directory telephoning, the next day interviews with those calls which had been receptive enough to progress that far. Generally the replies were negative, occasionally the company was not offering what we sought, and, every now and again, we and they would be successful and happy.

It was hard and soul-destroying work. If only we had the money to be able to walk into a store and buy what we wanted straight off the counter like anyone else. It is incredibly difficult to sit facing a total stranger and sell yourself to the extent of making him believe that you will succeed with the same conviction that makes you know it, and then to convince him that he has something to gain from your success. How we wished someone could do it all for us, but David Llewellyn had been suddenly recalled to London before even our food supply was settled, and Ivan had his own business to attend to and had already made far more than his fair contribution to our caper.

There came a weekend when we decided to play truant. Anyway there is no business at weekends, so why not? We drove up to the famous Yosemita National Park and within four hours we had left the chill city of San Francisco, passed through rolling cattle country, continued into really hot orchard valleys and finished in deep snowy mountains. Beautiful majestic mountains, with sheer cliffs soaring up over seven thousand feet, cut by glorious waterfalls which cascaded down channels in the granite to the wide, rocky rivers bubbling through the valleys below.

We saw hardly a soul, so that even the little tourist village, with its low log information centre, warders' huts, motel and other buildings, seemed deserted. We liked it so much that, instead of returning that night, we talked ourselves into staying overnight and continuing to the Sequoia National Park on the Sunday.

If possible, this was still more beautiful as, not only was it mountainous, but it was heavily wooded with great thick pines and the awesome straight red trunks of the fabulous giant Sequoia trees, the world's oldest and biggest living things, including the celebrated General Sherman Tree, over three thousand years old. The road was bordered by all kinds of pretty shrubs and flowers and, in spite of the two feet of snow covering the higher reaches, we walked comfortably around without coats. To conclude our little tour we returned to San Francisco by the coast road through the impressive Big Sur State Park which wound across hair-raising gorges and round cliff-hanging bends till we were slowly re-absorbed by the sprawl of the city.

The following morning it was back on the job for the pair of us. Although it was not apparent, progress was obviously being made, since what had begun as a little pile of oddments in the corner, had grown into a great mass of weird objects which now sprawled happily across our huge double room

obscuring Viv's beautiful handwoven Mexican rugs completely. We seemed to arrive back with our little Austin
American loaded to the roof every time we went out, and the
packaging of so much gear had grown into a mountain of
rubbish beside the dustbins in the backyard. It was beginning
to look as though our tiny boat would be overflowing
already, and still we had no food. What a terrible mess it all
looked, yet not a murmer of protest nor a hint of concern,
from our heroic hostess. Not only that, but we would usually
arrive home to be greeted by a whole list of telephone
messages which poor Viv, after a hard day teaching mal-
adjusted children had painstakingly accepted on our behalves.

One by one our problems were slowly dissolving, but we
still had one major item outstanding, one which could not be
ignored or brushed aside. We still had no food.

Vacu-Dry at Oakland were most helpful and enthusiastic
and offered us unlimited supplies of their products, which
proved delicious, but one cannot live on fruit, soups and
green beans for a year. Roos Atkins (in co-operation with
Rich-Moore camping and trekking foods), and The Ski Hut at
Berkeley also contributed generously towards our larder, but
we still had to find the bulk of our normal everyday diet.
Eventually Ivan spoke to the Oregon Freeze Dry Company,
manufacturers of Tea Kettle instant meals and Mountain
House foods. They were willing to provide as much food as
we would need for cost price less ten per cent.

Marvellous! Arrangements were even made for us to collect
samples before ordering, to make sure we liked it. By then we
were so desperate we would have taken cat food had it been
offered, but, fortunately, their products are really whole-
some, tasty and ample portions, besides being incredibly
simple to prepare — all one has to do with the vegetables and
complete meals is to add boiling water, wait five minutes and
then eat. The meat has to be soaked in warm water for ten
minutes and then fried for one minute on either side.
Nothing could be simpler. We could hardly believe our good
luck. We were really scraping the bottom of our financial
barrel now and the time to leave beautiful San Francisco was
imminent.

During most of these preparations *Britannia II* had remained in Sausalito undergoing repairs but the time came when she had to be towed to a mooring in San Francisco, one where we could comfortably load and stow our vast accumulation of necessities before we could start our journey. Film producer, Alex de Renzy, with his crew on the *Euphrates* volunteered to tow us to the *Alert*, a converted coastguard cutter owned by Barry Brose, who had kindly offered us a mooring alongside at Pier 47. Barry told us that we could load from the security of the *Alert*'s deck, where we would be afforded unlimited space.

Moored alongside the *Alert*, *Britannia II* looked very small indeed and I could not help comparing that view of her with my own very first sight of John's tubby Atlantic boat, *Britannia I*. By comparison our Pacific rowing-boat looked very streamlined, her long pencil-like shape broken only by the Plastazote blisters, or covers, at either end. I remembered seeing her at the various stages of her construction and being struck by her apparent enormity. 'How ever,' I remembered thinking, 'can they expect us to *row* that thing?' But now, knowing how easy she was to row, she looked so small and frail that, had I not known how solidly she was built, I would only have wondered how she could be expected to stand the sort of weather we were bound to encounter.

At 13.00 hours on 15th April we were met by the somewhat unusual crew of the *Alert*. Commanded by Barry, himself the owner of a film laboratory, the crew were all voluntary and part time, their livelihoods ranging from an engineer to an insurance conveyor. In spite of, or more probably because of, this, the *Alert* was spotless and ship-shape at all times except when, arguing that green was an unlucky colour and therefore insisting on repainting ours, I had inadvertently allowed a can of brilliant blue paint to blow over onto her smart black deck. Her crew, particularly the youngest members, seventeen year old Chip and his pal, Ernie, seemed so much to enjoy helping with our preparations that, far from feeling intruders, we felt they might even miss us when we departed the following day.

Whilst John was busy loading *Britannia II* with the mounds of provisions piled on the deck of the *Alert*, I went back to Viv's to clear her rooms and finish packing what still remained there. It was far more than it looked and ended up as a number of large boxes which Viv helped me carry downstairs and drive to Pier 47. It was with the final margarine box that I missed the last stair and fell in a most unnatural heap with my left ankle creased painfully beneath me. In the tumble I broke the chain of a very pretty St Christopher medallion which I had started to wear an hour earlier in readiness for the start of our crossing. This had been given to me by my great friend Val Austin, who had sacrificed most of her spare time the previous summer in a vain effort to teach me to swim. Viv found the medallion, repaired the chain, and we drove to the *Alert*.

By 10 p.m. there was still a huge heap of our equipment lying around the *Alert*'s deck and it began to look as though we would have to work all night in order to leave the next day. Midnight came and the pile looked no smaller. Because there was very little anyone else could do, and because there was only room for one person at a time on little *Britannia*, one by one our helpers retired to their bunks below, till only Ken Crutchlow and I remained to pass one of the longest, coldest nights of our lives, in shivering attendance waiting the odd request from Johnny.

Dawn crept upon us unnoticed through the icy wind and electric lights, but morning was declared by the appearance of Barry and some chummy teasing from Ron Mathieson at the sight of the colossal sprawl of still unstowed gear littering the deck of the *Alert*. At 7 a.m. we encountered more good-natured bantering as the first pressmen started to arrive for our departure, and to witness that not properly stowed being unceremoniously checked into any available space aboard *Britannia II*.

Everyone stood around shivering while Johnny rushed about slinging half our stores haphazardly on to our deck. Terry Zabala brought along a huge lemon cake she had baked to start us happily on the trip, and Lieutenant Commander J.D. Caldecott, on behalf of the officers of The Royal Yacht

Britannia (paying her first visit to San Francisco), presented us with a bottle of champagne to drink on the Equator. Then, suddenly, at 07.50, the whole thing was called off. Barry had telephoned for a weather report and discovered a twelve knot wind to be blowing, which would have made it impossible for us to clear the Golden Gate Bridge.

Everyone was very nice about it, especially considering what a ghastly day it was and how early they must have risen to be there at that time. Secretly I was delighted at the postponement which, because of our contract with the *Sunday People*, had to be for a full week, as the boat was really in a hell of a mess and we ourselves were dog-tired and in no fit condition to face what we knew would be one of the worst stages of the whole crossing, the start. John's thoughts were roughly parallel to my own, so I guess everyone was happy. By eleven the visitors had all left and we returned to Viv's. John slumped on his bed and fell instantly asleep and I, for the first time in my life, fell asleep in the bath, was awoken by Viv, and promptly repeated the performance, although this time Viv didn't leave me till she heard the water running out!

Whilst undressing for the bath I discovered the chain to my St Christopher had broken again and was tangled up in my underwear, but I couldn't find the medallion. It was not till a couple of days later, when Johnny asked what the chain around my neck was, that I told him the sad story and he gave me the even sadder reply, 'Oh, was it a pretty little blue thing? I found that in the boat and threw it away.' I was speechless with fury at his utter thoughtlessness. I had been the only person other than himself to board *Britannia II*, and he had not had the sense to realize it must have been mine — besides, any man worth his salt would have kept such a pretty trinket for his girl regardless of its origins, had there been no chance of finding its owner. Strangely I wore the empty chain during the entire crossing and it never broke again.

The very next day, out came all our hastily stowed stores, as we now had a whole week in which to properly arrange our boat in a truly seamanlike manner. My ankle got steadily

worse, instead of better, so we were afraid that some small
bone must have been broken and had it ex-rayed and
examined. Fortunately, nothing was broken, although it was
swollen to three times its normal size, and I hobbled around
whilst doing the incredible amount of shopping we still found
wanting.

One near oversight in our last minute shopping was the
kettle, an item which we used more than anything other than
oars throughout our journey. When all was as ready as could
be, Johnny was reminded of a ship he had met during his
Atlantic row and remembered begging that most essential of
culinary equipment from them. It was a Saturday morning and
Marilyn Clark of the *Alert,* insisting that there was only one
reliable make of kettle and that she knew it and where to
find it, whisked me off to downtown San Francisco in search
of the wonder kettle. With us I took our gimbals and we
dashed from store to store waving this strange iron contraption and picking up kettle after kettle in search of the one
which fitted. The two pint was too small, the three pint too
large and, believe it or not, the two and a half pint in this
particular brand seemed to have disappeared from the face of
the earth. But Marilyn, bless her heart, because it lasted and
whistled the entire trip, would hear of me having no other.
We were about to rush off on a tour of suburban stores when
it occurred to Marilyn that she had just the thing, still in its
box and brand new, sitting in her temporary flat awaiting the
move to her permanent home, so we rushed off there (a mere
couple of hundred yards from the *Alert*) instead, and I was
duly presented with our greatest treasure!

Our stay in San Francisco was drawing to a close. We had
all we needed neatly stowed and were just waiting for the
right weather to arrive on a Friday. Considering we had
earned our freedom, we now accepted as many of the kind
invitations which had been bestowed on us during out visit as
time would allow. We enjoyed enough memorable meals with
the kind folk of that delightful city to provide nostalgic
mumblings almost every time we ate at sea. I, true British and
all that, was even missing hamburgers, instead of steak and
kidney pudding, during my first months on the Ocean.

Amongst our most colourful evenings was one aboard the friendly *Kamperdyk* with Captain Dobbimba and his guests.

The Captain, who had been our host on two previous occasions, is big, straight, and bearded, with a twinkle in his eye, in fact looking so much like a sea captain that it is difficult to believe he really is one.

The result of all this festivity was that when the next scheduled departure time arrived, we again had a rush to meet it. This time we spent the preceding night sleeping aboard the *Alert* and were feeling fit and ready by the time the press began to arrive about eight o'clock.

Three hours later we cast off from the cutter, not expecting much success, because the weather seemed the same or worse than the week before, but feeling obliged to provide some entertainment, story, call it what you will, for the gentlemen of the press who had so valiantly and patiently turned out yet again. Within an hour we were moored alongside the *Alert* back at Pier 47. I have honestly forgotten how many more false starts there were but, as John will now relate, eventually it was for real.

3. The First Stormy Weeks

At last, at 02.47 hours April 26th, we left our mooring alongside the *Alert* and everybody knew that, this time, there was no turning back.

The night was cold but windless and the outgoing tide, one of the strongest of the year, was carrying us towards the open sea at a rate of nearly six knots. We were escorted by the *Bruin*, a little tug owned by Barry, and a motor boat chartered by the *Sunday People* and I.T.N. with only a handful of friends and reporters on board. We made excellent time and at 03.33 I took the tiller from Sylvia to give her the pleasure of rowing *Britannia II* under the Golden Gate Bridge. By then our little party had been joined by a Coastguard cutter, probably to give a hand in case we ran into trouble.

Getting out of San Francisco by rowing boat, even with a tide as favourable as we had, is certainly not what one would call a piece of cake. Terrific currents and counter-currents form under the Bridge, the coast on both sides is steep, peppered with treacherous rocks, and I knew that our chances of getting through were about even. For her size *Britannia* was an extraordinarily easy boat to row, but under certain circumstances she could also behave like a bitch, which is exactly what she decided to do shortly after we left the shadow of the bridge.

There was no wind to speak of, yet, quite suddenly, we found ourselves in the midst of four to six foot waves, *Britannia* was tossed about like a toy and, with total disregard for our efforts to keep her in mid-stream, she began to drift towards the shore to our starboard. Sylvia was doing her best, but, good as she was, she simply did not have the strength for the job. We switched places. It could not possibly have taken more than a few seconds yet, by the time I was manning the oars, *Britannia* had swung broadside to the waves and stubbornly refused to be turned back on course.

Shipping in the port oar and grabbing the other with both hands I feelingly cursed the day I had come up with the idea of San Francisco as starting point.

Pulling on one oar only finally did the trick, although by then we had lost so much ground that our predicament was only just beginning. As far as I could judge in the darkness we were only about two or three cables away from the cliffs and, at the present rate, it would not take long before we drifted into their prongs. Already we could see, here and there, the white splashes of the sea as it grinned with malicious anticipation over the nearest rocks. Suddenly the dark silhouette of the press boat materialised almost alongside and we were blinded by the flare of the powerful searchlights they switched on. Unaware of our trouble — I had not requested help and, after all the fuss and bother about leaving San Francisco unaided, I would be damned if I would — they were happily filming what, presumably, looked like a nice piece of action.

Hollering at them to get the hell out of the way, I caught sight of Ivan, leaning over the side, pale as a corpse and shaking like a leaf as he spilled his dinner into the Ocean. I have never been seasick in my life, but I have spent many days and nights in the company of some wretched beings who have been and felt a twinge of remorse and commiseration for them. The poor bastards were only doing their job and I was cursing them as if they were responsible for my problems. To keep station with *Britannia* in those choppy waters was no easy task for a motor boat and, being so much higher on the water than we were, they swayed like a pendulum, making life miserable for everybody on board.

Their pictures taken they withdrew, taking up position a cable away from us, as before.

Meanwhile, in the grip of a vicious eddy *Britannia* went on drifting towards the cliffs. Huddling over the tiller Sylvia never said a word and I was sure that she too was a bit under the weather. As a non-swimmer she must have been a little frightened as well. Maybe things will look brighter in the morning, if we manage to stay afloat that long, I thought.

To those who will ask why we did not request a tow to clear the coast I would like to point out that to do so would have been against the entire principle of the exercise. We had not chosen to row across the Pacific because of our love of rowing. Personally I don't even like it as a sport. The idea was to row because that is the ultimate, hardest way of crossing an ocean. Skipping one of the most difficult parts, getting away from the shore, was tantamount to negating, from the very beginning, the spirit of the whole thing. To a mountaineer the challenge of a peak, regardless of height, is not reaching its summit by way of the easiest path, but by the most improbable. Failure to succeed only means that one has the opportunity to try again. In all fields of human endeavour the greatest satisfaction lies in the struggle rather than the achievement itself, rewarding as that may be. We *had* to get under way on our own or not at all.

After two hours non-stop slogging during which, somehow, we managed to prevent a pile up on the rocks, I was beginning to feel the strain. *Britannia* was so overloaded as to be positively sluggish. Although reasonably fit, my training had consisted of eating as much as I could — both Sylvia and I were more than twenty-five pounds overweight — and fifty press-ups every morning. The theory behind this unorthodox training method was based on my Atlantic experience. Then I started my journey without an ounce of fat to spare with the result that, as I began to lose weight, I grew weaker instead of stronger. By the time I reached Florida I had lost over twenty pounds of muscle, literally eaten up by the body, and with it, half of my original strength.

It must be remember that the more strenuous the exercise the more calories one burns. Unless they are replaced by an appropriate diet, something else must take their place. With the food we carried, supplemented by fish, we were unlikely to starve but we could not restore all of the 3,500 calories our daily toil was likely to consume, with the result that we would gradually, but inevitably, lose weight. Since ours was a marathon, not a race, I figured that hard training prior to departure was unnecessary, as two weeks at sea would make us as fit as we would ever need to be.

While this proved to be sound thinking it didn't help much during the first gruelling hours. All the same we finally made it, thanks to a change in the current, which pushed *Britannia* back on course at the eleventh hour. At dawn we were in very calm waters, fifteen miles or so off shore. Ivan and Ken Allen came alongside once more for a last farewell, asking Sylvia, *en passant*, if she had had enough and wanted a lift home. She was in no mood for foolishness and told them to go jump in the lake.

'I'm cold, tired and seasick. Never been so miserable in my life. Leave me alone.'

Then, rather sweetly, I thought, she added:

'Anyway Johnny told me that soon everything will be much better and I'm looking forward to it.'

How is that for a vote of confidence?

Our friends departed but we were not left alone. The coastguard cutter crept nearer until they were just beyond hailing distance and started circling us, like a hen protecting a stray chick. We had not asked for any help but, presumably, they wanted to make sure that we were not rammed by a ship, being, as we were, on the outskirts of such a busy port as San Francisco. We thanked them with a wave and, taking advantage of their vigilance, crawled under the 'rat hole' and went to sleep. The first day is always the worst and we could certainly use a few hours of untroubled rest.

At ten o'clock the din of a helicopter hovering above made us jump with fright. Luckily it was only the Press. By leaving at night we had given them all the slip but, apparently, not for long. More noise and a hovercraft zoomed in. A fine show of British ingenuity at its best, I decided with usual modesty, from the most modern to the most primitive, all in one picture, as far from home as one can get. Ere long they left and we were back on our own, except for our patient escort. Matter of fact their solicitude was beginning to get on Sylvia's nerves and she was rather peeved about it. You see, on *Britannia II* the calls of nature were answered by squatting over the gunwale and hanging on a line, or 'loo rope' which

I had fixed to the opposite bulwarks for that purpose. When alone we simply asked the other to 'turn around, please'. Now, with the American Navy on watch at such close quarters, Sylvia could not bring herself to show her bare bottom over the side.

'Suppose they chose *that* moment to take a closer look with binoculars?' she wailed.

The coastguard remained with us throughout the day and Sylvia's first insurmountable problem at sea was logged as 'those blasted sailors won't let me go to the loo!'

Darkness brought relief, at last, and by midnight we were left on our own. I let Sylvia take the mid-watch which, according to her log, she thoroughly enjoyed in spite of her misgivings.

'Never had I seen so many stars in my life. Within five minutes I saw two enormous shooting stars and, only having seen my first ever two months ago, began to think I must be seeing things! The sea was incredibly glassy and, I don't know whether it was the reflection of the stars, or plankton, as star-spangled as the sky. This was the moment I was so sure would be my first fright, my first night alone at sea with Johnny asleep. Johnny had warned me about the noises, and there were two or three lights from lighthouses, so land was still not that distant, nevertheless we were alone and I was happy to find I was not afraid. The sound of whales or dolphins breathing seemed almost continuous for those four hours, there was also a great deal of barking and croaking from seals, sundry bird noises and some squeaks from I know not where! I was amazed at so much activity but suppose it was because we were still so near to land. The thing that did momentarily scare me was a big bird — looking enormous in the dark! — gliding about six feet from my head. As the end of my watch approached a deep purple curtain appeared to grow out of the sea, obliterating star after star, making half the sea black and gradually spreading its gloom over all my newly found fairy land.'

During the next two days an unseasonal southerly wind pushed us thirty miles north of our intended course. It was bitterly cold and more than once I had to reassure a very worried Sylvia — feeling too seasick to row she was chilled to the bones — that, in spite of appearance, we were not heading for the North Pole. Eventually the wind changed back to normal and all was well except for the cold. For a week we made excellent progress. My lovely First Mate found her sea legs and began to take a lively interest in what went on. She took to seal spotting and squealed with delight every time a dark little head bobbed near the boat. If it happened to be a whale however, and there were many around, she would beat a hasty retreat into the 'rat-hole' and wait for me to give the all clear before venturing out again. Schools of dolphins were great fun also, providing they kept their distance, which they almost invariably did anyway.

Gradually we established a sort of routine and were reasonably happy although life was not, by any stretch of imagination, easy going. For one thing there was not a single place in the whole boat where one could rest in reasonable comfort. The open deck between the fore and aft blisters was so crammed with gear that finding a couple of square feet to sit without trampling on, or being prodded by, something or other, was in itself a major undertaking.

As for our sleeping quarters under the forward blister . . . well, we didn't call it 'rat-hole' for nothing. With a vertical clearance of less than two feet we could, at best, crawl under. The four feet width at the entrance tapered to nothing at the bows so that, for all practical purposes we could only use six of its ten foot length, which meant that when sleeping together one of us always had our feet and ankles sticking out and, when sleeping alone, one rolled about. Our bunk was the hard deck, our bed a sleeping bag. The entrance was covered by a bit of transparent plastic which we could roll up or down, quite effective against wind and rain, but absolutely useless as far as the sea was concerned. *Britannia* was self-bailing but it took several minutes before she drained herself through the scuppers and by then the water had found its way under the 'rat-hole' and we would be drenched from head to toes as thoroughly as if we had been sleeping in a bath-tub with the taps fully open. Needless to say, with a

14 inch freeboard, it did not take much of a sea for it to happen.

Generally speaking, matters were a lot worse for Sylvia who, aside from not being used to a rough life, was very much afraid of falling overboard and, to minimise the risk, dared not walk upright. When I was asleep she always wore a life-harness. Then, since she had not yet learned to keep her balance without holding on to something and a ducking was bottom in the list of things she fancied, especially at night with 'all those horrible monsters lurking out there', every time she moved she did so on all fours. Also she had the frustrating feeling that the sea had a very personal grudge against her. Pure coincidence of course, but it was true that I could sit for an hour at one end of the boat without getting splashed while Sylvia, at the other end, would collect spray by the bucketful. Always a gentleman I would eventually offer to change places and, — would you believe it? — the same thing would happen in reverse with my hitherto dry spot at the receiving end, while a most indignant Sylvia spluttered her disgust to all and sundry.

No, life was not all fun but at least it was bearable. However a very great problem had arisen. Our radio had never worked, and I had not the slightest idea of what could be wrong with it. I was very surprised because it was the same Marconi CH 25, I had used in my Atlantic Row when it had never failed. Since then it had been completely overhauled and a radio technician recommended by the manufacturers had been in charge of the installation on board *Britannia* in San Francisco. Ivan Sharpe was supposed to keep in touch with us throughout the journey with the co-operation of KMI, a marine radio station in Oakland, with whom we had arranged a schedule prior to departure. P. & O. liners in the Pacific had also promised to listen and relay our messages in case we got out of range from KMI.

Naturally I had advised everybody concerned that it would be most unlikely for the radio to go on working to the end, but I had certainly not expected it to fail at the very beginning, to the point of not being able to send a single report. What the world would make of our silence was not difficult to guess and the last thing we wanted was to inconvenience the Coastguards by being responsible for them mounting a search and rescue operation.

Finally I made up my mind that, painful as the idea might be, we had no choice but to attempt to land somewhere along the American coast and have the radio repaired. In all fairness to our parents, not to mention the *Sunday People*, we could not possibly disappear for a year without letting them know that all was well. I was sure that, sooner or later, we were bound to be sighted by the odd ship, but not enough to rely on it. After all the Pacific is a mighty big ocean and we were unlikely to be in a shipping lane more than a few days at a time.

Deciding to return was one thing, doing it quite another. Since our departure I had only bothered to fix our position once. To know where we were I depended entirely on astro navigation, the only practical way in our situation. To shoot sun and stars from a little boat with reasonable accuracy takes a lot of practice but so does anything one wants to be good at. Personally I'm very disappointed if I cannot fix my position within five miles, therefore, knowing where we were was seldom a problem, although it did happen every now and then, if the weather was too rough to take sights or the sky totally overcast for long periods. The latter was the case at the time and my previous fix being four days old I could only guess that we were some hundred miles offshore, slightly NW of Punta Conception. To make for Santa Barbara, or Los Angeles, was our best bet. Mind you, I would be more than happy if we hit *anywhere* along the American coast as, short of a miracle, that would be the best we could hope to achieve. A rowing boat in the open ocean is at the mercy of wind and currents, mostly wind, and for all practical purposes can only be steered about ninety degrees ahead of it. The stronger the wind, the smaller the choice. Ideally we would have liked a ten to fifteen miles an hour westerly but were quite prepared to make do with what we had, a north-westerly of the same force. Providing it stayed there we would make it. If not . . .

The very next day after deciding to return we met a ship,

the *Export Courier*, and took the opportunity to send a message to Ivan, saying that the radio was on the blink and that we were attempting to reach Los Angeles. Our position, as given by the *Export Courier*, was 34° 15′ N 22° 15′ W, so we hoped to make it in five or six days at most, weather permitting. Two days later we were hit by a gale.

Britannia II was designed and built to survive a hurricane if necessary and I had no doubts that she would, as she was truly unsinkable. What could happen to her crew, however, was an altogether different proposition. That gale lasted for ten days, with winds gusting to forty knots, and waves up to twenty-five feet. Ten days of sheer, undiluted hell, and that's praising it.

On May 13th the wind veered from the north-west to north, steadily increasing in force so that by sunset it was gusting at 25 knots and the sea became too rough for rowing. Other than that there were no signs of impending bad weather as the sky was absolutely cloudless and the stars shone in all their glory. Nothing to worry about, I thought, a bit of a blow that will soon pass. So, instead of unshipping the rudder, I lashed it at such an angle as to keep the waves coming from our port quarter, crawled under the 'rat-hole' with Sylvia, and went to sleep. Round about midnight, there was an almighty thump as *Britannia* lurched and seemingly jumped right out of the sea, then fell on her beam ends and lay there, at an angle of 60 or 70 degrees, showing no inclination of righting herself again.

Still in a daze my first reaction was 'Hell and damnation, we've been rammed!' Under the rat-hole things were a shambles. Sylvia had been thrown on top of me and in her fright was wriggling like an eel screaming, 'Oh God, we are sinking darling, we are sinking!' Cursing and telling her to shut up, I tried none too gently, to push her aside so as to scramble out and see what had happened.

Hampered by the fact that we were crammed like sardines, still inside our individual sleeping bags, in pitch darkness, sloshing about in so much water we were almost floating, it was not an easy thing to do against *Britannia's* almost impossible list. Luckily, in spite of her fear, Sylvia didn't panic — not that I would have blamed her if she had, I felt quite jittery myself — and, after I raised my voice a couple of times, swearing with a bit more feeling than usual, her screams subsided into tears and at last I got out.

The wind was truly howling and I figured the waves to be all of fifteen feet high but the stars were as numerous and as brilliant as ever and aside from her list *Britannia* appeared unscathed. However her bows were pointing in the opposite direction to which they had been when I left her to look after herself, my conclusion being that we had been hit by a freak wave with such violence as to swing her round 180 degrees in a single, mighty blow. Sitting on the windward gunwale and leaning as far out as I could to counteract the weight of the water accumulated against the opposite bulwarks I gradually helped her to get upright. Once the deck was level it was a matter of seconds before she bailed herself out.

Britannia's bailing slots were along the fore and aft line, and served the double purpose of housing the rudder and two dagger boards as well. In bad weather we would unship one or the other, or all, leaving the slots free for the water to drain through, which, the deck being raised above the water line, it did quite simply by gravity. The space below deck was divided into ten separate water tight compartments where we kept most of our stores and gear. Access to them was through individual hatches, also theoretically watertight. This was the first time we had been really and truly swamped. That wave must have broken right on top of us. I have no idea how many tons of water *Britt* could hold above decks at one time but in any case this did not matter since, in practice, she would immediately lean to one side or the other and spill most of it over the gunwales. What happened was that apparently the bulwarks were too high and the water that remained inside after she tilted over was too much, and, its weight kept her listing. Since the scuppers were amidship the list not only prevented the water from sluicing out through them but kept the gunwales below sea level with the result that *Britt* could not return to an even keel on her own. So far no more than a nuisance but in very bad weather it could

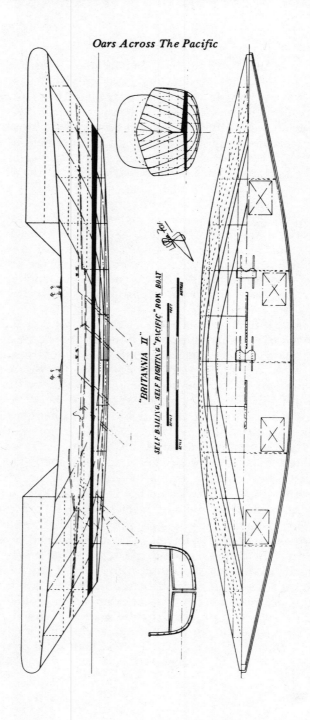

"BRITANNIA II"

SELF BAILING, SELF RIGHTING "PACIFIC" ROW BOAT

prove to be a dangerous one.

For the rudder to have survived a turnabout as sudden and violent as we had suffered would have been a blooming miracle, which was not to be. The tiller was still lashed but that was all that was left. A very good example of the consequences of rotten seamanship, made worse by the fact that I did know better. My only excuse was that with the rudder shipped I had hoped to go on making progress in the right direction by retaining at least a small measure of control over her drift. Not much, as a boat that is not under way cannot be steered, but, if one is rowing every little bit helps.

Now she lay broadside and to keep her head on to the weather I had no other choice than to stream the drogue.* We had two drogues, four feet diameter, which was rather big for a craft like *Britannia*, except that their main purpose as far as we were concerned was their braking power. Since we could not row against unfavourable winds we had to have something that would prevent, as effectively as possible, loss of conquered ground. In that context the drogues were as important to us as the oars.

Once the drogue was out and working properly, I lashed the remains of the rudder and the dagger boards, checked that everything was securely fastened in its proper place, then crawled back into the rat-hole. There was absolutely nothing else I could do.

Sylvia had obeyed my orders to remain under cover and we huddled together in an effort to get warm. We were soaked to the bones, and so cold we could not control the chattering of our teeth. Ivan had presented us with a bottle of brandy and, deciding that there would never be a better occasion, we drank his health with enthusiasm. Gradually we stopped shivering. Two hours went by and we were almost beginning to feel comfortable again when another bluster of a wave came crashing in.

This time we knew the drill. I was to go out and sit on the gunwales to straighten *Britannia*'s list while Sylvia did all she could to help by shifting her weight from the inside. In my

* A tapering canvas bag, open at both ends, also known as a sea anchor.

mind there was no great danger to the situation and I went about it in my usual parsimonious way. Sylvia thought otherwise and in her haste to push me out gave me a no nonsense 'hurry up' kick just as Britt rolled heavily under the impact of another big sea. Losing my balance I landed in the drink with a yelp. The water was as cold as ice and in spite of being thoroughly drenched already I nearly went stiff with the shock. All sluggishness gone I grabbed the gunwales and shot back on board with such impetus I almost went over board again from the other side. Sylvia never realised what happened until I told her and she is still not quite convinced that I am not fibbing. That's women for you!

Dawn's frigid greyness did little to dispel our gloom. *Britannia* was riding the drogue well, if jerkily, but the weather, which had degenerated into a moderate gale, looked as if it would get a lot worse before it got better, and we were swamped so often that cooking was out of the question. Hot soup, or even a cup of tea, became luxuries, something to dream about. To assuage our hunger we ate California Raisins and chocolate. To keep warm, Ivan's brandy, and when that went, whisky. Mostly, we starved and froze.

The gale increased in strength until my hand anemometer registered forty knots. After that, I stopped bothering with it. Twenty-five foot waves, looking twice as high, as they always do from a little boat, swamped and battered us without pause. Most of the time we spent cowering under the illusive protection of the rat hole, wet and shivering. Next, salt water boils sprouted all over our bodies, proliferating on those parts that chafed most, backs, buttocks and the inside of our thighs. Poor Sylvia, whose skin was naturally a more delicate texture than mine, was so badly affected that her backside became one big, red sore, hurting and, above all else, itching so much it nearly drove her round the bend. As long as we remained wet there could be no cure against it. In spite of the intense cold we took to stripping, once or twice a day, and smothering each other with Vaseline Petroleum Jelly, which gave us a measure of relief, lasting until the Vaseline was rubbed off by our soaked garments. Ideally, we should have remained naked to prevent any unnecessary friction but that would have turned us into solid blocks of ice.

So it went, on and on and on, until we completely forgot what it was like to live as human beings. Every day brought a new misery to be endured, a new problem to solve. Because of my stubborn refusal to wear a life line I was washed overboard several times by enormous seas breaking with irresistible force over *Britannia*, sweeping off the deck anything that was not firmly lashed. I ·didn't worry over much because riding the drogue kept *Britt* almost stationary on the water and gale or no gale I was more than confident in my ability to swim back to her.

Sylvia, however, did not share my optimism and was rather worried about the possibility of being left alone. Irresponsible, cocky little twit, was, if I remember rightly, one of the mildest things she called me. Perfectly justified too, I would have thought the same in her place, but I simply could not bring myself to live, on top of all other discomforts, permanently attached to a line that would tangle itself on to something every time I wanted to get from one end of the boat to the other in a hurry.

By the sixth day we were so ravenous that Sylvia decided to brave the elements and, come what may, boil a pint of water, so that we could eat one of the ready prepared Mountain House meals, which only needed the addition of boiling water to become as tasty a dish as any home cooked stew. Crouching in front of the galley she had been trying to keep the flame of our little gas stove alive long enough to bring the water to the boil for nearly two hours without success when, at last, there was a lull in the weather. Syl was a minute from victory when *Britannia* gave a little lurch, rose to the top of a wave and slid down the slope at the other side, crabwise. She behaved like this, sometimes, but always, in the end, responded to the bite of the drogue facing the next sea bows on.

Now she wallowed in the trough, her side utterly exposed to a mammoth breaker seemingly born out of nowhere, and tumbling towards us in a rage of spume. I was sitting near the rat hole and barely managed to yell a warning to Sylvia when I was sucked into a maelstrom of unbelievable violence, squashed, trampled and carried away like a bundle of straw.

Eventually I came up twenty odd yards from *Britannia* and for a while all I could see was her red, glistening underbelly. Thinking that she had capsized and failed to right herself, with Sylvia trapped underneath, I damn nearly surfed back, but soon realised that all was well. She was listing, as usual after a bad swamping, and I was looking at her from the wrong side. Our sleeping bags and a bundle of clothes had been washed overboard and I grabbed them before they sank. This time Sylvia was scared out of her life. The hapless little thing never saw it coming and was hit from behind while on her knees, with head and shoulders into the galley hole. It must have been a terrifying experience which she can better tell herself.

The first I knew of any crisis was a warning yell from Johnny at the far end of the boat. 'Look out, darling!' pierced high above the thundering of the waves with such obvious urgency that I grabbed the closest secured objects, lowered my head and huddled to the deck, as nearly inside the galley as its entrance would allow — in the hope of protecting my carefully nurtured flame from extinction. This time, peeping under my arm as I knelt, and seeing nothing other than the usual mountains of foam seething around us, I turned back to the galley thinking it was a false alarm. Suddenly a tremendous force overwhelmed me from behind and, as my knees were floated from beneath me, I was swept helplessly towards the valiant little flame, still struggling to produce our hot meal.

The picture of that tiny open flame rushing to within an inch of my face before mercifully being extinguished by the swirling water around us, will never fade from my memory, but then, neither will the darkness which followed as, my legs entangled in a large heavy bag of clothing, I struggled to surface from the turmoil of black salty sea.

Eventually it was light again, my head and shoulders were above water level and I was hanging on with all my might wondering what on earth had hit us and looking frantically around for the invisible Johnny. I finally saw him clutching for the gunnels at the far side of the boat. As usual after an exceptionally large wave, the sea was relatively calm and he climbed easily aboard and set about comforting me by explaining exactly what had happened. I was shaking with cold and with shock and, as he finished telling me the story, I dissolved into tears. It really was too much. It was all so miserable, and I was so frightened, and it had been so bad for so long that, at that precise moment, I felt I just could not go on.

As I sat weeping on the deck, I looked up and there, within a hundred yards of us, was a ship. She was quite small, painted a dull mid-green with white, and some of her crew were on deck waving to us and signalling if we wanted anything. Really a very ordinary little ship, but to see how horribly she wallowed in those ghastly seas, to see her cheerful crew, and to realise she had turned off course in such horrible conditions just to come and see how we were, was a real tonic. The way she yawed and rolled made me almost feel seasick to watch, and I felt so sorry for those aboard her that I forgot how frightened I had been ten minutes before, and stood up to wave back and signal that we were OK and that we didn't need a thing! She'll never know it, but she was the most important ship of our whole crossing, and left the fondest memories.

Now, having told all I ever knew of the incident, I had better pass the narrative back to our seaman so that he can explain the causes and describe the remedy.

The reason *Britannia* copped that one fully broadside was that she had lost the drogue just before we were hit. Whoever had fixed the eyebolt that carried the line of the drogue (or anchor) at the bows, forgot to strengthen the pin with a brass plate from the inside. As a result the whole thing was wrenched away and two hundred feet of line were lost as well. Luckily we had spares and, *Britannia* being a double-ender, it made no difference to her whether the drogue was streamed ahead or astern, and as long as the aft eyebolt was stronger than the one at the bows had been we would be all right.

Actually it did make a great difference, to us, because with the wind blowing from astern the galley was more protected and Sylvia was able to boil her water and fix a hot meal after all. That she had the heart to do it that very same day speaks volumes for her fortitude, and my admiration for her grew immensely. Unfortunately what was good for the galley was not good for the rathole, now at the receiving end of wind and spray. At that stage of the storm it was hard to imagine that life could become even more miserable, yet it did and what the remaining days were like is best forgotten.

Except, maybe, for one last thing. May 21st was my birthday, the second I had spent rowing in the middle of nowhere. In the Atlantic I had been washed overboard, in 180 days the only time it ever happened, and, sure enough, the Pacific was not to be outdone and swept me away twice within ten minutes. As a birthday treat Sylvia had promised me a cup of tea. She tried, but . . . oh, hell, forget it!

4. Ensenada

The gale over we were able to open the hatches for inspection. As I said before, theoretically, they were supposed to be watertight. This was of paramount importance as all our stores and equipment were stowed below deck. Finding three out of the ten compartments absolutely flooded came as a terrible shock, especially as almost everything in them was ruined beyond hope. Transistor radio, I.T.N.'s camera, film, half our stock of perishable food, sugar, rice, etcetera, to mention but a few items.

We usually kept things in polythene bags but the tiniest hole in them was all the water needed to get through. Badly fitted hatches were responsible because the hatches of *Britannia I*, my Atlantic rowing boat, had been a perfect fit and not a drop of water ever got passed them. If it had been possible to get a decent fit once, why not a second time?

More than ever now we had to reach the mainland. Without a rudder, *Britannia* was extremely hard to control. We wanted to go east and the wind, blowing from the north-north-west was not particularly helpful. The sky remained totally overcast and for once — our last known position had been the one given by the *Export Courier* — I had not the slightest idea of our whereabouts. The gale had certainly pushed us south, but how far was anybody's guess, depending on the effectiveness of the drogue, it could have been anything between one hundred and two hundred miles.

At this point Johnny passes the narrative back to me — seems to have got tired — a not infrequent occurrence ashore but, I am glad to say, a rare happening at sea. In fact our respective roles were reversed as soon as we stepped aboard. It became Johnny who was telling me to tidy up and do this, that and the other, and I who was comparatively helpless. At home Johnny never lifts a finger, never knows where anything is, and doesn't know one end of a screwdriver from the other. After showing me the full range of his skills at sea, even to the point of dissecting the generator and fiddling about with the battery leads, I swore his home days of idleness were over, but now it seems as though I went to sea with a different person. My energetic mechanical genius of days gone by has long departed, leaving me with the same comfortable, easy-going 'don't knower' with whom I was so happy with before the trip.

Now, with the ravages of the gale to contend with, Johnny was a very worried man. We were not quite sure that we had even seen the end of the gale. The whole time we had been afloat, the weather had been cold, the wind had come and gone without warning and the condition of the sea had changed only from choppy to very rough. The sun being out made it worse than ever. It seemed to mock us from a cold blue sky, whilst the seas crashed around us and the wind roared and screamed across the ocean's vastness, whipping up the spray in swirling white sheets.

Before the real gale, we had gone through a couple of mini-gales, with only a few more moderate days between. It was a nightmare but I told myself it could not always be this way at sea. Actually, I had no idea what it could be like but consoled myself by thinking if it were always that bad no-one would ever leave the coast. After four weeks I cheered up a bit by calculating that, if the journey were to take ten months, which is forty-three weeks, this meant that we must have done nearly a tenth of it. Continuing in the same vein, I convinced myself that it was sure to get warmer as we neared the Equator and, in that respect at least, it must get better.

The one nice part of these weeks were the seals. They always seemed to be alone, drifting in their sleep as much as a hundred miles from land. They slept afloat, looking like an open triangle of driftwood, and when disturbed would dive immediately, resurfacing for a quick look before swimming away. Once we were very close to one before she woke up and, in her fright, she did three beautiful curved leaps forming a crescent about thirty feet from us.

One afternoon I was sleeping when a funny short, croaking bark woke me. Slowly I crawled quietly out of the rathole and there, within ten feet of the boat, was the bewhiskered face of a young seal, craning her neck to see what *Britoo* was all about. She had absolutely huge black eyes nearly bursting from her head with curiosity. She swam and dived around us for a while, pulling herself up from the water, and making a weird hoarse bark as she stretched her cute little round nose as high as it would go in her efforts to see inside *Britoo*. Finally she became so bold that I swear she was on the verge of jumping in, which would have proved injurious, if not fatal, so I made a sudden movement and noise and away she went.

Otherwise the only interesting feature of the trip so far had been, for want of a better name, my 'face in the water'! What it was I had, and have, no idea. It was on one of our calmer days and, as I washed a teaspoon over the side, I watched this strange face coming up towards me. I continued to watch it, rather as one watches flames flickering in a fire, not really registering that it was real. It had a much bigger head than mine, with a large round face encircled by a ruff something like a circus dog's. Its nose was big and dark and it had huge round eyes. Somehow it looked furry but was definitely not a seal, or anything I have ever seen a picture of. As I was vacantly watching its approach, it must have been watching me in the same way for, as I moved, it suddenly turned — giving me the shock of my life as I suddenly appreciated its reality — and I screamed. Looking back, it had gone. What on earth was it?

There was little else worthy of mention. It was just a dreary slog for land coupled with a constant longing for better weather. If it had either become more comfortable or even if the wind had co-operated a little better, we would have been happy. But no, the misery continued. Birds were few and far between, the seals were no more, and we had no idea where we were.

Eventually we saw the welcome grey smudge of land far away to our eastern horizon. It seemed as if we would be

ashore within a couple of days and we could hardly believe
it — which was just as well, because it was another ten days
before we actually landed.

Miserably cold, wet and sore, with a north/north-easterly
wind blowing at about fifteen knots or more, we struggled
towards that elusive coastline for the next five days. Our goal
was the glow of a distant town which we wished to be Los
Angeles, assumed to be San Diego, and which turned out to
be neither. Slowly the coastline grew nearer until we could
see the outline of the rocks separating us from the lights of
the town, but it was a sheer, deserted stretch of cliff without
a sign of life. One night we were close enough to distinguish
tiny individual points of light, two stationary and two
moving in a most mysterious way, drawing together, then
parting to continue their own erratic courses. We watched till
about midnight when three of them vanished, leaving a
solitary static pinpoint of light till morning.

I got quite excited about all this and decided they must be
smugglers rendezvousing in the dead of night, but we later
discovered they were nothing more sinister than little sardine
fishing boats.

As the town's glow receded to our north, the cliffs to our
east became clearer until we could see their rich redness and
distinguish weird craggy shapes, whilst watching their splendid hues changing from flame to crimson in the reflection of
the setting sun. Very beautiful and all that, but where the
hell were we? It was still too overcast to take sights and there
was still no sign of life. The next day we made for the shore,
apparently only an hour or two's rowing away, to our east.

We had our first big row that day. Rowing separately we
were making no headway whatsoever, so we decided the only
solution would be really hard rowing together. Problem was
we both had our own ideas on the best tactics, and our own
styles of rowing, so we sweated and cursed and almost came
to blows. Even so it wasn't until dusk that we were close
enough to examine the possibility of anchoring thereabouts.

The sea had huge patches of thick floating weed lying in a
belt quarter of a mile offshore and, having navigated around
these with reasonable success, once we were inside the water

seemed to go right up to the cliff with no beach whatsoever and, as far as we could tell, no shallow water suitable for anchoring. We scanned the cliff with our rather mouldy pair of small binoculars until we saw what could have been a little fisherman's hut in a small bay. As this was the only sign of life, we headed for it as best we could, desperately hoping there was a bay, even if the hut was an optical illusion, so that we could anchor for the night, rather than drift around, the aimless prey of rocks and desolate cliffs.

We made it just before dark and dropped anchor about two hundred yards from the little gaily painted fishing dinghies lying on the beach. The fishermen came and went from their hut but paid us no attention whatsoever, almost as if they were used to boats like *Britannia II* anchoring on their doorstep. We watched them light a beautiful cosy fire on the clifftop and, whilst we sat cold and miserable, sit around chatting and taking their evening meal. Then they drove away — an odd set-up, cars but no electricity, primitive wooden boats, but outboard motors — but how sad they had gone. Would they be back tomorrow, or next week?

A very funny thing happened that night. Due to the proximity of the fishermen and their ladies, I had been obliged to postpone using the loo-rope until after dark, which seemed to upset my metabolism altogether, because I had to crawl out a couple of times in the middle of the night to hang over the side. On the last of these occasions I was holding on quite securely, with my poor pimply backside hanging overboard, listening to the snorts of distant dolphins, as I thought, when there was a loud violent snort to beat all snorts right beside my left elbow. I hurled myself amidships, and fled stumbling along our cluttered deck to arrive breathless and bruised beside a most incredulous Johnny, anything but amused at having been so unceremoniously woken from his most blissful sleep in weeks.

The next morning the fishermen were back and we watched them launch two boats, start their outboard motors and chug off without a word, passing less than a hundred yards from us and nonchalantly weaving their way through the school of porpoises which had caused my horrible scare of the previous night. A third boat was launched and, apparently unable to start its motor (from mechanical defect or curiosity, we shall never know!), drifted towards us with a cheery '*Buenos dias*!'.

The speaker was a handsome Mexican in a diving suit who informed us that the lights we had seen were those of Ensenada, sixty miles south of San Diego and forty miles north of our present position. He told us that it was a tuna and sardine fishing port with a sizeable boatyard and that it was our nearest town. He could offer us no advice on how we could get to Ensenada, other than to tell us that there was a large cement quarry a mile or so up the coast. At noon he returned with a boatload of abalone and gave us a couple and instructions on how to cook them. A real delicacy, what a treat!

All that day we stayed at anchor in the fishermen's bay unwilling to attempt reaching the quarry in the strong wind still prevailing. The next day, being Sunday, we decided the quarry would be deserted, so we stayed at anchor again. I must confess that I behaved very badly and spent most of these days watching the cars coming and going from the fishing huts, watching the two resident women walking about with their buckets and their washing, and, to put it bluntly, generally spying on the little fishing fraternity through our misty binoculars. I never did manage to make either pattern or reason of their activities. I excuse myself on the grounds of having been isolated for what then seemed so long, and never having seen people living in such a basic way before. It was naughty and fun, but never did make sense.

At dawn the following day we lifted the anchor and rowed to the cement quarry which, to our surprise, we reached after a couple of hours. There was a very sheltered bay beneath the cliff and here we anchored. Johnny put on his wetsuit and swam to the shore and I watched him climb out of the water, amidst the huge sharp rocks bordering the bay, with some trepidation. Then I took out the binoculars to watch him climb over two hundred feet of jagged cliff to the path winding along to the quarry.

I sat huddled in the shelter of the rathole, dry but

shivering whilst poor Johnny had dived into water so cold, he later told me, that it had hurt his head, and was now plodding along wet, cold and barefoot over a dusty, unmade-up path, still wearing his rubber suit.

'He's gone plodding off into the unknown, looking like a ruddy Martian, to return God knows when, and I'm stuck here like a lemon,' I thought ungraciously. 'What the hell shall I do if the anchor doesn't hold?'

Deciding there was no reason why it shouldn't. I got the binoculars again, this time to watch the goings on of the cement plant. They were pretty few and far between, so I soon got bored and started to think about the anchor again. I didn't like what I thought so got out the transistor and tuned into a Mexican station in an attempt to improve my few words of Spanish. My few words were not enough to enjoy anything so, once again, I drifted into thinking about the anchor. This time I resorted to my infallible solution to worries, I went to sleep.

Shortly after midday Johnny returned saying that he had approached a worker at the quarry with a kind of 'take me to your leader' remark and had been ushered into the manager's office. The manager had kindly telephoned his head office in Ensenada and explained our circumstances to Sir Albino Huerta, the Company's Personnel Officer, who had asked that a car be put at John's disposal and that he be offered every assistance.

Johnny had now returned to *Britoo* to tell me he was off to Ensenada to arrange for *Britoo* to be towed back there and to cable London to send some money for boat repairs, a new rudder, and living expenses whilst these were being carried out. With him he had brought a huge bundle of foil wrapped tortillas which he had carried over his head during his swim back to *Britoo* and, when he left again fifteen minutes later, that was how he carried his city going clothes drily ashore.

Once he had left I tried the radio again but gave up in disgust and went back to sleep. I woke to find it was getting dark, that I was still alone, and, worse still, the boat seemed to be at a different angle to the cliffs than it had been all day. I leapt up out of the rathole to take a better look. Horror of horrors, the wind had changed! Now it was beginning to blow offshore and I was going with it.

'Now, don't panic, Keep cool. Find a spot ashore, line it up with part of the boat, stay still and watch it,' so I counselled myself, wisely.

The problem was that I only proved my worst suspicions well founded, the boat was moving quite fast, definitely dragging the anchor, if not completely free, and was inevitably bound, as far as I could see, to either wreck on the rocks fifty yards away or else just miss them and be blown out to sea for . . . how long?

'Well, if she drifts out she won't go far before Johnny returns and alerts help and then they'll find me. What I must prevent, at all costs, is piling up on those vicious looking rocks.'

So, I grabbed the ,oars and rowed like a maniac in an attempt to turn her, but she and the wind were too much for me to handle. I tried and tried. It was a desperate situation, and I couldn't cope. We were sure to wreck any minute. I began to cry, from fear of wrecking, fear of failure, and fear of the wrath of Johnny. A couple of lorries from the cement quarry were manoevering on the little path above and one of their drivers was signalling me to swim — but if I did, assuming I could, what of poor little *Britoo*? I had to get her round. More crazy, frantic rowing to no avail. Then, quite suddenly, I realised it was hopeless, I could do nothing so I might as well go back to sleep.

The next time I woke up it was completely dark and I could hear voices. I was still at the foot of the cliffs and there were a couple of torches moving on the rocky beach. It was midnight, and Johnny was swimming back at last. Thank heavens I had gone to sleep, what a long, long evening I would have passed waiting alone with my fears.

Johnny enjoyed a good laugh at my expense when I told him of my imagined crisis, and he explained that onshore winds often become offshore at night, due to the land cooling faster than the sea and hot air rising, and that the change of position had only been the boat swinging on her anchor line as a result of this and the changing tide. I then heard how he had been driven to Ensenada and how kind and helpful Sr Huerta and his company had been, but that there was no possibility of a tow the following day because he had arrived in the town too late and found the Port Offices closed for the night. Furthermore, they would not open on the morrow, this being 'Sailors Day' and a National Holiday.

Another complication had arisen because the telephone exchange had refused to accept a reverse charges call to England and Johnny had no money. We would have to remain at anchor all the next day and, in all probability, the following day too, before the tow would be forthcoming. What a dreary prospect, but at least we had contacted civilisation and it was now only a question of time.

The next day passed with binoculars, tortillas and jam, lots of extra sleep and more boredom. The following day we were awake bright and early and Johnny dived into the icy water and swam ashore with his tightly packed clothes over his head. I doodled the morning away until I heard the chug of an outboard motor around mid-day. It was our fisherman come to check on our progress. I told him, in my miserably broken Spanish, and he presented me with another abalone and went his way.

I couldn't resist asking him his name just as he was leaving, probably atrocious manners for Mexico but we'd been calling him Pedro all along (Pedro the Fisherman la-la la la-a . . .) which seemed rather unfair. It turned out to be Enrico, but as we never saw him again, I suppose it doesn't matter much anyway.

Scanning the horizon with the faithful binoculars around four in the afternoon, I saw a ship, seemingly anchored a couple of miles away and a raftlike contraption carrying about eight men heading for me. I didn't associate the two but wondered what on earth those men were doing on a raft out there, I even began to worry that they might be shipwrecked, pretty arrogant for one sitting in a powerless, rudderless boat waiting for help. They came within a few yards, coiling a rope which they were about to throw to me. Eight swarthy, happy-looking Mexicans all speaking at once, loud, fast Spanish, and all gesticulating at me to co-operate.

To be honest they had me worried, they certainly seemed friendly but what on earth did they want?

Eventually I managed, 'Thank you very much but I do not need any help. All is well. I am waiting for my friend.' A trifle inaccurate under the circumstances, but the best my Spanish could manage. During the stunned silence, head scratching and muttered conference following my astounding remarks, a sudden shout and pointing drew my attention to Johnny swimming back to *Britoo*. It was rather like the Mounties to the rescue.

The solution was that Johnny's visit to the town had been so promptly acted upon that the radio message of our plight had reached our rescuers before Johnny had reached us. The men on the panga (flatboat carried aboard some fishing boats for the purpose of setting the nets) had come from the trawler I had seen through the binoculars, in reply to the call for aid. Johnny's fluent Spanish soon had all our problems sorted out and we were taken to the Santa Isabel who towed us into Ensenada.

Johnny refused their invitation to go aboard during the tow, as he felt the Captain must stay with his ship, but insisted that I travel on the Santa Isabel because for me to remain on *Britannia* would be too dangerous. Once we were under way, I began to see why, she really did seem to be taking punishment as she dipped and swung in the trawler's wake. In fact it became quite a joke for the crew to say, 'Oh, yes, the boat is there, but John . . .?'

They were a jolly bunch and, although only their Fish Captain,* Manuel Aguirre spoke English, were very friendly so, besides treating me to my best meal since San Francisco, gave me a thoroughly enjoyable ride. I will never forget that meal. Whether it was a special celebration, being their last aboard after two months at sea, or whether they always ate that well, I will never know, but it was a feast indeed.

Another reason I have for remembering it was that it was my first temptation to smoke since stepping into *Britoo* in

* Trawlers generally have two Captains, one who looks after the ship and another responsible for the fishing side.

San Francisco with a cigarette in my mouth, smoking forty a day, five weeks ago. The fishermen all produced their cigarettes after eating and courteously offered them to me, one by one, but I decided that, after abstaining for so long, to accept at the first provocation would put me back on the road to ruin.

About eight o'clock men began to re-appear, cleanly shaven, combed hair and smartly dressed, whilst the ship took on an air of eager anticipation. Captain Aguirre took me up on the bridge and there was the cause of the excitement, the pretty little coloured lights of Ensenada flickering out of the night across the bay. We had rounded the point and faced the town across the harbour. These men were coming home to their families after more than eight weeks hard fishing.

Perhaps this would be a good time to explain why we had needed a tow in the first place, and why the town's lights had receded from us the nearer we had rowed to the coast. Because we were a heavy rowing boat with little draught and much windage, we were at the mercy of the winds and had very limited manoeuvrability. Losing our rudder had left us even less control than usual. As we had rowed eastwards towards the coast, the wind had steadily blown us south, so that, although when we had first seen the flow of Ensenada, it had been directly east of us, by the time we arrived at our anchorage off Punta China, we had been blown forty miles south.

At this rate it was obvious that in trying to reach the town under our own steam, we would only be blown further and further from it, and there were no other towns for over a thousand miles south along Baja California's desolate coastline.

As the Santa Isabel approached the harbour, I discovered the explanation for the two stationary lights we had seen on the night of the sardine boats. They were lighthouses, one situated on the south-western tip of the bay housing Ensenada, at Punta Banda, and the other was sitting on the Island at the entrance to the bay. As we had gone south-east, the point itself had completely obscured the light from the Island.

It was past ten on 3rd June, our thirty-ninth day from San Francisco, when we had tied up alongside a panga in Astilleros Rodriques, S.A., the government-owned shipyard of Ensenada. Captain Manuel Riveros Rotge, Captain of the Port of Ensenada, had turned out with his wife to welcome us and guide us through the embarking formalities. Smartly dressed in his full gold-braided uniform, the Captain was now clambering over the oily barges and fishy pangas as he kindly helped us to tie up. Having done so, he drove us to the Cortez Motel, managed by Don Fernando Kellenberger, the brother-in-law of Sir Huerta of Cementos California, S.A., who had made the booking for us. With such kindness and efficiency, even before our arrival, and the quick glance of the town I had during the ride, I knew I would like Ensenada and the Mexicans.

Amazingly we checked into the hotel to find a message waiting for us from Ivan Sharpe, already on his way to Ensenada from San Francisco with a photographer. They arrived at 1 a.m., which I considered pretty fast going, even for journalists, and we sat around and chatted until about two. Johnny and I, deciding enough was enough, chucked Ivan and Ira out, then had a lovely hot shower before going to bed, feeling clean for the first time in weeks, although my hair remained so filthy that I covered the clear white pillowslip before I dared to lie on it.

Next morning, my hair still wet from its first wash in five weeks, we went straight to Captain Botge's office to clear the customs and shipping formalities, as we had promised the previous night. I would swear we each signed a minimum of eight copies of two enormously long, hand-typed official documents before we left to visit the shipyard.

On arrival we were introduced to Mr Nichicagua, the manager, who took over poor leaky little *Britoo* and advised us where to shop for our lost or ruined gear. After that we went to the town to buy some clothes for Johnny and myself, still walking around in our rowing togs which were hardly suitable for strolling about in civilisation. Ira Block, the photographer who had come with Ivan, took lots of pictures of us both parading around stores in various outfits before making our final selection and the whole expedition was fun. I did have one problem, in that I had jettisoned my bra because it chafed, and those in the store were exaggeratedly stiff and pointed so, from the less of two evils rather than choice, I went without for a couple more days.

Later in the day we were joined by Ken Allen who had come down from San Francisco on behalf of I.T.N. Ken wanted us back in our grimy old rowing clothes for an interview in *Britoo*, so we didn't wear our smart new regalia for very long before going back to the boatyard for more talk and pictures. Whilst there, we thought we might as well hand over to Ken all the film and still pictures we had taken on the trip so far but, when we looked in the pocket lining the rathole, where we had left the movie camera and exposed films the night before, to our horror the case containing the whole lot had gone, vanished without a trace. Obviously, in spite of the night guard at the gated entrance to the yard, some light fingered body had been there before us. We felt rather bad about this because, already having ruined one of their camera by salt water, we now had to tell I.T.N. that the other had been stolen.

Before *Britoo* could be taken out of the water for repairs, we had to empty her completely of all stores and water. Mr Nichicagua had put an empty lock-up shed at our disposal so we had somewhere safe to put it all, a great weight off our minds, but nevertheless it was arduous work. The miserable weather had left us now and Ensenada basked windlessly beneath a typical Mexican sun, while we trudged backwards and forwards with our mountains of gear. There were a few privately owned pleasure boats around and it wasn't long before we were on nodding terms with several of their occupants, mostly Americans.

It was in this way that we became friends with Ken and Lupita Gunderson, who were rebuilding a huge yacht moored the other side of our pier. They were a great help to us. Ken seemed to possess every tool and gadget we ever thought we needed, whilst Lupita seemed to be constantly offering cups of coffee.

Just before we left Ensenada, Ken mentioned that raw eggs

can be preserved for months by a sealed coating of wax, and Lupita added that it would be great for Johnny and I to eat fried eggs on the Equator, so she would make them for us. Some time before our arrival at Washington Island, I noticed a very strong smell coming from one of the hatches and asked John to check that no leaking gas canisters were inside. He reported that all was well, but the stench continued, and I was constantly shouting at him not to open the hatch when smoking, just in case.

It wasn't until he was re-arranging the stores off Washington Island, over three months later, that he discovered the source of the foul stink was a dozen bad eggs! How bad they must have been to have penetrated their own wax, and box, and all else, I dread to think. Poor Lupita, all that trouble! And poor us, no fried eggs on the Equator!

Ensenada is called the Cinderella of the Pacific, not because she was riches turned now to rags, but because she is so full of cinders. I think this has probably been vastly improved recently because, although many of the town's roads are still little more than dust tracks, the main streets are well maintained and there are good roads leading out of the town. Even so, joy-riding was a precarious business as one never knew when the nice smart road one was travelling would suddenly become a boulder strewn track interlaced with foot deep ditches; not the ideal situation for a huge low American car. However, this all added to its charm in my eyes and I loved it.

The houses were generally small single-storeyed and brightly painted with tiny windows and set in little gardens or yards, but if one drove up the bordering hills, they became grand Spanish style mansions with swimming pools and magnificent views overlooking the town and harbour. There didn't appear to be the great mass of extremely poor ruled by the élite few enormously rich that one is led to believe of South America, but maybe things are changing fast nowadays or, possibly, the American tourists who flock to Ensenada at weekends, have given the town an economic boost. It seemed a happy place and even the tiniest hardboard constructed houses frequently had a television, refrigerator or car.

After the feverish activity of our first day ashore, my legs and hips ached horribly from the unaccustomed walking, but I was dying to get to the shops. Normally I am not a very enthusiastic shopper — I can never find anything I like, and the crowds make me bad tempered after half an hour, but here I had seen such beautiful things I was itching to have a closer look, and it did seem that I had been missing clothes and the niceties of life for quite a while already.

Actually I had even dreamt of clothes and the strange part was that I had seen a dress exactly the same as one I had dreamt I was buying in Sydney after our arrival. It was off-white cotton, floor length with a high neck, long sleeves and covered with lace and tucks. Not at all my type of thing but perfect for someone delicate and pretty and, after all that mess, I felt like trying to be exactly that. Eventually I dragged Ivan, Johnny and Ira to the shop housing this masterpiece of femininity, and they all said it was quite impractical and utterly ridiculous for someone like me. I was most upset at the time, but they were, I am sorry to say, so very right.

Other than all sorts of gorgeous hand embroidered or lace worked clothes in any style or colour imaginable, Ensenada was rich in beautiful pottery, jewellery, leather goods and onyx, all painstakingly made by hand and for sale at, by our standards, unbelievably low prices. The great tragedy was that we had no money and no facilities for transporting our purchases home.

With the arrival of Ivan, our immediate money problems were solved. Don Fernando was letting us stay at the Cortez Motel free of charge and *The Sunday People* had authorised Ivan to look after our day to day living expenses until our departure. Ivan also had a huge car which solved our transport difficulties. Even so we needed money to replace ruined equipment and restock our larder, besides making one or two additions to *Britoo* which, in the light of recent experiences, seemed like a good idea . . . Johnny had telephoned George for some cash as soon as we had arrived, but a week had passed without sign of the promised money. Apart from the discomfort of walking around penniless and dependent, this meant that we had been unable to do one jot of the long list of *Britoo* shopping we carried around. The boat repairs were well under way and, in spite of liking the place, the last thing we wanted was to be waiting around for cash; once the boat and radio were ready, we wanted to leave.

When he had heard, via the *Export Courier*, that our radio was not operating and we were returning to Los Angeles for repairs, Ivan had been pretty busy. Aside from alerting the coastguards and staging a full scale search on our behalf, including chartering planes to circle the area, he had sought out the one man everyone said would be able to repair or amend our set.

His name was Butch Mason and he came especially down from Los Angeles to get our Marconi working. With him came his wife who was roped in for several jobs to help the cause, but never seemed to mind, and stayed patient and smiling throughout the four days or so of their visit. Butch decided we had been fitted with the wrong crystals and given the wrong aerial and that we hadn't a hope in hell of it working like that. He changed both and spent and awful long time dissecting our little box of tricks, finally concluding that 'it's a can of worms. Anything can happen at any time or it could go on for ever – which is unlikely'. As Butch is one of the foremost marine radio experts, we had to take his word for it and keep our fingers crossed.

There was still no sign of our cash so Johnny phoned George to find out whether it had been sent. The news was bad. George had cabled to Oliver Swan in New York for him to send it but there had, unbeknown to him, been a cable strike in New York at the time so that, when Johnny telephoned Oliver Swan, he had said, 'Money? What money?' and knew nothing about it. At the same time Ivan had announced at dinner, completely out of the blue as far as we were concerned, that he didn't know where we thought the following morning's breakfast was coming from because he had no more cash, there had been a delay in its reaching him from London. Finally Johnny and Ivan both arranged for funds to wait for them over the border in San Diego. Ivan's arrived two days later and ours the day after that.

Weekly bullfights were advertised in Ensenada and, never having seen one, I suggested we went along. Ivan's wife, Ann, had joined him for the weekend and the four of us trooped along to what must have been a typical small town Mexican bullfight. The first bull to appear looked pathetically little and young and certainly had no intention whatsoever of fighting anyone. He just wanted to be left in peace and quiet. The matador was an American girl, blonde and pretty but as hopeless as the bull where the fight was concerned. By the time the picadors had managed to drag some activity out of the by now half dead bull, she looked more terrified than he ever had, and made a really long drawn out butchery of the kill. In fact it was so bad that the crowd were booing unmercifully and shouting abuse at her, including advice for her to go back to her kitchen and wash dishes!

It was a rather nauseating performance and the only reason I stayed after this was in the hope that one of the bulls would put a horn through someone's backside but, regrettably, they were far too stupid. The amazing part of the whole business was that there were girls with their girlfriends, mothers with their daughters, and whole family outings, complete with toddlers, attending the spectacle, and that, poor as we might consider them, they had all managed to find their two dollars per head admission money.

An hour or so later I watched a small open van drive past below our hotel window with the body of a young bull lying stiff with his legs up in the air, slung in the back of it. An ignoble ending to what could have become a noble beast had he been allowed to grow.

We have another Mexican friend, so far unmentioned, who threw all his spare time into our caper, a seventeen year old schoolboy called Antonio Rosales Green — Green because his paternal grandfather had been Scottish. Antonio had been part-time bell boy at Ivan's hotel and had shown interest in Johnny's diving equipment as we moved it into the room. He told us that he was starting a diving club in Ensenada and he was very enthusiastic about our trip and offered every assistance. I asked him how he had come to get his job, to

which he had replied that he had just hung around and
started doing it for the tips. One day the manager had
noticed him and asked him what he was doing always hanging
around the lobby and Antonio had replied, 'I'm the new
bell-boy', to which the manager had nodded his approval and
Antonio had stayed, unpaid but well-tipped. And enterprising
schoolboy who should go far!

During the weekend Ann Sharpe was with us, we asked
Antonio whether he knew of any local tourist attractions or
beauty spots. He told us there was a blow-hole nearby so we
invited him to come with us and off we went. It was half-way
to where Johnny and I had been at anchor and was a spot
where the sea crashes between rocks against the cliff. The
blow-hole is caused by the waves being driven under cliffs
and rocks at great pressure until they reach an open topped
cave, where they explode in great spurting jets of water,
fountaining up sixty or more feet above the rocks. A strange,
rather frightening place, full of thunderous roars and
rumbles.

To make our expedition more interesting, Johnny clambered up the wet cliff above the water spout to a horribly
insecure looking ledge far, far above any other spectator. Ivan
followed part way, but at least had the sense not to go that
far. Antonio had more sense than either of them and stayed
with Ann and me on the concrete and railed observation
platform. Ann and I got so nervous and angry watching our
two men playing goats that we left them and stalked back to
the car in a big huff.

One very nice thing about Ensenada was the musicians.
They wandered around, usually in threes, with guitars and
suchlike, making a tour of the restaurants, bars, swimming
pools, and anywhere loungers could be found. Apart from
their lovely Mexican music, the very pleasing part is that it is
the Mexicans themselves, rather than the tourists, who ask
them to play and keep them for hours at their tables. In this
way many enjoyable sing-songs grow. Surprisingly in Ensenada we heard incredibly little American or English pop music,
they have better taste and prefer their own tunes and lyrics
with a tale to tell.

We had our own memorable musical evening at a country
bar one night during our stay. It all happened through Sparky
Green and his girlfriend, Joy, who were staying in a large
caravan just outside the town. Sparky had breezed into our
hotel room on the third day of our stay intending to write
our story for the *Los Angeles Times* but, due to some
internal mix-up beyond our control, we had been interviewed
by a reporter from that paper the previous day, and poor
Sparky, having come down from Los Angeles especially for
that, had no story. He had shrugged that it didn't matter,
refused our offer of a drink and returned to Los Angeles
immediately. A couple of days later, when we were working
at the boatyard, he had re-appeared asking if we would mind
being interviewed for other papers instead. He was twenty-
three, bright and breezy with curly blonde hair and bags of
enthusiasm. A couple of minutes after arriving at the
boatyard he took a sharkstooth necklace from his neck and
gave it to me. He had worn it for good luck for years but now
said I needed it more than him. It seemed to have been a
good omen because I wore it all the way to Australia and
arrived in one piece.

Johnny and I hit it off pretty well with Sparky and Joy
and one night they came along and said their landlord had
told them a friend of his, a bar owner, had caught a forty
pound yellow-tail and was hoping for some volunteers to help
him eat it up. Ivan had gone to San Diego and Ken was back
in San Francisco so, together with Ira, we drove out of town
through some of Ensenada's famed roads in the country for
our fish supper. The fish was lying on a charcoal barbecue in
the backyard, smelling out of this world. Our host was the
only other diner and the six of us set about demolishing it
with our bare hands, a glass of wine, and such gusto that half
an hour later only the head and spine remained. It was the
most delicious fish I have ever tasted.

Once the fish was gone we drifted into the deserted bar
and started playing pool but Joy, who is a professional night
club singer, spotted the owner's guitar and asked if she might
give us a song. The two of them had fine voices and spent the
rest of the night passing the guitar backwards and forwards

playing and singing delightful ballads and folk songs, whilst the rest of us got blissfully tight, continuing to play crazier and crazier pool.

Many of our requirements were not available in Ensenada so Johnny and I had to make several shopping excursions into San Diego, completing our list just about when *Britannia II*'s repairs were in order, but then Johnny noticed that the boatyard had not fixed a reinforcing plate behind the eyebolt which was to hold our drogue and anchor. A very serious oversight since, without this, it would not be strong enough to stand the terrific pressure likely to be put upon it during use. This delayed us yet again, but eventually we were ready to go.

Departure eve we went to an Italian restaurant where we all got a wee bit tipsy and played a rather cruel joke on Ivan, who was footing the bill. After the meal Ivan popped off to the loo, leaving his wallet on the table. With the full co-operation of those present, I took the wallet and sat on it, so that when our victim went to pay the bill he discovered the loss. Poor Ivan, took it all extremely well and a great deal of horseplay ensued, culminating in Ira being thrown, fully dressed, into the hotel's swimming pool around midnight.

If this was our English farewell party, our second time in Ensenada we had a Mexican adieu, Johnny's birthday party of 24th June. Mexicans have two birthdays, the anniversary of the day of their own birth and the anniversary of the birth of the Saint after whom they are named. It came as quite a surprise to use when Sr Huerta and Don Fernando told Johnny that it was his Saint's day, so they were inviting us to dine with them and their wives. We were taken to a most attractive floating seafood restaurant in the harbour and, after a delicious dinner, a beautifully decorated birthday cake, baked by Sra Huerta, was produced.

Obviously the conversation was all in Spanish and, although I managed to follow most of it, I said very little until Johnny made me so angry — babbling on about the English getting married one week and divorced the next, to the great expense of the husband and satisfaction of the wife — that I surprise them all, and myself, by coming out with a rather hot retort in perfect Spanish. It was very funny because it was only the wine that had given me the courage to say anything at all.

I hope I haven't given the totally erroneous impression that our stay in Ensenada was one long round of revelry. Most of the time we were rushing around working like slaves. In fact it was San Francisco all over again. We had emptied *Britoo* completely, bought much new equipment and fresh supplies which we had had to repack in waterproof containers. A lot of time had been spent looking for a few difficult articles and regular visits to San Diego, sixty miles away, had been time consuming and tiring.

Having finished with all this, we had to restow completely, refill the water tanks and relash our stores to the deck. In the middle of everything we had noticed some of our gas cylinders were leaking through rust, and Ken Gunderson had given us some anti-rust paint with which Ivan and Ira had painted the whole blooming lot. One way and the other we had been busy the whole time and it had been hard work, but the evenings had been our own, as the boatyard was locked and guarded with strict security controls after sunset.

Despite difficulties and mishaps, eventually we were ready to go, and I feel it fitting that our departure be described by the Captain.

5. Settling down to life afloat

We left Ensenada at last at 16.30 on June 17th. The Mayor of the city came to see us off and all of a sudden a mariachis band appeared on the quayside and played Mexican music. The whole show had been planned in great secrecy by Sparky and it was really quite moving, but it was all a bit much for Sylvia.

The Mayor presented us with an envelope of adhesive Ensenada pennants and the Chamber of Commerce brought a large red and white banner — all totally unexpected, very gay and typically Mexican. Sparky, Joy, Ken, Ivan, Ira and Antonio came along with us for a couple of hours in hired motorboats taking pictures, and before they turned back we tested the radio by calling KMI.

Sylvia cried a bit and felt very sad. She never likes leaving people, especially if they have been kind to us, and the emotional farewells had left her depressed and irritable. When I tried to cheer her up she snapped my head off, asking me what made me think I was so great that no-one else mattered. It must have sounded daft even to Sylvia, for she had to laugh at herself and that cheered her up anyway.

I wrote in my log:

'At night light west breeze stopped and we were able to row out of the bay without effort. Everything seems OK. About time. Time we were off anyhow.'

I should have known better. I certainly shouldn't have written, on the fourth day out:

'Spent a couple of hours sunbathing. Starry nights. Beautiful. Maybe our problems are over for the time being.'

From John's Log

21.6.71   57th day
'Shortly after breakfast Sylvia suddenly yelled, "We've lost
our rudder!" Of course I thought she was joking. She wasn't.
How could it happen? A brief inspection showed that
whoever did the job at the boatyard forgot to put a pin in the
bolt and the rudder just slid into the sea. My comments at
this stage are unprintable. There was nothing to do but turn
back for Ensenada, by now between 80 to 100 miles to the
N.E. of our present position. To go without rudder would
make things so difficult it's almost impossible. Got in touch
with Ivan by radio and explained situation. He will phone
boatyard to ask for new rudder to be ready by the time we
get back, so we don't lose too much time. As for us, we feel
extremely bitter about it but there is nothing we can do.
Hope to sight trawler going towards Ensenada to ask a
tow — we'll see. Weather calm but overcast; cannot take
position.'

We didn't have any luck for a couple of days, which was
depressing, but on June 23rd a new trawler, the *Mazatlan*
spotted us, turned round and took us in tow. She had been
bought in Spain and was being delivered to Ensenada, and it
was very good of her skipper and crew to put themselves out
for us. Considering they had been at sea for more than two
months and were all anxious to return to their families, here
we were slowing them down and delaying their homecoming.
    Sylvia went aboard for a good meal of bacon and eggs
('Delicious!' she said) but I stayed on board *Britt* to look
after things. Planing along in the wake of the *Mazatlan* was a
change from rowing! Sylvia said our little boat looked like a
submarine at times, and there was no knowing if I was still
with her or not. Sylvia's log tells what happened next.

'The tow had begun about 6.30 and we arrived in the harbour
about 2 p.m. The *Mazatlan* slowed to take the rope from
Johnny, but pulled *Britt* alongside too close. I could see her
sharp Plastazote bow coming straight for the iron side of the

Mazatlan. Johnny shouted to me to push her off with my foot, but the side was too high and, thinking it would be all right if I were quick enough, I used my hand instead. My hand really got a bad squash and I'm lucky it didn't break. To add insult to injury it was a useless injury as poor *Britannia*'s bow acquired yet another dent. I climbed down into *Britannia* and, once free, Johnny rowed her round to our dock of last week. We had arrived in Ensenada for the second time with twenty dollars in our pocket, and once again everyone was fabulous.'

Back in London they apparently thought we had had enough and wanted to give up. What rubbish! Don Fernando very kindly let us stay free at the Hotel Cortez, and we rested up while the new rudder was being fixed. I also got a spare in case the same thing happened again. The only untoward happening was that we were robbed – again – this time of our two Nikonos II cameras. We had to borrow a car and drive to San Diego for a replacement, and that wasted another day. Then we were off again – and this time it was for real.

From Sylvia's Log

'Our scheduled departure time of 5 p.m. yesterday went awry in typical Mexican style. Finally we were towed out of the harbour about eight by a different boat. They left us at 9.15 well past the point and past the island. My hand is still rather swollen and discoloured and can't take any kind of pressure yet (which is partly why I wanted a tow past the point), but I hope to be rowing after a couple more days. I can only write because the soft tip of my Pentel writes easily at the slightest touch.

'Johnny's back seized up on him during the night but seems to have cleared itself now.

'Been overcast most of the day. The mist cleared mid-afternoon, giving us a lovely view of Punta Banda and the island, even "My" hills (behind Ensenada!).

'Really got scared this morning . It was one of those steely coloured, smooth eerie mornings and there was a sudden snort, just behind my left shoulder. Few moments later there was another snort, this time to the right, and there is a dark grey whale about ten feet from the boat. That was her closest, but after that she popped up around us at least two dozen times and it was pretty unnerving. Johnny thought I was mad, but I insisted on my safety harness, I don't share his confidence in the near misses of whales and I guess it flapped me to see it so close and not know where it would be next time. As usual, we had just got the camera out when she vanished for good.

'Sandwich time is here again but now I have peppers, tomatoes, celery, sandwich spread, cucumber, etc. to moisten them up — hope we get through them before the complaints start pouring in!'

From John's Log

27.6.71   63rd day
'Overcast but very calm. Whale surfaced very near *Britannia*, scared Sylvia who insisted on putting on safety harness in case whale bumped us and we capsized. Silly girl. By mid-afternoon mist cleared and land still in sight.'

Sylvia's hand stayed very painful and she couldn't row for about ten days. It was a handicap with her cooking too, although at first we seemed to exist on a diet of nothing but sandwiches to use up the fresh food and vegetables we had stocked up with. By now the routine was beginning to settle down, although the deck of *Britannia* was still cluttered with gear and there was hardly room in the tiny galley to use even one saucepan. Sylvia found that a jar of cooking oil had lost its top and threequarters of its contents were swimming around the hatch. It was a mess and made the deck as slippery as hell, but fortunately she'd bought some detergent and managed to get it cleaned up.

On the third day out we had the first of a number of similar narrow shaves. We had already seen two ships who veered off course and passed close by, people lining their decks to stare at us. The third ship, a trawler, damn nearly collided with us. Some lookout they were keeping. They must have been on autopilot and nobody noticed our presence. Apparently we couldn't relax even during the daytime with good visibility all round. Even so, I could write, much more confidently now: 'All goes well.'

For the first week the weather wasn't too bad — overcast and with a big swell. We seemed to be making good progress but it was too cloudy for us to get a fix. On the sixth day I was giving Sylvia a bit of a meteorological lesson for, as well as the customary blanket of clouds, there was a light hazy patch in the north-western quarter about the horizon.

'Look,' I told her. 'Now that could be land, but it isn't.'

Five hours later it was still there, joined by two other humps and, so much for my expertise, was definitely land! It could only have been the island of Guadalupe, for there was nothing else showing on the chart, and that made our average 36 miles a day. This was fantastic considering that Sylvia hadn't rowed until then because of her hand and I wasn't exactly overstraining myself.

Britt did indeed go very well. I calculated that when Sylvia's hand had mended and she began to row again we might be able to step it up to 50 miles a day. I couldn't help comparing the difference with the Atlantic trip — then I made only 83 miles in the first 17 days, *not* in the right direction.

I was delighted with Sylvia. She was adapting to life on board exceedingly well. A couple of months more and she wouldn't remember she'd ever had another existence. She made no complaint about the chores that were her share of the voyage and was always cheerful. Of course we did have the odd spot of bother, like the time when the anti-rust liquid spilt out of my toolbag and stank out the galley. According to her, the galley was no place for my toolbag, and this had been a bone of contention since San Francisco. The anti-rust liquid did it, and I had to find another home for the whole kit. Perhaps I was a bit blasé, after the Atlantic row, and what I was waiting for was the real sport — sharks and big fishes so I could go over the side with my spear gun.

From John's Log

10.7.71   76th day
'Lost our Union Jack together with flag pole last night. I glanced up as I was just about to pull my pants up following nature's call to the gunnels, to have this small wave break full in my face, throwing me completely off balance. My chin hit the flag pole and snapped it off, and somehow I ended up athwartship, my face down under water, one hand grabbing a jerry can handle and the other a loose and broken part of the flag pole. My feet were in the air on the other side of the boat but at least I kept myself more or less on board. An egg came up on my chin, slight cut lip, bruise and grazed thigh, but nothing that will cause any bother or affect rowing. To-day is still very rough and it's sunny but cold because of wind, anyway better this way. I'm not looking forward to a nocturnal existence.'

From Sylvia's Log

11th July, Sunday   77th day
'Suddenly saw a big grey fin right by *Brit*'s now while having breakfast. Seconds later it was the other side of the bow and so on. Johnny had his back to it and just as I yelled him to look one way the dolphin popped up the other! At one stage five in a row were leaping straight for *Brit* broadside and I was so sure they were going to jump over her and through me that I rushed for the shelter of the galley! Instead they either dived or turned within a few moments not a dolphin in sight. I think it's incredible how they bound up to investigate, with all that splash and show, something – to them fish or what? – as enormous as us in our boat, whilst other animals investigate with silence, secrecy and caution.

'There are some "things" which look like bubbles in the water – about one to two inches diameter supposedly jelly fish of a sort. Then some one to two feet trailing jelly-looking stuff, rather like a white chiffon scarf, just below the surface (not connected with bubbles at all). Also on the surface are pin-head sized silvery blobs darting erratically in all directions. Saw a small, shilling-sized, green crab swimming on surface and assume other opaque splodges of approximately the same size seen below surface are the same. For the information of Stanford University's Department of Oceanography, the only plastic debris so far sighted was to-day and highly questionable, two white objects within an hour, each about one and half feet squarish and below surface, could have been plastic bags, or rays of some sort. Quite a lot of wooden debris, a few large logs and plenty of smaller pieces, all have barnacles growing to a greater or lesser degree.'

12th July, Monday   78th day
'Sea still lousy and rough, rowing and everything else uncomfortable. To make it worse it seems to have a personal vendetta against me. The moment I start cooking it really bitches and the boat goes crazy, lurching, pitching and rolling irregularly everywhere, so I can't even pour the kettle where I want it to go. Then, during my rowing stint I'll get splashes galore, Johnny, at the stern end will be bone dry. The moment we change over, the stern and I get all the action, rowing seat and Johnny remain dry! Another irritation is Johnny seems to fit anywhere and be comfortable. I have yet to find a single place where I can be comfortable on this whole damned boat.

'Apart from these generalities, this morning I had just filled the kettle for breakies, looked up to see three gigantic waves approaching (that is a funny thing, the real whoppers always seems to come in twos or threes). Somehow I just knew it, so said to Johnny, "This one's for us. I feel it in my bones!" Sure enough, the middle one broke full over the boat, kettle submerged, galley awash, myself in water to hip level (kneeling as usual). The worst swamping since Ensenada and Johnny only slightly more wet than a normal splashing! Charmed life! The kettle is a whistler with only a tiny hole in the lid so not much salt got in and we used the water.'

13th July, Tuesday   79th day
'Seems to be calming down gradually, wind dropping. Real

solid looking clouds around now — am beginning to believe the wind and sun come together and the clouds block out the wind. Few days ago there was not a cloud in the sky and one started to grow, right up in the middle of the blue. Began as a streak then swelled up, never seen this before and had always thought clouds broke off and moved around, but to actually see them developing in an empty blue sky is quite something. For the past few days there have been "wavy" semi-transparent clouds, and the streaky type, with that wind. Now big solid clouds and no wind.

'Found out where we are yesterday and seems very good.

'Been suffering with my feet at nights, little red spots across the fronts of my toes, I say salt-water sores and Johnny says it's my stomach!

'During our stay in Ensenada I tried to improve on our Great Northern sleeping bags by covering the last couple of feet of each in a rubberised waterproof fabric. Reason being that we tend to drag the ends out of the rat-hole on to the wet deck, or just kick them there, so our feet were often wet. What I did just ensured that our feet were always wet, since the rubber stopped them from breathing, condensation built up inside and the things were a permanent soggy mess. Have now cut away my addition and everything is greatly improved, they dry incredibly quickly in any case, being Dacron filled, so we'll just try to take reasonable care.'

Eighteen days out from Ensenada (and about 500 miles) we had sighted another ship, the *Toyota Maru 12*, which circled right round us. The crew waved, we signalled we needed nothing, they whistled three times and got under way.

Sylvia was very pleased with them.

'It's nice to see a ship out here, especially if they whistle,' she said.

'It makes me think somebody cares.'

So long as the simple things in life could keep her happy, we'd be all right.

From Sylvia's Log

14th July, Wednesday   80th day
'Johnny said, "What's the most important thing round here?"
I said I didn't know. He said, "Seawater. Without it we'd sink
like a stone."
   'Think that's enough for to-day!'

   Actually I'm not the sort of guy who goes around making
corny cracks like that — especially at sea. This often irritated
Sylvia, because she would prattle away at me and then get
cross because I hadn't answered her. There was just nothing
to say . . . I usually had something on my mind anyway.

From John's Log

14.7.71-18.7.71, Wednesday-Sunday   80-84th days
'Afraid I've not been keeping the log up to date in the last
four days. Actually nothing at all worth mentioning has
happened. The weather became increasingly calm, and to-day
we have absolute calm although the overcast is still there.
Alto and Strato Cumulus mainly with the sun shining
through every now and then. Without wind the heat is now
quite noticeable but at night it freshens most pleasantly.
Barry [the barometer] is as usual steady as a rock. I'm
watching it like a hawk. We are almost in the middle of the
hurricane season and that's anything but reassuring. I've been
thinking and re-thinking on what to do when and if a
hurricane eventually strikes us and finally came to the
conclusion that there is damn all one can do. Whether we
survive or not will depend on the strength of the winds. I
think we stand a good chance of getting away with it if the
wind doesn't blow at more than a 100 knots, providing as
well that we are not caught in the dangerous quadrant. Ivan
told me there was a hurricane last week near Hawaii with
winds of 125 knots. If anything like that hits us it will be
touch and go.
   'Still, I have faith in the boat and properly lashed we might
be able to stay with *Britannia.* She will probably capsize

more than once and then the big if is: will she right herself in time or at all? We'll probably lose most of what's on deck as it is impossible to lash every single item to withstand the fury of a hurricane and I must give priority to the oars and water jugs. Oh well, we can be hit any time from now till the end of October, and it's no use to speculate too much about what will or will not happen. *Que sera* and all that.'

'We are beginning to get a tan, about time, but there is still no sign of fishes of any kind except the occasional school of porpoises.

'Our average has increased to 40 miles per day which is excellent and everything is as it should be.'

By now the weather had really warmed up and was in the high eighties during the daytime. We still hadn't seen many fish, but as we had plenty of food this didn't matter yet. We hadn't seen any sharks and that, combined with a glass-like sea, persuaded Sylvia to wash her hair and have her first swim since setting out a month before. Perhaps she'd better describe it.

From Sylvia's Log

19th July, Monday   85th day
'I'm a lousy swimmer and don't enjoy the water at all, pools are boring and rivers and the sea always frighten me, but this morning it was so clear and blue that one could easily see its emptiness for at least a hundred feet all round, so in I went, complete with flippers, mask and snorkle. Climbing out of the boat into the water was a real exhibition, which I'm glad was only witnessed by Johnny who knows my clumsiness inside out and therefore was not in the least surprised. Once in I started kicking, intending to swim once round the boat and then back in. Looked up when I was level with the blister, suddenly realised there was nothing to hold on to and no way back on board till I reached the other side, panicked and shot back to Johnny begging to be hauled back on board and assuring him I would be better at my next attempt!

'He insisted on rinsing the remains of the shampoo out of

my hair and then began the tussle to get me back on board, in the middle of which I had another minor panic because I felt "something" (the rope actually) touch my leg. Feel quite ashamed of myself, but being in a boat is an entirely different feeling from "free floating" in all this water.'

One thing Sylvia forgot to mention: it was the first day that we were able to sunbathe in the nude! Looking back on it all now, this part of the trip — from Ensenada to Washington Island, where we took a breather in Paradise — was the happiest part of the whole voyage. It wasn't hot enough yet to be forced into our 'night routine' when for weeks on end we had to row by night and rest as best we could by day. We hadn't yet succumbed to the incredible boredom of ten months of being cooped up in a space fifteen feet by five, and the 'minor' physical ailments like salt sores and tropical boils (about which more later) hadn't yet begun to get us down.

All our troubles, for the moment, were little ones, like the day when Sylvia lost the knife. It was only a cheap one, but I annoyed her by remarking (as we watched it slide down through the clear blue water hundreds of feet below us) that we couldn't afford to do that once a month. (Which was a little unfair, as it was the first time it had happened in the eight weeks since we left San Francisco.) It happened like this.

Among her odds and ends in the galley Sylvia had a box of miscellaneous items for the kitchen, and one of them was a box of margarine. She noticed that the marg had melted in the eighty degree heat, and was running out of the corner of the packet, covering everything in grease.

She decided to put the margarine in a plastic jar, but everything was like melted ice-cream in her hands and soon everything — the knife, the jar and the deck was reduced to a slippery mess. She was trying to clean it all up with a sponge, when suddenly the knife just 'slipped from her hands' and over the side. After she'd mopped up the slimy mess I relented and cheered her up by giving her a lovely little Gerber knife she'd had her eye on for weeks, in a smart leather sheath. Uncharitably I still wonder sometimes whether she did it on purpose, but she was always so wonderfully keen and cheerful that I know that's not true! I lost the Gerber knife myself later, but that's another story.

While we're on the domestic side, I think it's about time for some of the recipes Sylvia regaled me with during this period when the weather was calm enough for her to cook. Remember it's before we began to run out of the canned goodies we had bought on shore, and before we started to supplement our diet with the fish which we both (he says generously) caught later on. Here they are, courtesy of Sylvia, who took an immaculate note of everything when I couldn't be bothered to write a word.

From Sylvia's Log

21st July, Wednesday   87th day
'Breakfast: 8 tortillas — few corned beef, rest honey or Chabacano (?) Jam. Tea.
'Main meal: Fried last fresh onion, added most of corned beef, packet of Vacu-Dry tomato and veg soup, 3 packets Vacu-Dry cheese sauce mix, water, 2 cups Mountain House freeze-dried cooked corn and a dash of Worcester Sauce. Success: Eaten with 3 torts. each and tea.
'Extra: 4 cu. inches choc. fudge. Drink of Tang orange.

22nd July, Thursday   88th day
'Nastier, wind about 12, no sun.
'Breakies: 8 tortillas with clover honey.
'Meal: 1 pint jug full of inst. mashed potatoes, 2 cans (3 in each) of Wilson's Certified Pork Patties (fried), 2 cups Mountain House beetroot (diced). Nice but had to open 3 hatches to do it — for extra pan and frying pan and Ronson Table Chef for frying. 3 torts. each and coffee.
'Extras: 4 Rich-Moor fruit buns (I like, J. Doesn't much) 2 Mugs Vacu-Dry bouillion packets — beef, very good indeed.'

Interspersed was the occasional bitch about the conditions. I don't blame her.

From Sylvia's Log

23rd July, Friday   89th day
'Rougher than yesterday but begins to calm this afternoon. Still grey and overcast, never rains but always cloudy. When I think back to what *I think* they told me at school it should be like around here, I can't help feeling someone, somewhere along the line, made a dreadful mistake. Since leaving San Francisco I should say the most we had of completely sunny days would be 9. It's warmer now, but not nearly as warm as it would be in London at this time of year under a similar overcast. Anyone thinking London looks grey and dismal under cloud, should come and look at this little lot for a week or so, this is what greyness is all about! Ugh! To liven things up we saw a bird to-day, one miserable little bird, so far away we couldn't even see its colour, so that too was grey.

'Breakfast: 8 tortillas stuffed with one packet of Mountain
                     House Chili and Beans — lovely. Tea.
'Meal: 2 packets Mountain House Beef Stew, with ½
                     cup Minute Rice and ½ packet Vacu-Dry Soup
                     and Gravy Base (Beef Bouillon) added. 6 tortil-
                     las and tea.
'Extras: 2 mugs V-Dry Beef Bouillon. 1 Rich-Moor fruit
                     bar. 2 cu. inches choc fudge.

'The Mountain House meals are a real godsend, especially in roughish weather. They taste excellent, the servings are very generous (15-16 oz each), and all one needs to do is pour boiling water over the packet contents (still in packet), wait 5 mins and eat. No cooking and no washing up. At first we added nothing and found them plenty but rowing and the air have an accumulative effect and we find we get increasingly hungry.'

'24th July, Saturday   90th day
'Overcast but calmer.

'Saw another bird this morning, one of the big, brown duck-looking gulls we used to see a lot from San Francisco to within a week of our anchorage. Only difference was they used to come right close and sit on the water almost within an oar's length, this one kept its distance. Sometimes they came singly and sometimes in pairs, they seemed to like the company and would stay for hours. Johnny used to say this'd make a good meal one day but they look so soft and trusting I don't think I could bear it, unless there was absolutely nothing else to eat.

'Breakfast: 8 tortillas, 4 filled with sardine mashed in vinegar and the rest with clover honey. Chocolate to drink. We tried drinking chocolate once in the S.F. − E trip but it was a disaster. This time I used about 3 dessertspoons of milk powder and 1½ of choc. to each mug and it tasted fabulous. Don't know if I've mentioned it but I always warm the torts over the bare flame, it freshens and softens them.

'Meal: M-House dried beef, 2 cups, in pan with packet V-Dry green pea soup and 4½ cups water. When boiled add 2 cups M-House peas and 2 cups Minute Rice. Unfortunately put too much rice and the whole thing was too dry as a result. 6 torts and tea (which is always with lemon extract and sugar for J. honey for me.

'Extras: 2 mugs choc.'

So you see, we didn't exactly starve. But if it sounds too easy, cast an eye over this detailed entry in the log for a 'special' meal on July 31st, somewhere in mid-Pacific:

'Main meal was a lot of bother but worth it. We had 2 packets Rich-Moor beef patties fried, mounds of mashed potatoes and green peas. At home this would be the simplest kind of meal but here, mainly due to water conservation, it's the most complicated. The meat has to soak in warm water

20 mins before cooking, in order to rehydrate, so heat kettle and cover meat in large jug. Then open hatch to take out frying pan and small cooking pot, close hatch. Open different hatch to take out small cooker for frying, close hatch. Unleash stand for cooker from deck and assemble cooker. (Meanwhile kettle is getting towards boiling on big cooker for peas.) Light small cooker with frying pan and fat, remove patties from water, pat dry, and fry, put same water into small cooking pot for potatoes. Put peas in jug just contained meat, cover with boiling water. Remove patties and place small cooking pot on flame, when boils start adding potatoes, strain water off peas into potatoes, stir in more potato till enough, then remove from flame, replace meat on flame to re-heat, strain fat off meat into potatoes and serve the lot.

'Whew! All the while these little bits and pieces have had their own ideas on where they want to be, and a constant watch is essential to avert a serious landslide. Afterwards all the greasy dishes, etc. are washed over the side in cold sea water, then all the same hatches have to be opened and closed as before. Beginning to end — two hours!'

6. Fish

We'd struck the winds we were looking for, the north-east trades, in the third week in July. By the end of the month we were at 25° 24' north, 132° 37' west which was excellent. So far it had been a milk run, and now our course was set — south-west for Australia the whole way. One day followed the other, smooth and uneventful, so that it was in danger of becoming a real bore. I'd decided to make for the Line Islands, Christmas (of atomic fame), Washington, Palmyra or Fanning, whichever was easier, for a brief stop and a change, particularly to pick up fresh food and water. They are atolls, about 2,400 miles to the south-west of us, and I looked forward to both the challenge to my navigation and to some spear-fishing among the reefs.

The winds helped us along beautifully, blowing with utter reliability day after day. *Britt* was proving herself to be a beautiful boat after all, and the big iron rudder I'd had fitted in Ensenada made controlling her a piece of cake. We were even able to adjust the direction of our drift by as much as 30 degrees by setting the rudder at the right angle, and this helped enormously so far as speed and course were concerned. In the Atlantic while drifting, *Britannia I* lay absolutely broadside to the waves regardless of what I tried to do to prevent it, short of streaming a drogue which slowed her down. Now, when *Britannia II* was drifting, I had to swim like mad to catch her up, even with the flippers on, and, when the wind got up behind us to fifteen or more knots, she went like a torpedo. When we were rowing I reckon we were making a good two knots.

The maddening thing, especially for me, was the absence of marine life. It was not until the 38th day out that we spotted our first flying fish, and then there were only two of them. Sylvia found a little grey crab, no bigger than a farthing, crawling round the deck by the daggerboard, and made a pet of him.

Unfortunately he didn't last long as one day we found him squashed flat — one of us must have trodden on him without noticing.

We got out the cameras to take some films for I.T.N. and the *People* of our life on board. Filming was quite a performance — we'd spend hours trying to get it right on the cramped boat, what with rewinding the camera and moving around to get the different angles. It was not just a question of one shooting and the other carrying on normally. It was all part of the job and had to be done some time, but it did cut into our rowing schedule. I was doing ten hours a day and Sylvia five, and her being there made all the difference to the Atlantic run. Then I was rowing twelve hours a day (or night) and doing all the chores myself, with the result that I got very little sleep and by the end of the journey was desperately tired. Across the Pacific I was getting more or less a normal eight hours' sleep daily. That is, if you can call normal our tiny rathole.

Since we completed the trip, people have continually asked us about our sex life on board. How did we manage, and so on. They seem surprised (and not a little disappointed) when we answer, like the hardy captain of HM *Pinafore*,

> 'What, never?'
> 'No, never!'
> 'What, *never*?'
> 'Well, hardly ever' '

As Sylvia told one persistent questioner from a woman's magazine: 'You try it in a crummy little boat like *Britannia* at sea.'

I know it sounds absurd, but it is absolutely truthful to say that we didn't see all that much of each other, even though we were rowing naked most of the way through the tropics. The fact was, that while I was rowing Sylvia was either sleeping or doing the cooking or pottering about. When she was rowing, I was trying to rest.

It was too hot most of the time to sleep together in the rathole, which had almost no ventilation, and when we did the whole night would be spent bickering at each other. Even to turn over you had to ask the other one to move too.

We didn't row the Pacific in order to make love. We spent nearly all our time on the business of living — or maybe existing is a more accurate word. And, positively my last word on the subject, much of the time Sylvia's lips were so blistered by the sun that she couldn't even kiss!

We didn't row naked for aesthetic or any other pleasure either. It was a case of practical necessity. Both of us suffered from time to time, particularly when the sea was rough or when it was raining — in any case whenever we got wet for any length of time — from salt water sores. Sylvia's soft skin was worse affected than mine, but I know how bloody painful they were. At times the back of her legs and buttocks were one painful red mass of blisters joined together — she used to say they were like red hot needles sticking through her skin. We've mentioned before the vast relief that Vaseline brought, but the only complete cure was a dry spell, which cleared things up almost miraculously.

We never had any trouble with our hands — the design of the oars and wearing gloves saw to that — but the constant backwards and forwards movement of rowing means that your backside is subjected to permanent friction, even though *Britt*'s rowing seat slid to and fro as we did. Wearing clothes only added to the chafing, and so we took them off. Simple as that, but it still didn't stop the salt sea water and the sweat from our bodies running down and collecting between our buttocks.

As I've mentioned, Sylvia's lips became split and sore from the sun and wind, so she took to wearing a handkerchief round the lower part of her face, making herself look like something out of a Grade B movie, but on the whole we kept in good health throughout the whole journey. I had an eye infection for a while, but it soon cleared up, and for a couple of days I had a headache and a bit of a fever. I only record that because it occasioned one of the (few) flattering references in Sylvia's log.

'He's adorable when he's sick, unbelievably polite and considerate, really sweet. Strange because that's when most men seem to become monsters.'

On second thoughts, perhaps that's not so complimentary!

Sylvia bought a large drum of powdered yeast from a San Francisco Organic Food Store before we left. She'd remembered reading in Robin Knox-Johnston's book that it helped to prevent the salt sores. The problem was it was impossible to eat, being a thick, choking powder. She solved the problem by mixing it with honey, and she said it did her good, which was half the battle, I wouldn't touch the revolting stuff.

On August 7th, 41 days out of Ensenada, we managed to get through to Ivan on the radio. We had been unable to erect the aerial for some time due to the choppy seas and brisk winds, and he thought we had been hit by a hurricane which passed within two hundred miles of us. We asked for information on the Line Islands, for I was cursing my lack of foresight in leaving my Pilot Books behind, which would have contained all the dope I wanted. I was worried by their weight, but it was a stupid thing to do.

From John's Log

7.8.71   104th day

'For a change very hot, calm day. We spent it filming aspects of everyday life, having decided to stop the next ship. Fortune sends us we'll unload the exposed film and get some fresh fruit and vegetables, also re-fill our water jugs so that we don't have to worry about making any. I have decided it will be easier to have some extra weight than spending 8 hours every day to distil the gallon we need. We'll get more water on the islands if they have it. Getting there will be a real challenge to my navigation and I'm really looking forward to see if we can do it. Also by accident heard on the radio (transistor) that the same station that I listen to every day or so for my time signals transmits weather conditions in the North Pacific at ten minutes to the hour every hour.

Apparently we are hemmed in by hurricanes and tropical depressions. Sylvia says it would have been better not to know! Anyway we seem to be in luck and so far avoided bad weather. We'll see how long this lasts. Still overcast but managed to shoot some stars through holes in the clouds. At sunset we were at north 24° 05′ west 39° 11′. An average of some 40 miles since the 1st August but apparently we have lost only 1° of latitude, while I had figured 2°. From now on we'll let *Britannia* drift S. when we are not rowing, instead of W. as up to now, otherwise we'll end up in Hawaii. Extremely pleased with our speed which I hope we'll be able to maintain as long as the N.E. stay with us. All in all a very pleasant day, but still no fishes.'

From Sylvia's Log

11th August, Wednesday   108th day
'Another windy, wet day like yesterday with bigger waves (5-10 ft). Lots of splashes, usually on me not J., who laughs and makes me even madder. Sat down to eat my meal on a completely dry piece of deck, half way through a big cold wave slammed right into my back. As if that wasn't enough, ten to fifteen minutes later, drinking a nice hot cup of tea in the same place, boof! another, same way. I was so angry I only just managed to stop myself throwing my tea at the sea! It's hard to understand how angry this kind of thing makes you. Johnny told me that during his Atlantic Row the sea made him so angry once with this sort of thing that he shot at it with his speargun, thereby losing a spear. Until I got here I had always thought this was kind of daft and out of character, but now it's all too easy to understand. We are not cold any more and when the sun's out it's even rather pleasant to be splashed sometimes, but when one is doing something else, not thinking about it, and all has been dry for some time — and then a real big soaking, that's when the anger rises.

'J. baled out leaking hatch again to-day, got about 6 gallons of water out. This is hatch No. 5 and has been like this since before Ensenada, so that is another extra job every

few days. Found another jar of crackers, I always thought we
had more than two and wouldn't be surprised if we find yet
another somewhere.'

That leaking hatch was a bit of a problem. I went
overboard but couldn't find the leak to patch it up. It didn't
worry me overmuch, as the boat was made of watertight
compartments, but it was really annoying to find that all the
batteries I had for our watertight torches were ruined. We
only had one torch left that would take ordinary batteries,
and that was worrying. The nights were moonless by now and
if either of us had gone over the side and missed grabbing the
trailing line it would be very easy to lose sight of the boat.
Britannia drifted too fast for Sylvia to catch up with anyway,
but fortunately she was always far too cautious to fall
overboard!

There must be something magic about the figure 23. That's
the latitude of the tropics, and Sylvia and I have often
wondered since whether anyone actually drew a line round
the earth and told the fish to stay inside it. Anyway, we must
have been spot on the Tropic of Cancer on Thursday, August
12th, as Sylvia's log reported.

12th August, Thursday   109th day
'Thought I saw a dorado close to the boat whilst J. was
preparing radio. Got through to Ivan who told us there is no
radio-activity around Christmas Island now and that there is
ample water and a population of about 250. Also told us
there is limited water on Fanning (whatever that may mean!)
and that he had not been able to gather any information on
the other two islands, Palmyra and Washington, as yet,
neither had he been able to locate the French nuclear tests
being carried out at present. Everyone laughed at me before
we started because I was concerned about all the nuclear tests
in the Pacific; it might be a pretty big place and all that, but
in my opinion it's worth finding out the whereabouts and
extent of these tests, after all it would be a stupid way to go
under our circumstances!

'Johnny moaned on to Ivan about the lack of life round

here, in fact listed every fish we have seen since Ensenada, put the receiver back, turned off and thereupon discovered us to be surrounded by a school of dorado. This is what he's been waiting for, no time to pack the aerial away properly so it's just shoved into the rat-hole, on with the diving gear and, after one shot from the boat (which got away) into the water. Returns after a couple of minutes with speared dorado.

'This is where I'm still not sure whose side I'm on. It was a female, about two and a half to three feet. She was wearing her golden yellow dress with the little royal blue spots, and she was shiny, sleek and beautiful, but she had this horrid spear through her gills and she was struggling and thrashing herself against *Britannia*'s side as her combatant climbed aboard. He pulled out the spear and her lovely soft black eyes seemed to see and understand everything. Then she had a last surge of energy, whipping and flapping on the deck, after which she was still. For a few more minutes she remained very beautiful, even her gills were beautiful — like scarlet anemones — then her skin turned grey and her eyes dulled and she was just another fish, and I didn't mind any more.

'Johnny asked me to help hold her over the side while he cleaned her, all went well until he told me to hold her by her eyes, pushing them in with my forefinger and thumb, then the sick feeling I had whilst she thrashed on the deck returned, and I couldn't. Made up my mind next time he asks me I will. Ridiculous being squeamish out here, and I've never said no to fish, or meat, or leather etc. in my life for sentimental reasons, so what it boils down to is that I'm quite happy to let someone else do the dirty work as long as I don't have to watch or think about it. Well, out here that just won't work, so I'll have to be a little more realistic. Maybe this is another of the lessons I'll learn from this voyage.

'Ate her without qualms. We (even Johnny who has refused to eat it ashore since his Atlantic experience) have both been craving for some fish for a couple of weeks now, just to have something fresh and a change, I guess. Now we had it, but we wanted them to stay around so we would always have it when the fancy took us.

'The best way of encouraging them to stay is to feed them, and the only suitable food to hand was another dorado (after all, fish aren't that clever so they'd never know!) We decided to try with hook and line and we were both a disgrace!

'Using parts of the first victim as bait, Johnny had first try. Those fish came within four feet of the boat and were easily visible taking the bait. First he threw pieces with no hooks, then with the hook, dorado approach, nibbled and "Yank"! No fish, I called J. a few names as I'd only just pointed out how they always had a little nibble before swallowing.

'Not unjustly, J. handed me hook, line and bait. This gorgeous fish bites, swallows, and I also am in too much of a hurry and, like a fool, just keep winding in. We had a fight for about a minute, culminating in the dorado leaping out of the water in a backward somersault, thus breaking free. Biggest fish I've ever hooked and I'm going back for more!'

13th August, Friday   110th day
'Forget to say we've been seeing flying fish, more and more every day. They're very pretty, pale silvery blue, and they seem to be from one to ten inches, and appear in anything from singles to schools of a couple of hundred. I'm amazed how long they stay airborne, how high they fly, and that they can change direction in mid-air.

'There seems to be only one dorado left now. Hardly surprising since, out of the original dozen, three suffered near misses by John's spear, two nasty shocks with the hooks, and one her end. What is surprising is that the survivor is minus the fore part of her dorsal fin, thanks to the spear. However, she doesn't seem to miss it much and it makes her easy to spot through the water. We are feeding her scraps of yesterday's victim and we've christened her Spooky.

'Pleasant weather. J. swimming every day. I suppose I am missing quite a lot by not going in but I'm a weak swimmer and if some shark came up to me, I don't know what I'd do. It's unlikely, but being a poor swimmer doesn't inspire the confidence to want to find out! Then there is my hair. I hate the feel of wet hair dripping on me for hours. Maybe when it becomes really hot I'll take the plunge but, although warm,

S.C. obscured by the spray from a wave breaking over *Britannia*.

Launching *Britannia* at Cowes : Mrs Fairfax and Clare Lallow are standing by the stern. (*Photo The People*)

Britannia moored alongside the cutter *Alert,* our mother ship in San Francisco. (*Photo Syndication International*)

J. F. showing the drogue, or sea-anchor, used to slow down *Britannia's* drift in contrary winds and to keep her head into the waves in stormy weather. (*Photo Syndication International*)

What was left of the rudder on arrival at Ensenada. (*Photo Syndication International*)

J.F. equipped for rough weather.

Britannia was so low in the water that she would ship water even in normal weather. (*Photo Syndication International*)

One of the few absolutely calm days. (*Photo The People*)

Sunset at sea.

A booby bird settles on the blister.

S.C. (*Photo Syndication International*)

To save drinking water S.C. washed her long hair in the sea. (*Photo The People*)

S.C. making bread outside the galley which can be seen in the background. Normally she had to crawl inside to cook.

there are too many clouds around and I don't want to chance sleeping with wet hair.

'We had a lovely big tin of beef roast for our meal to-day, in honour of Johnny's Mum's birthday. With it mashed potatoes, beans and corn mixed.'

On August 16th, we saw what Sylvia described as a rotten lousy horrible ship. She was on the Bilbao to Honolulu lane and she passed three cables away. We saw her coming for miles and parcelled up all our film and letters home for her to take. She didn't see us, although I lit two orange smoke flares and, with the little wind there was, the smoke spread almost across her bows. My opinion of the kind of lookout kept by many ships in the open seas was getting lower by the minute. I wrote in my log:

'I hope we never really need them. What a real castaway in the last stages of exhaustion must think if, in broad daylight, a ship goes by at arm's length without spotting him can only be imagined by actually living through a similar situation.' Prophetic words, they nearly turned out to be.

In fact we really cursed that ship later on when that blasted hatch, No. 5, leaked again a few days later. We found that every one of our ten casettes of carefully thought-out documented film were ruined. Each was in its original foil wrapping, resealed with waterproof adhesive tape which was also used to patch any weak or broken spots in the foil. The whole lot were then inside two large polythene bags together with letters home, all an illegible soggy mess. The water had softened the paper on the foil and the movement of the boat had caused constant friction to rub through the foil. Damn and blast!

However, the fish were still with us, including Spooky, so I oiled and cleaned all my spear guns and shafts so as to be ready for action at any moment.

But it was still slow to come.

From Sylvia's Log

18th August, Wednesday   115th day
'Perhaps slightly calmer, definitely sunnier but not hot.

'Dorados still about. They now swim under boat and much
closer than before. They are beautiful. J. went in the water
and only saw five, including Spooky. Forgot to mention the
beastly start to yesterday. Awoke to hear rain hammering on
roof and big breakers surging about. Put kettle on and the gas
expired almost instantly. Got a fresh canister from hatch, but
it wouldn't screw in so I threw it away, went back, reopened
hatch and tried another one. This time I pressed really hard
and the gas wouldn't stop coming out so I had to throw that
away too. Tried two more with no success.

'By this time I had been up in the pouring rain, subject to
constant splashing, for over half an hour to absolutely no
purpose, so I was anything but happy. I had to ask J. to look
at it, which I hate doing as so often the moment one asks
someone else in on these mechanical mysteries, they immediately function perfectly; not so, however, in this case. This
time the thread was broken on the tap and where the spares
might be was anybody's guess. Finally I produced the
Ronson Table Chef and boiled the kettle on that but had to
hold the kettle the whole time to stop it sliding off, since the
Table Chef is not designed for this kind of life and has no
gimbals. Found the new tap and changed it, so the Calor
Cooker is now in perfect order again. There should really
have been no problem but with all the damp inside the
hatches, the cans of Calor Gas had rusted rather badly, in fact
we found ten empty whilst in Ensenada,

'To prevent further rusting Ivan and Ira had kindly painted
all the tainted cans with rust prevention paint. Unfortunately, half way through the job they had tired of dipping
each individual can into the paint, diligently holding the valve
with a pair of pliers, and had resorted to chucking the cans
into the paint, half a dozen at a time, and then fishing them
out again. Every time I need a new can I have to scrape the
paint (sometimes two layers, as someone produced a better
paint halfway through, so the first ones were redone with

this) from the top, inside the valve, and from the fine, screw sides of the nozzle, the only suitable tool has been a pair of scissors but I'm now going to try a fish-hook. Each time I feelingly curse Ivan and Ira, which is hardly fair since neither of us stopped it or considered the consequences.

20th August, Friday   118th day
'Was doing my first stint at the oars, gazing vacantly at the sea with an equally vacant mind, when I saw a splash and, as I looked a beautiful dorado, wearing their hunting colour of Royal Blue, leapt out of the water after a flying fish, disturbed the whole school of flying fish and sent them soaring, dorado in hot pursuit. Very exciting.

'Johnny speared one for lunch later, hope not the same one! I did fillet it but wasn't asked and didn't offer to clean it out first, next time I must do that too. I curried it with rice, much the same as the chili recipe.'

22nd August, Sunday   119th day
'Saw a ship late last night but distant so nothing happened. Still rough, wet and windy with less sun and very big waves here and there, usually in groups of three for some strange reason.

'Had a can of corned beef for lunch as a Sunday treat. Ate it cold with beet, mashed spuds, mustard and barbecue sauce. Later disposed of more tinned pineapple. Whilst on the subject of food, I have to confess that hamburgers are what I most miss, gets quite obsessional sometimes. Expect my poor Dad'll be well and truly ashamed of me, an English girl, missing American hamburgers. Well, sorry Dad, but until you've had them you don't know what you're missing! Maybe later on, when their memory has faded (hopefully!) I'll start missing steak and kidney pudding or roast beef and Yorkshire!

'Had visitors late this afternoon. Dolphins again. Only yesterday I had been thinking we should be seeing some again soon since we are nearer land now. They fooled around for quite a while, born exhibitionists. I'm sure they come to show us what they can do, rather than to investigate. In spite of this, or possibly because, they are welcome visitors at any time and I wish they would stay longer, but I guess they are too intelligent and know they've seen all there is to see in twenty minutes and that there's nothing in it for them, so off they go.'

23rd August, Monday   120th day
'Ghastly day! Colder, windier and rougher than ever since Ensenada. In fact horribly reminiscent of S.F. to E. stage. Heard on our weather station there is a "disturbance" here! That's no news, last night was the violentest red sunset, and the low clouds were shooting off our way whilst the high ones were going in completely the opposite direction. Two hours later our weather people informed us we were the centre of a Tropical Depression. What next? Swamped quite a few times.

'J.'s spots are increasing, and so are mine to a lesser extent. He never usually complains so these must be real misery. In this weather, with clothes and sleeping bags permanently wet, there seems little chance of improvement. I still wear my yashmak, got very wet to-day and the salt came through to my lips and rubbed my nose, both painful, so I took it off later. Hope this weather doesn't last long, to-day's really grim. J. saw his biggest dorado to-day (from inside *B.II* — no swimming in this), was a good five foot. Nice to know the dolphins didn't slaughter or frighten them all. On the other hand he may have been a loner who came after the dolphins. Had a drama, in the late afternoon, from an unexpected source. A white gull, with black markings under wing and below head, was swooping and diving amidst the waves, a really beautiful flyer. Suddenly a flying fish appeared and the gull chased it, it fell back into the water, closely followed by the gull. The whole school of flying-fish took off, the gull chased them, caught one, and then, after swallowing, resumed the chase. Amazing how exciting this sort of thing is out here, the fact that it was mild weather and that both the gull and the flying fish were so pretty enhanced the spectacle still more.'

From John's Log

23.8.71   120th day
'A rough day. Last night at sunset I thought there were signs of coming bad weather, as I explained to Sylvia. The sky at sunset was a most violent red — any violent colour at sunset or sunrise usually indicates moist air in the distance which sometimes is a forerunner of bad weather. Also there was very poor visibility, which again sometimes happens when there is moist air in the upper levels in front of a warm front, and then the clouds were quite obviously racing in opposite directions, the low ones with the N.E., the upper ones, mostly cirrus, from the S.W., clear indication that two fronts were crossing. Also Barry fell steadily throughout the night to its lowest yet. Well, there was little to do except check that everything was lashed properly and hope for the best. By morning the wind was 20-25 knots and eventually reached 30-35 knots, swamped continuously but *Britt* is now much lighter and things were not as bad as they had been in the S.F. — Ensenada run. Weather conditions in the North Pacific, from our Colorado station, said there was a tropical depression in the area and, by our respective positions, it was clear we were near the centre of it. Luckily it was supposed to move away from us so maybe things will improve soon. Hardly did any rowing as sea conditions were too bad. Miserable day and night.'

From Sylvia's Log

24th August, Tuesday   121st day
'Remarkably calm morning, considering all the bangings and hisses of the night. However, in the afternoon it became rougher again, but not much to worry about.

'Poor little flying fish, they are so pretty and everybody but us seems to eat them. One was being chased by a dorado from below at the same time as by a gull from above. Didn't see the end because of waves. Must be millions of them, they seem to be everywhere. One did land in the boat, it was half inch long at most!

'Had a lovely dream last night. I was in an English country town, something like Marlow. I came out of the Post Office, having been advised to go to an excellent baker's next door. The baker's had a delicious new-bread smell and was half a baker's and half cabinet maker's. The whole thing was run by a darling little white haired man in an apron, who was really just closing but told me not to hurry and he was sorry there was so little choice at this time of day. He proudly showed me some of his beautiful furniture then recommended a particular loaf to me, it was white with fruit inside and a little sticky icing on top. I bought another type as well, because he'd been so nice, then woke up — cramped, wet and thousands of miles from any bakers!

'Quite often dream out here, suppose because it's so darned uncomfortable I sleep poorly. Mostly I dream I'm shopping, buying really pretty things at bargain prices. This surprises me because I always say I don't like shopping, maybe it's just the pretty things I like. In the last one I was in a draper's with my mother and they had a Sale on, and we chose four very pretty embroidered tray cloths at half a crown (bit out-dated my dreams!) each. We were just about to pay for them when I spied a real beauty, palest pink embroidered with lily-of-the-valley in deeper pink and white, it was in the 2s 6d tray but had an 9s 6d ticket, but we checked with the assistant and got it for 2s 6d. Generally the objects of my shopping dreams are clothes; exaggeratedly feminine type things, all lace, frills and embroidery, not at all what I usually wear. Then I had a dream that someone gave me a dachshund puppy and a pure white kitten. The pup nearly ate someone's guinea pigs, and the kitten kept being lost and found over great distances.'

From John's Log

25.8.71   122nd day
'Two months today since leaving Ensenada for the second time. Nice weather, sunny and hot. Cannot row during the daytime any longer: by 10 in the morning the temperature is almost in the 80s and if there are no or only scattered clouds

the sun is beastly. I swim and sunbathe, got quite a tan and so has Sylvia. She used the ladder today but came up right away. I really can't understand how she can be so afraid of the water considering what we are doing. There is simply no logic in women.

'Up to now it's been a milk run, that is to say from Ensenada to here, but things are bound to change sooner or later. I have absolute confidence of course that whatever happens we'll cope. Morale is high and the only disturbing thing is the monotony of having to row so many hours every day. Still, there is not much else to do and having a companion improves things enormously as one has a lot more time to rest.

'Got through to S. Francisco on the radio after trying for half an hour when I was just about to give it up for the day. Ivan was not there again which is rather infuriating when one goes to so much trouble to get through. I think I'm going to tell him what I think of it next time. After all, he only has to do it twice monthly! Sylvia gave me a much needed haircut to-day but I'm afraid she overdid it. However by the time we reach Australia I should be all right again. Speared a dorado for lunch and dived to 40 feet.

'Sylvia has indigestion! Or so she says.'

If my agitation at Ivan's absence seems unreasonable, as it most likely was, maybe I should explain exactly what was involved every time we made a radio call. Far from being a question of pressing a button and lifting a receiver, to prepare for a call took us over two hours. The weather had to be splashless, as the tiniest drop of water in the generator electrics would finish the calls for ever more. Two hours before the scheduled time I would uncover the generator, unlash the petrol jerrycan and fill her up, start her and let her run till we were ready. Then we had to unlash the aerial mast, pull the two aerial prongs out from their home in the rat-hole roof and screw them into the aerial.

Meanwhile Sylvia had to clear the galley of all its storage jars, kettle, pots and pans, dismantle the gimbals and pull them out in order to reach the radio situated, for dryness, at

the far end of the galley blister behind all this junk. I would
then pass her the aerial leads to plug into the radio and she
would switch on to 'Receive' whilst the set warmed up for
ten minutes or so and I, at the far end of the boat, erected
the twelve foot aerial. I had to clamber over all her galley
stuff littering the deck and, propping myself up on one
elbow with my head and shoulders in the galley, constantly
repeat, 'Calling K.M.I. . . . Calling K.M I. . . . If you read
come in please.', wait hopefully, then repeat the whole
shebang until we got an answer.

After the call another twenty minutes or more would pass
as we pulled the lot down and put it all away again. It was no
joke and cancelled any other activities for the entire morning.
When we started to do it at night and everything had to be
stowed by torchlight, it became even worse, when we
received no reply then, our language was unprintable.

From John's Log

26.8.71   123rd day
'Beautiful day, but very hot. Sylvia says she definitely has
indigestion and won't eat to-day. We'll see what happens
later.

'As I thought, she couldn't resist the temptation and ate as
usual. Complained all night but rowing did her good. She got
scared again to-day when some very big fish or mammal —
presumably whale — jumped three or four times some 300
yards from *Britt* making tremendous splashes. It will never
cease to amaze me how she can get so afraid about certain
things and not care much about other far more dangerous
ones. A whale or whatever feels in a happy mood and jumps,
and she gets the jitters. A hurricane might hit us any time and
she shrugs — what can we do about it? Women are mad.'

From Sylvia's Log

26th August, Thursday   123rd day
'The day of the Monster and two months from Ensenada.
Yesterday's fish was far too fatty and I probably ate it too

fast because have had indigestion ever since. For lunch to-day had our first steak (Mountain House freeze-dried Beef-Steak, very good and a nice "real meat" chewy texture). Seems to have worsened my troubles, have never had it so badly, and rarely at all. The radio station answered just as we were giving up after 25 minutes calling. I had said to J. that I'd like to bet Ivan wouldn't be there, because J. had made the mistake of telling him, last time, not to worry if we didn't get through as we'd be going through a bad weather zone. Needless to say he was out and we were 'dealt with' by a stranger, who was very nice but still a stranger, who recorded our message. Makes me hopping mad, apart from anything else, what about the information we asked for? He doesn't know how vital it is, or its urgency. Besides, when I remember all the trouble John Parker and John Mahoney at I.T.N. in London went to during J.'s Atlantic trip, not only to talk to him but also to enable me to do so, I think who the hell does Ivan Sharpe think he is? We don't speak to a soul apart from ourselves except for once in two weeks, and then he can't bother to be there.

'I even asked him after the first time this happened if he could arrange for us to speak to someone we knew if it was likely to happen again and he said he'd leave a message with the answering service and we could call the following day. We don't just pick up a receiver and dial, the whole operation takes us a good two and a half hours, weather permitting, and he talks about his darned answering service. Maybe I just have to get mad at something, and poor Ivan's it to-day. Really makes me feel very guilty, having written all this, to remember what a great help and good friend Ivan was in San Francisco.

'Sitting on deck after lunch I saw the biggest head I could ever imagine pull itself out of the sea and flop back with a most gigantic splash about 250 yards away. Almost paralised with fear, I told myself I'd imagined it, witnessed a repeat performance, and called J. He saw it twice — while I was fastening my safety belt! It was dark brown and about 1½ times the height of the blistered end of *Britannia.* Its return splash came higher than itself. J. said I was crazy to be afraid;

he was hoping it would come closer to us, so he could get some good pictures. I was hoping it would keep right on going and not even know we were there. That's the difference between Johnny and I, he's an adventurer, I'm a tourist. The way I see it, anything with a head that big, must weigh tons and be of a size which doesn't bear thinking about. A creature that size need not be hostile or aggressive, could be the most friendly soul beneath the sun, but one playful mistake could be the end of us.'

From John's Log

28.8.71   125th day
'Calm almost, incredibly hot. Shaved. Sunbathed. Cursed the heat. Sylvia can kiss again. Midday and all is quiet.

   'Sylvia couldn't resist the heat and used the rope ladder I made for her. It was the most hilarious performance I have ever seen of anyone going into the water for a swim. Well, she didn't swim really. Never let go of the bloody ladder and after a couple of minutes was back on board. I got a mind of giving her a good push one day and see what happens. Trouble is she may go down like a stone.'

From Sylvia's Log

28th August, Saturday   125th day
'Johnny's absolutely cheesed off with rowing and I keep telling myself rowing isn't always like this. Anyone who has ever rowed in a badly balanced eight will understand if I say it's that way all the time out here, and any amount of juggling of hands and pressing of feet isn't going to have much effect on a ton and a half of boat. However critical I might have been, and other rowers, of Johnny's style — or lack of! — during the Atlantic trip, I can now appreciate how absolutely powerless the finer points of the game are in conditions like these. It's backbreaking, to say the least. I doubt if I'll every row for St George's Ladies again after this lot, any style I might once have had will surely be gone for ever.

'The other criticism is that we have a booklet on identification of fishes, and have only seen three or four species, but nothing on birds, of which we have seen many varied species. Forgot to mention another happening on the day of the Monster.

'Sometime between the phone call and the Monster I used the ropeladder Johnny made for me for the first time. It was hilarious. To start with instead of hanging vertically, because of the drift on *Brit II*, it more or less floated horizontally so that, having one foot on the top rung, I found no lower rung for my other foot. Having overcome this and with both feet on the bottom rung and both hands on the gunnels, it is now me who is almost horizontal as, for some strange reason, my feet and legs are raised before me right against the hull, and I'm getting a ducking with every wave as the boat rolls. I never had intended to let go, and soon had had more than enough. With the aid of a strong pull from J. I was soon safely back on board again — but what a performance!'

29th August, Sunday   126th day
'Last night's sunset was the most colourful yet. The entire sky joins in the sunsets round here, not just the part around the sun, and it is frequently the side opposite the sun which is the more colourful. Last night it was everywhere, the most unbelievable colours, green, a real definite apple green, muddy greeny-grey, mushroom, pale peach, deep plum, gold, dove-grey, turquoise to almost peacock, and a whole range of blues, flames and pinks, a really incredible sight. Even the cloud shapes are weird and unreal so that almost any tiny section, if accurately reproduced, would make a beautiful abstract painting which no-one would ever associate with the sky!

'Dreamt a very good girl friend of mine phoned to tell me she expects her second child in March and it will be a boy. I queried the boy bit, but she said, "Oh, yes. They can tell you now." Putting this in so I don't forget, time will tell! [It did: she has not had one.]

'Have a new trouble now. During the night the gum on my lower right jaw, behind all the teeth, swelled up and is very sore and soft. Doesn't feel like an ulcer. Hope I'm not cutting a wisdom tooth, can't remember if I have them all or not, because there doesn't seem much room for it. Besides, out here? What a place to choose! And cutting teeth at my age? Ridiculous! J. said he'll dig out some antibiotic to-day and try to get rid of all my mouth troubles — hope so.

'Became ever so still during the night and to-day the sea is barely audible. Also it's incredibly hot, very little wind but, luckily, quite a few clouds and little showers which are a joy.

'This is the first day we have not discovered a flying fish in the boat at first light, for five days that is. For the past four days there has been a small, solitary flying fish on deck each morning. Each has been twice the size of its predecessor so we were getting hopeful for breakfast but, regrettably, the last was only three inches, so we have a long way to go. I've never tasted them and everyone says they are delicious.

'So hot and calm that I actually had a swim! Got J. to go in first and fight off the beasties for me, then I went down the ropeladder, complete with flippers but easily. J. said I was to swim in front, not behind, the boat, so I could not lose it and he kept an eye on things and soon I was very comfortable and unconcerned. After a while he said he'd bring the school of dorados round from the other side of the boat for me to see; I laughed — how on earth does one herd a school of fish? Well, sure enough, after a moment or so he appears, swimming slowly backwards beckoning with his hands, followed by the school of dorados, just like the Pied Piper of Hamlyn. There were six or seven of them, rather disappointing under water as they had no colour, just silvery, and they looked at me, I looked at them, then they went.

'After a while I climbed back on board then J. came later. Very enjoyable. Half an hour or so later J. says, "Look! The whole sea's full of dolphins. Or whales? Where's the camera?" I saw them heading straight for us, about a hundred yards away. They looked very big, and were mouldy brown numbering twenty or so. Before I knew what was happening (in fact while I was fastening my safety belt!) J. had dived in and was chasing them. As they neared the boat, the whole school veered to the left and swam past altogether.

'Interesting that they didn't let the boat come between them, as would have happened had they kept to their original course, with some to her left and others to her right. J. said they dived beneath him very deep rather than get near and the closest he managed for his photograph was about ten feet — close enough, I say! He said they were only about fifteen feet long and had short snouts like a bottle-nosed dolphin, but shorter. Watching them in the distance I saw one raise its head, like the Monster only in miniature, lighter coloured and making no splash on return. I also heard them make a noise I've heard several times in the far distance, a sound like elephants trumpeting. This time it was much closer and very loud and they just made two hoots. Pleased about this because J. never seemed to hear it and I didn't know what it could be.

'As if this were not enough, as I sat on the stern chamber watching them disappear, I glanced into the water beneath me and there was an eight-foot white-tip shark! Complete with his entourage of pilot and sucker fish etc. J. grabs camera and knife and is back in the water again, leaving me to sweat it out till he came back ten minutes or so later, feeling rather pleased with having got pictures of dorados swimming round shark.

'Otherwise, for Sunday treats we had a can of German potato salad, a tin of Zucchini, with Pork Chops, and I mixed a double portion of Fruit Galaxy. This is a really fresh, crunchy fruit salad and the jar was lying around, and J. seemed pretty indifferent so I kept dipping in, till suddenly realised there was hardly any left and he had had the tiniest little taste! Gave him the remains and said I was sorry, which I was. He said, "That was rather unfair of you," which it was. That was the end of a matter which might easily have become a major row. In the afternoon a squall came with delightful, soft refreshing rain.'

31st August, Tuesday   128th day
'Saw a strange fish beneath the boat whilst preparing breakfast. Later J. dived and tried to spear it unsuccessfully. During the day he dived two to three times more but each

time the stranger outdived him by disappearing into the deep,
only to come right up under the boat again the moment J.
was safely aboard! Later in the afternoon he speared a
dorado, mainly to use as bait for hooking the Stranger, but
also, in case the Stranger should not be hooked, as a standby
meal. This is where the trouble starts. He is already putting a
lump of dorado on a hook at the end of his great thick line
wound round a cylinder of wood with nails stuck in it, as he
turns to me and says, "Would you like to try?"

'I told him I'd have to change the hook on my reel, and he
said I couldn't use my reel as the line was too thin. Rather
than a make a major issue of it I said I didn't feel very
interested in fishing or anything else as my gum was making
me miserable. So far so good! J. throws pieces of dorado.
Stranger rushes out and grabs them unhesitatingly. Then J.
throws hooked dorado. Stranger rushes out, steadies, swims
round, then back to boat. This performance is repeated three
or four times, and he had no need to be a particularly
brilliant fish to see the lump of cord that bait was dangling
on.

'Eventually J. says to me to get out my reel and try the
finer line. I wish I could say I caught the b. but the nearest I
got was for him to bite on two occasions, run a while and
both times free himself before the action even started. Then
J. said I was casting all wrong (so what? I'd got nearer
the damned fish than he ever had, hadn't I?) took my handle,
reel and tackle, took it back over his shoulder and gave a
mighty hurl, thereby sinking the hook about three feet from
the boat, and my beautiful intrepid reel about a foot away.

'My anger had been steadily mounting throughout this
whole episode, and now he'd lost my precious reel, my one
symbol of independence in this entire boat. It was too much,
I had never wanted to get involved in the first place, I really
did feel under the weather, and I am very bad at being
helped — if I'm doing something I like to do it on my own, in
my way, win or lose — besides which, I am very possessive
about my personal belongings; all this added up to tears.
Also, the reel had been given me in San Francisco by Ken and
I had rather hoped to be able to return it in good condition

at the end of the voyage as a kind of souvenir.

'Of course Johnny was sorry, but I was in no mood for sympathy, it seemed to me he could and was doing everything on this trip and I was just a useless passenger and the one thing I jolly well was going to learn to do better than him, he'd now lost and ruined. The more I thought, the more I cried and the more my accursed gum hurt, then suddenly Johnny lost his temper. Swore at me, threw our delicious dorado fillets in the drink, I screamed at him that it was our dinner and I couldn't eat much else with my gum, he said he wasn't eating, so I said I wasn't going to bother either, etc. etc. etc., till the carcass of the remaining dorado followed the fillets. 'Pity we have no neighbours, they missed a treat! Ended up with me eating the little fillets put aside for bait and him eating chili and beans and promising to raise hell and high water to get me another reel on Christmas Island — which I said was a pipe-dream we would never see, thereby rekindling the whole scene! Meanwhile the Stranger slowly swims alongside, about a foot below the surface.'

1st September, Wednesday   129th day
'All is forgiven. The Stranger has left us. The sky is just cloudy enough. A few pleasant showers. The sea whispers and rocks. Peace reigns once again.'

7. We aim for land

On September 2nd we got through to Ivan, who redeemed himself by giving us a mass of detailed information about the islands and also put some of Sylvia's fears at rest by telling us that the French nuclear explosion tests had been cancelled due to pressure from Peru. Apparently the biggest island of the group was Christmas, which had 250 inhabitants and plenty of water, so we decided to head for that. I had wanted to try for Fanning which I thought was uninhabited. Ivan said the prettiest was Washington, which didn't worry me, but if we missed Christmas, we could always try for one of the other two. We needed a rest and some more water and supplies, for our diet was beginning to bore me stiff.

I was getting more swimming time in, but the only shark I'd been able to tempt near to the boat and lasso was a tiny five-footer which I shot through the head.

Sylvia said it all sounded very evil in the dead of night, with me chuckling and talking to the beast: 'Thought you'd got away, eh? Ha, he, he, he!'

In the morning I asked her if she wanted to see it, tied alongside as the dorado had been to bait it.

'Ugh! No!' she answered, shuddering all over, so I let it sink to the bottom. Its teeth were too small to keep.

'Why don't you want to see a dead shark'. I was curious to know. 'You're a funny one.'

But Sylvia couldn't see it that way.

'Why?' she asked logically, 'If I'm afraid and would rather not see them living, should it be strange that I don't want to see them dead?'

A few days later the action I'd been waiting for came in earnest.

From John's Log

8.9.71   136th day
'Quite a day. Totally becalmed and impossible to row
because of heat. Sylvia got up to make breakfast at dawn and
after five minutes she yelled that we were surrounded by
sharks. I didn't really believe her but she kept saying that
there were at least ten sharks around *Britt* so eventually I got
up to have a look myself. Sure enough there were about
seven or eight medium size sharks around and in the calm it
was easy to spot them. Rowed till it became too hot, then
went over the side to take pictures of our sharks. I started
with the Nikonos II and, after taking a few shots of the ones
that came nearest to me, I asked Sylvia to pass me the
underwater movie camera. The blasted thing didn't work and
I could hardly try to see what was wrong with the shutter
under water as the sharks became increasingly bolder and
were starting to take passes at me. Being so many I had a job
to keep an eye on the lot.

'Finally I gave the movie camera back to Sylvia and asked
her to pass me the spear gun with the power head (bullet)
attached. Then I went for the biggest and boldest shark and
let him have it right in the head. The more I use the power
head the more I'm amazed at the tremendous power it has.
The shark died almost instantly and sank to the bottom
followed by the rest swimming greedily after the trail of
blood. Thinking that that would keep them busy for a while,
I swam back to the boat and changed spear guns, this time
for one with the normal spear head as I wanted to catch a
dorado for bait. I also took the Nikonos. A minute later all
hell broke loose with me in the middle of it. Sylvia was
leaning over the gunnels and suddenly screamed as a school
of at least two hundred little tunas and dorados swarmed
round the boat, right at the surface and in such panic that
Sylvia was drenched with the splashes, I thought they were
about to leap into the boat. As for myself, for a moment I
didn't know what was going on. I was so utterly surrounded
by darting fishes it was like being hedged by a living wall.

'Then suddenly an enormous blue fish whooshed through

it like lightning. The tuna and dorados scattered only to regroup again in the next second and I was once more jammed in the middle. However, I had had time to see that the cause of the commotion was a swordfish at least nine feet long. For the next five minutes or so I was able to take a few still pictures of the swordfish hunting, but must confess that I did so with some apprehension. If that son of a bitch decided to attack me, even by mistake or through irritation, I wouldn't have stood a chance, as most of the time being in the midst of that cauldron the sea around *Britt* had become I couldn't even see what was going on.

'Let me say that that was one of the few times in all my years of diving, in all kinds of water and among all sorts of fishes, that I felt scared. On the other hand it was an opportunity that may never repeat itself of taking pictures of a swordfish running amok in a school of tuna and dorados and I just had to go on snapping shots. I can only hope something will come out of them. The swordfish disappeared as suddenly as it had arrived and soon everything was normal. The sharks were back but kept their distance and I spent a couple of hours swimming around as it was too hot to do anything else.

'Another kind of fish came around, either wahoos or very similar to them, but these also never allowed me to get within shooting distance. The little tuna by the way are according to our booklet on fish identification, Skipjacks or Ocean Bonitos. While swimming I came upon an inflated porcupine fish and pushed along until Sylvia passed me a bucket and caught it on that. The porcupine fish became Sylvia's pet for a couple of hours, then she released it.

'Later took out Ronson's Camp'n Glow Lantern so that we were able to row at night in spite of continuing overcast. That's the only way of making light still left to us now our compass light and torches are all on the blink.'

9.9.71   137th day
'Rained all day, got 1 gall water. As I was rowing in the morning and Sylvia was cooking there was a commotion alongside *Britt* and the same thing as yesterday happened

again. A dark big fish was chasing bonito and dorados when all of a sudden something did jump into the boat and began to flap madly at Sylvia's very feet. This time I can hardly blame her for screaming! Anyway, it was a three-foot silvery blue dorado who, in trying to get away from the jaws of whoever was after him, had jumped from the pan into the fire. I let go the oars and tried to hold him but he was so slippery it turned out to be almost impossible and eventually he escaped over the side, presumably to his doom as by then he was rather stunned. Shortly afterwards the commotion ended.

'It is very funny how these fishes group around the boat when they are in danger, as if we could help them. Particularly in the case of the dorados being, as they are, among the fastest of all fishes, their attitude is completely incomprehensible. The same thing had happened during my row across the Atlantic although only once. It was when a school of bottle neck dolphins attacked my school of dorados, mine because they had been following me for over three months, instead of swimming away they all grouped around the boat — this only to be slaughtered by the dolphins. I thought at the time they were so used to the boat and me feeding them from it that they considered it a safe place, but obviously the same cannot apply to the present ones and least of all the bonitos which always stay deep and never come near the boat in normal circumstances.

'Anyway, the same thing happened again in the afternoon, only this time the big one was definitely a swordfish, maybe the same one as yesterday. I didn't go over the side this time but took advantage of things by spearing a bonito from the deck. Knowing that unless I was very quick I would lose it to the swordfish, the moment the spear struck the frenzied bonito, I pulled it in. As I pulled, the swordfish singled out my victim from the rest and streaked for it like a torpedo but I was fast also and got it out and into the boat in the nick of time.

'Once on deck the bonito flapped with tremendous energy and with blood spurting from the spear wound, made an appalling mess of things, to the horror and disgust of Sylvia.

Must say that she hates the whole business of my going over the side when I do, or otherwise fooling around with sharks and messing up the boat with fish. She likes to eat it though.

'Just before sunset as I leaned over the gunnels the strap of my Rolex wristwatch broke and before I had time to do anything, the watch disappeared in the void below. It was such a maddening stroke of bad luck I could hardly believe it. I'll never know how it broke, I have worn Rolex watches all my life and never had a strap break like that, but for it to break just as I leaned over the side . . . God dammit! This is the second Rolex I've lost in this caper, the first one was stolen from our hotel room in New York. Luckily I have another one. Hope this will last the journey.'

10.9.71   138th day
'Another day of action and Sylvia, poor thing, is beginning to wish she hadn't come! I don't really understand how she can get so scared about certain things, like a whale suddenly blowing a hundred yards from the boat. "So what?" I keep telling her, "they are harmless, as safe as houses", but what's the use! Things started moving in the afternoon when I decided to lasso a white tip shark so we could have pictures of the proceedings. In the morning I had gone for my usual dip, and noticed there were 2 white tips among the normal school of brown and, up to now, unidentified ones. I shot one with the powerhead and decided to keep the other for lassoing. Duty comes first and I had to row my schedule. Then catch some sleep. Then in the afternoon was ready.

'Sylvia was supposed to take the pictures. She wasn't very keen about the whole idea but eventually agreed to co-operate. To lasso a shark is really extremely easy and when done from a big boat like ours, it can be done with little or no danger. By using a big chunk of fish as bait, this being tied to a string, one tempts and eventually brings the shark alongside the boat. Once there it's child's play to guide it into a loop previously prepared and, once the head has gone through, one has to be quick in tightening the noose before the shark realises what has happened. After that it will go mad and start pulling, but the more it pulls the tighter it gets and eventually it drowns itself, as sharks must be able to swim freely if they are to breathe.

'Unfortunately the white tip proved itself a tough customer and twice got away after getting into the noose, this mainly because I was using a line that was too thick and did not run properly. The second time the shark was thrashing to free itself, an enormous whale surfaced and, making a terrific noise at it blew through the blowhole, it sounded like a ship's horn and poor Sylvia nearly went out of her mind with fright. The whale came up once more much nearer this time, only about a hundred yards from us and blew just as noisily. To make things worse, the white tip had got some funny ideas into its mind and started bumping the boat and that I didn't like in the least, so to put an end to it I shot it in the head with a bullet next time around and it went to the bottom like a stone; a shame really as I was looking forward to collecting its teeth. Oh well, there will be others. At last things quietened down and the beastly routine of rowing started all over again.'

There are two sides to every story, and here is Sylvia's:

10th September, Friday   138th day
'Another nightmarish day. I really am beginning to think I should have stayed at home knitting in front of the television and confining my rowing activities to England's peaceful inland waterways.

'As usual we had a little following of sharks of varied size (I am beginning to consider my swimming days part of a gentler past); as usual J. dived in to count them and shoot one, and see the lie of the land. We still have the bonitos and dorados with us, and one solitary trigger-fish who seems to have lost his school.

'Besides the usual brown sharks we had a couple of white-tip join us to-day, one must have been a good seven feet, this one dear Johnny decided to bait and lasso, inveigling me into taking pictures of the proceedings whilst sternly warning me not to panic or drop the camera when the shark starts to thrash and pull the boat! Well, I crouch beside the gunnels about 6 ft. from J. and the action, determined not to panic but to just keep pressing that button. White tip nears bait several times but doesn't seem to like the look of all that rope. He looks gruesome and enormous. Evil. I feel myself shaking and take myself firmly in hand. A few more passes and he takes the bait. I'm clicking steadily and feeling rather pleased with myself. The noose is round him. He doesn't know it. Noose tightens. White tip suddenly wakes up and thump! I do drop the camera (still held by neck strap). He thrashes. I'm drenched. J. struggles with the rope to hold him. He bangs and twists. Rope is round his tail, but too loosely. I am again in control of camera. J. is sweating and cursing. The beast has broken free. Apparently the rope used was to thick to tighten up fast enough but, if we were to be sure of this particular demon, there was no time to change it.

'We took up our positions for the second time. Personally, I was sure that whitetip would be many leagues away, but J. was confident its greed would win over and it would be back for a second go at the bait. The whole ghastly spectacle was repeated. Whitetip eventually fell neatly into the trap. I did not drop the camera at the first sign of life, water everywhere, J. sweating from exertion, me from fear, the shark fighting like fury, when suddenly . . . *sshoooo.* I looked away from the shark to see the most enormous, shiny black back of a whale about three hundred yards away. Look to change distance on camera and the whale has dived again. Back to shark in time for his freedom leap.

'At this point I really did think I might pass out. The whole shark ritual had had me shaking and the size of this newcomer, coupled with the proximity of the shark scene, made me feel completely dry, very dizzy and rather sick. J. gets powerhead, lures whitetip back and shoots him. I don't see him sink for his blood in the sea. I think it's time the whale resurfaced, but where the hell is it? The loudest blow-hole I've ever heard. J. said it sounded like a ship or steam train's whistle. Suddenly I want to go home: every-thing seems so huge and brutal. I reckon 100 foot for that whale, a friendly creature, but who wants friends that size? The sharks, a four foot one is hell to hold, a seven footer pulls the boat. As for swordfish, a prod clean through the boat, or worse a little stab straight through Johnny. Jumped out of my skin, there it was again, this time the same distance in front as it had been astern. Must have been at least eight minutes in between the two blows, just long enough to have forgotten. The last appearance was about a hundred yards, astern of us so she must have been having a friendly look around without us even knowing. She must have been pretty colossal to have got out of sound range before her next breath, because we never heard her again.

'This is a horrid thing out here, the feeling that one is being investigated by God knows what all the time. At night this is especially so as the locals seem to be much bolder and cheekier after dark, the situation is worsened when we have to use a lamp because we can then see absolutely nothing outside its glare, all is black, although anything but still and silent!

'We ate the bonito to-day, the first time I've ever tasted it and the first time I've ever seen fish of dark red meat. J. said it is best and delicious crispy fried, so I went to enormous bother with flour, egg, breadcrumbs and my Ronson Table Chef and produced the best crispy fry I have ever managed anywhere. Really was very good. We couldn't eat it all so I made fishcakes with the remainder, tasted good but looked a bit messy.

'A fair sized dorado came around last night after the slaughter and whilst J. was filleting the bonito. We fed him scraps and he came very near to the boat. He brought a friend round this morning but friend was rather cool and aloof. Our dorado has a small white scar on his neck so we know him (not J. inflicted). He now has a name, Jo.'

From John's Log

11.9.71   139th day
'It rained so much to-day that we collected nine gallons of water. I'm very happy about this because it begins to look as if we might not make it to the islands after all. The weather here in the doldrums is absolutely horrid from the rowing

point of view as the wind keeps changing around the card, never being the same for more than a few hours, and I'm afraid our progress is seriously handicapped. We are not going in circles but damn near to it. What is worse, however, is that we are getting too many S.E. winds, and this is pushing us to the west and we seem unable to lose latitude as fast as we should. I'm guessing because I have not been able to take accurate sights yet due to permanent overcast, but I'm afraid that that is what is happening and will be surprised if it turns out to be otherwise. Some lightning and thunder during the afternoon and Sy got all jittery again, but luckily it didn't last.'

12.9.71   140th day
'Sy has three pets now, which she made me promise I would not spear. They are a dorado — Jo, and two trigger fishes Porgy and Bess. These last two are quite fun to watch but a damn nuisance every time I try to fish as they go after the bait and pull it off the hook, their mouths being too small for them to get hooked. And Jo, of course, I have to watch line and hook as, if I ever get him, either with the line or the spear, I should never hear the last of it, especially since the business of the lost reel. Hundreds of bonitos around us but still have not been able to get near enough to one underwater to spear it. They are just too cagey to let me near. A calm day but wind S.E. God knows where we are! But I'll know tomorrow morning as I have been unable to take sights at sunset. I'm writing now under the Ronson Glow lamp but have to put it out because Sy doesn't like the feeling of being in bright light when all around us is absolute darkness.'

The fix was a disappointment, but much as I'd expected. We had travelled only 120 miles in the past seven days, most of it due West. We were by now truly in the doldrums, and our only consolation was that we'd done better than a sailing boat would have done. I spent a lot of time filming with the underwater gear but it made me furious that the cameras wouldn't work properly — the cassettes kept jamming or not running at all and the end result was nothing.

The heat during the day was now between ninety and a hundred degrees and the only shade in the boat was in the rathole, which was more like an oven. But Sylvia was still bubbling over with enthusiasm and curiosity.

From Sylvia's Log

17th September, Friday   145th day
'Porgy and Bess were swimming happily around at dawn, Jo too. When I started to feed Porgy and Bess, at tennish, I could hardly believe my eyes. They had collected another trigger fish, promptly named Number 3. Trigger fish, or at least our species of trigger fish, are from six to ten inches long, eight to nine inches round at their fattest, have tiny round mouths, and an extremely tough, scaly skin with an overall diamond pattern of a colour ranging from pink to dark grey. Their trigger is a high triangular dorsal fin which constantly wiggles from side to side as they swim.

'We can easily distinguish our three from each other, not only by appearances, but by their characteristics. Porgy is the largest, and also the palest. He is inordinately curious, to the extent of swimming partly on his side to get a better view of what's happening up here. Bess is the smallest, she was also the darkest before the arrival of Number 3. She is extremely shy and except at feeding times, swims under the boat out of sight as soon as she realises she's being watched. At feeding time she stays respectfully behind Porgy, taking only pieces he misses or drops at first. Then she seems to wake up towards the end of mealtime, realises she's still hungry and likely to stay that way, so she chases after everything, grabbing tit-bits even out of Porgy's mouth. They both behave like a pair of starved pigs.

'Now we have Number 3; he comes between the two in size but is by far the darker, and by far the bolder. The other two are only just becoming brave enough to necessitate us taking care of our fingers. Number 3 at his first feed, zooms straight in and takes his stand six inches from the hand that feeds him. I tossed the fish scraps to the other two, so he swam off towards them, but arrived too late. I had my face outside and level with the gunnels to watch them, Number 3 turned about, swam straight up at me, looking me square in the eyes, stuck his head out of the water six inches below me, and blew me a kiss — or was it a raspberry? In any case, the cheeky newcomer, six inches distant from a strange monster, put his head out of the water and blew a fountain of water three inches high! They are hilarious, even when not doing anything; just their shape and way of swimming is comic.'

19th September, Sunday   147th day
'Our lucky wind still blows but it was a hell of a miserable day. Wet, drizzle from above, splashes from below. Clothes wet, sleeping bags wet, hands and feet soggy, white and peeling. Windy, my lips in trouble again. Have to cook outside as have been unable to repair gimbals as yet. Actually, didn't cook at all, just boiled water, but had to hold kettle the whole time to stop it sliding off gas ring. Had a tin of Prem and a tin of macaroni salad for main meal.

'Caught only two gallons of water. Whenever the rain was hard enough to make the effort worthwhile, the wind was too strong and our collection would have been ruined by salt water splashes.

'Rowed quite a bit during the day as it was pretty chilly doing nothing, and what else can one do being that wet? More seriously, we want to take every possible advantage of this wind whilst it lasts.

'To-day is the birthday of my oldest friend, by which I mean I have known her since I was four. We were neighbours, went to equivalent, though different, schools, had the same kind of upbringing and background and, I supposed, were intended to develop into the same kind of adult. She now has a perfect husband, a model home and three beautiful children. Whilst I? I know that there is nowhere I would rather be and nothing I would sooner be doing at this time — I just hope I have not left it too late.

'Had a very funny dream — not so funny the way things are going at present. We arrived at a quayside which was wide and concreted. Standing to receive us were two gentlemen in white grocers' coats, before them was a large carton containing all the supplies on our list, behind them was a shack combining grocers and greengrocers. As we drew alongside they stepped forward and announced that they were from P. & O. Lines, who had gathered our supplies together to save us time. We asked where we were and they told us Marseilles! They hoped the supplies were adequate and was there anything else they or P. & O. could do to help us? We started stowing the supplies and I realized there was not quite as much of everything as we wanted, but it was all top quality and it was so nice of them that we decided to say nothing. The bananas were very large American ones, individually wrapped in cellophane, the salami was rectangular instead of round, the rest either didn't figure or I forgot.'

In the middle of September we got some more brisk north-easterlies, for a few days, which cheered us up a bit. It also rained, in bucketsful, which replenished our water jugs enough for two months supply. But it got both of us down.

From Sylvia's Log

25th September, Saturday   153rd day
'A big white bird swooped down at my face, about eighteen inches short, this morning after circling the boat several times. Have never been able to understand how people can have a phobia of birds, but this was pretty disquieting. On his next circle the bird landed on the stern chamber right beside me. Showed absolutely no fear of J. or myself. He was a rather scraggy specimen with a windspan of approximately 4 feet, back edges of his wings were brown and tatty looking. He had small grey webbed feet and a long straight grey beak with grim looking grey eyes atop. After ten minutes or so he left us and we never saw him again.

'Yesterday evening I had my first shot with a speargun — and missed. Telling Johnny how much and irrationally I hated sharks, especially the big brown at present alongside, he asked me if I'd like to shoot it. I stood with the bullet in the powerhead held about two inches above the water, whilst J. lured the victim elect alongside by means of the bonito's

head. At point blank range, hardly daring to breathe, I
squeezed the trigger. The rubbers sprang, the shark swam
coolly away, the bullet remained intact. J. then shot a smaller
one, to ensure the bullet was OK and asked me if I'd like to
have another try. Not to-day thank you! My jitters had been
steadily mounting since I first took the gun, so I was by now
quite shaky. After all, it was my first shot ever at a living
thing.'

26th September, Sunday   154th day
'Three months since Ensenada — most of this one having
been spent on getting nowhere fast. To-day is another rough,
wet, windy day. For our meal we had a tin of sauerkraut
mixed with a tin of corned beef and rice, eaten hot was OK.
    'The most miserable part of this spell is having to get up at
4 a.m. every morning to row. J. does from 12-4, wakes me, I
do a couple of hours rowing, then get breakies. The bad part
is that sun-up isn't till nearly six round here and the water is
very lively. During the northern part of our trip, i.e. before
Ensenada, the phosphorescence was minute little squiggles,
thousands all jiggling about in the blackness, now it is very
little like that and mostly big solid flashes, really brilliant,
frequently near the boat and often over four feet in length.
Like everything else, if I knew what was going on I would not
be bothered. Besides the phosphorescence, there is plenty of
noise, dorado leaping, other fish splashing, bird noises and
unidentifiable noises which I try to convince myself never
happened.'

27th September, Monday   155th day
'Still lousy, miserable weather. Better to say nought than
grouse for pages.'

28th September, Tuesday   156th day
'A small school of brown short-nosed dolphins stayed around
our bow for three or four hours this morning. They were
about eight feet long and most uninteresting, no frolics on
their part. Their sole contribution to the day's statistics was
the annihilation of a few bonito, thus causing great excite-

ment amongst our aviary (now grown to some two or three hundred birds of mixed species).

'We have a close little following of dorado now. Jo you've met, was shortly joined by Mark (for 'Marked by Johnny'), then Mangy came along (his flesh is all fight-torn like an old Tom cat) with his mate Jet (who always gets there first). There is one with his own small scar and, as there are always six to dinner, we assume the sixth is always the same too. There are another twenty or so, constantly lagging behind, who are too timid to feed yet, but we keep hoping. My lovely Gerber Knife is no more. J. used it to mark Mark on Monday, pulled the knife out and nine-tenths of the blade sank to the bottom of the deep, leaving the remaining stub in the handle in Johnny's hand. Must have been a fault in the blade but, as it was one of the few things I like in this boat, I'm sorry to lose it.'

29th September, Wednesday   157th day
'Hate! Hate! Hate! Hate being wet. Hate rowing wet. Hate sleeping wet. Hate the wind. Hate sore lips. Hate spotty bottom. Hate tangled hair. Hate pitted hands. Hate peeling nose. Hate the dirt. Hate tippy cooking.

'It must get better. The wind will drop and the sea will calm, and one day my nose will get used to the sun, and when we reach *our* island I'll clean everything and Johnny can mend the gimbals. And at least we know where we are and like it, which is the main thing.

'Made some super stodge cakes using wholewheat flour, sunflower seeds, California Raisins and mixed spice. The last ones I made were a corncake mix to which I added raisins, also good.

'I'm more sorry than ever that we have no bird identification book. By late afternoon there are usually over two hundred hovering about, yet in the early morning there are rarely more than two or three. I'm sure neither of us will remember where we saw which birds, assuming we get round to looking them up once home. High above the flock hang what I call the witches, numbering up to six. They are black with a white chest, have short necks but long forked tails;

however, the tail is usually two parallel prongs, as in a tuning fork, and rarely an open V. They seldom move their huge angular wings, except to fold them back to plummet down on some poor little bird who has managed to snatch some food from the sea, in order to terrorise him into relinquishing his catch. The witches dwarf every other bird here. They follow each other, usually in pairs, so closely that each turn and twist is duplicated exactly two or three feet behind.

'Once in a while one will dive and catch his own food, several times this has been a flying fish far too big to swallow, but nevertheless another witch will swoop down on the hunter and harass it till the catch is won or lost. They look sinister and I hate them in the same way as I hate sharks and that little parasitical yellow fish which is still under the boat. My favourite bird out here is the little stormy petrel, we only ever see them singly, the throng is ahead of us but they stay astern and at a distance, pretty and quiet. The bird which so scared me re-appeared yesterday for a short while. Actually I think a different one of the same species because he looked spruce and well fed and really quite pleasant.'

From John's Log

27.9.71–1.10.71   155th–159th day
'Been so fed-up these last four days. I just couldn't be bothered to write. It's really a pain in the arse this writing the log when nothing happens. Anyway Sy is doing an excellent job with hers. To her everything is still new, therefore exciting and worth writing or talking about. She is in a poor shape lately, what with a sore bottom, and lips, and her long hair matting up and a peeling nose and, hey . . . she really is getting the treatment. Don't know many women if any who could put up with and cope with life such as is out here. Yet she is always cheerful, well, almost always. I'm really proud of her. Already she has been in an open rowboat longer than any man except myself and, of course, no woman has ever even attempted to do what she is doing. Quite a girl Sy is, quite a girl!

'We cannot possibly reach Christmas Island. The wind just

keeps pushing us west but I'm almost sure we'll make Fanning, as was the original intention anyway, if the weather remains the same. Should get there in about eight to ten days in fact. But it is such a small island, roughly ten miles long and less than half that wide that it will be a real problem to navigate if in the last three days or so we get overcast and I can't take sights, and even if I can the slightest change or lack of co-operation by the wind and we'll miss. Oh well, we shall see what we shall see.'

From Sylvia's Log

30th September, Thursday   158th day
'No radio call to-day, too rough. I hope the folk at home don't get worried sick but realise that "Too rough" doesn't necessarily mean that we are going through hell, in constant peril of our lives, or being thrown hither and thither at the sea's whims. In fact, more often than not, it's just a little choppy and the irregularity of the waves endangers the electrics of the generator. Last night we witnessed a real comedy, it would have made a priceless film but unfortunately the light had begun to fade. It began with one of the white/brown birds that landed on *Britoo* before circling around, but pretty soon there were five of them. I must say they were all neat, clean and fine looking birds — the scruffy one which so scared me must have been a real freak. The five were circling closer and closer and there was no room for five birds on that size to land on *Britoo*.

'Luckily they left us after twenty minutes or so and we thought that was that, until one returned. He wanted to land on our aft chamber in the manner of his predecessor, but he seemed to be having a little bother. His first attempt stopped him short so he fell in the sea, sideways in a most undignified manner. We held our breaths to stifle the laughter, since I'm convinced animals know when they are being laughed at. His second effort overshot the mark so he flew straight over the target and once again fell in the sea. Third time lucky? Well, no, not quite; this time he landed on the smooth, curved surface of the blister only to slide straight off the other side,

and so back into the sea. This time we just had to laugh but
he was a very persistent fellow, not to be deterred by the
inane cackles of those who can't even fly!

'Round about his tenth serious attempt (that is, disregard-
ing those passes so distant that even he realised the
impossibility) he finally landed near the end of the chamber,
his little webbed feet skidding frantically, his wings raised for
balance, in fact hardly a comfortable position, yet one in
which he seemed determined to stay — however, someone
else had other ideas.

'Our friend had only been in position for two or three
minutes when his mate came back for him. She dived at him,
quacking and cackling as only a mate can, but he stuck to his
precarious perch. Mate circled, then attacked again, louder
and nearer, still no response. Her third and most violent
attempt failed, so she then decided "if you can't beat 'em,
join 'em."

'She was far more controlled than he, and soon had a nice
spot for herself on the wide, flat part of the blister where she
neither skidded nor needed her wings. The pair of them stood
swaying side by side, he ignoring her, and she turning to give
him the odd nag and bicker, until a bigger roll than usual sent
him sliding off into the sea again. Well, now he had less than
half the landing space available than on his first landing, so he
was circling and falling into the sea for a good half hour,
madame refusing to move and let him have more room, till he
finally flew off never to return.

'She stubbornly stood her ground but gradually one saw
the twitches of anxiety and surreptitious glances over her
shoulder, and eventually she gave in and flew off in search of
her lost mate.

'I think her behaviour was typically wifely in that she
leaves the flock intending to rejoin it with her erring
husband. Finding him enjoying himself and refusing to leave
she scratches and nags unsuccessfully till she realises they
have now both lost the flock. Now she decides to make the
best of things and stay with him, but he leaves her. After a
decent interval off she goes in search of him, to repeat the
same story so many times!'

1st October, Friday   159th day
'A big brown shark, nine footish, was following us and giving
me the creeps so. J. suggested I hooked him then he'd dive in
and shoot him with a bullet, and I could have the teeth.
Sounds fair enough and easy? Well it may, but the result was
a first class slanging match between J. and me, and no teeth
either. I've hooked a few sharks and never once have they put
up a fight until pulled out of the water. A dorado puts up a
far better show, and as for a bonito, well, you just can't hold
their line without gloves.

'J. said, "Don't throw the hook till I tell you", so I waited
obediently till the order was given, threw my line, hooked
my shark, pulled him in a good way and waited for the
bullet. J. hadn't put on his flippers, mask gloves, gun,
anything, just nowhere near ready and there was I dangling
this brute like a yo-yo.

'The shark slowly awoke to the fact that all was not well
and began to pull away, so I let him have more line and go.
Meanwhile J., still not ready, starts yelling at me to keep it
away from the rudder and not let him under the boat. I was
keeping the line as short as I could, but if it came to a tug of
war between me and a nine foot shark (even though he is just
steadily pulling and not fighting), I knew who'd be the loser.

'Finally the inevitable happened, shark lazily swam beneath *Britoo*, round the rudder back to the other side, neatly
snapping the line on the rudder. J. swore at me for letting
him get round the rudder, and I cursed him for telling me to
cast so long before he was ready, and we had a fine slanging
session ending with J. diving in the sea. He came out later,
having had to shoot my shark, rather than be beaten, and we
both apologised and all was well again. We really do get along
extraordinarily well. This doesn't surprise either of us, but
seemed to be the major interest of most people concerned.

'I appreciate that circumstances are somewhat confined
out here, but if two people are in sympathy under normal
conditions, why should they become aggressors simply
because of a change in surroundings? Also, neither J. nor
myself are wildly sociable, we have a few friends but don't
often see them, we don't talk much and we don't go to

parties etc. any more than we can help, so I suppose we are
not missing people as much as a more gregarious couple
probably would.

'One thing I wish we had on board a few music casettes,
not for all the time, but now and again, otherwise all is well
and I'm sure I could not be in better hands — after all, how
many girls can say, 'I fancy fish for dinner , and have their
man dive into the sea, returning in under two minutes with
dinner on the end of his spear?'

By the beginning of October it became obvious that we
were not going to make Christmas Island, because we had
drifted too far to the west, so instead we headed for Fanning.
For some unexplained reason — a current perhaps, which we
did not identify — we made 160 miles in three days. It was
hell on my navigation, but on the morning of October 5th we
woke to see Fanning two miles away . . .

From John's Log

5.10.71   163rd day
'Blast everything to hell and back! After all this work!
Bloody, filthy drogue fouled up during the night and we
woke at dawn to see Fanning about three miles to the
south-west of our position and the wind blowing too hard
from the south-east for us to make any progress against it in
spite of our efforts. I'll be goddamned, how can such a thing
happen? A white beach, so near we can see the surf breaking,
and we cannot reach it!

'We decide to go on to Washington Island, 70 miles to the
south-west of Fanning. Only a dot in the chart I have.
Chances of making it rather dim, and we are going back, so if
we don't get there I'll never forgive myself. No mood to
write. Hell and damnation, what have I done to deserve this?'

6.10.71   164th day
'Streamed the drogue again at midnight last night. Don't
want to be caught again with my pants down in case that
S.O.B. drogue fouls up. At dawn could only take a shot of a

single star, Capella, due to overcast. Shot the sun three hours later, thus getting a fix, but same unreliable. Position apparently only 25 miles S.E. Washington at dawn. 11.00 Z.T. Transferred second sun shot, result puts us 25 miles N!? of Washington. Can hardly believe it. If correct, we are now in a lousy position to make Island. How on earth could we have drifted so far north? Stream drogue again, must wait till noon to confirm position. 14.00 Z.T. In this latitude the sun changes azimuth so fast around mid-day it is possible to get accurate fix within an hour, taking sights at 11.30 hours, noon and 12.30 hours, and still get an angle of cut for the respective P.L. of nearly 45°.* Confirmed position, we are 20 miles north of Washington, but luckily still to the east of it, 16 miles to be precise. Question now is — with a S.E. wind, strength 7-10', can we row on a S.W. course for 20 miles while keeping our lee at less than 16'? What's more, having started an hour ago (Sy is at the oars at present), can we make it within visible distance of Washington before dark?

'23.00 Z.T. At anchor N.E. side of Washington Island in 50' water, moderate surf. All is well. Taking turns on watch in case anchor drags or line cuts against coral. Sy first, I'm dead.

'03.00 Z.T. My turn. Looks beautiful under moon. Cold. Very pleased with self.'

---

* Not so much Latitude, but declination of the Sun, being at the time only 2° or 3°.

8. Life on Washington Island

Verde que te quiero verde. Verde viento. Verdes ramas.
From *Romance sonambulo* by Federico Garcia Lorca*.

'Island looked absolutely beautiful, white sand beach and coconuts all over, green, green, green — I think green will be my favourite colour from now on.'

With this log entry the morning following our night arrival at Washington Island, John endorsed my own feelings. Until that daylight, I had never realised how must it was possible to miss a colour. It wasn't a question of missing foliage, or grass, or the smell of either, were were too far away for that, it was purely and simply the colour, the colour of life.

From where we were anchored, the only sign of habitation was part of the island's smaller settlement, Manounou, jutting out through the trees on the nearest point of the island. However, between the single-storey brick building visible to us and ourselves, stretched huge lines of breaking surf, so it was obviously impossible for us to proceed in that direction. Johnny had to dive to release the anchor, and then we set off rowing away from Manounou around the north coast of the island. We continued following the unbroken white beach till we came to another seemingly inpenetrable barrier of surf and here we anchored around 10 a.m. Johnny swam ashore, complete with mask, snorkel and flippers, to find the settlement and our best method of approach. I watched him plod unsteadily out of sight round the next point.

After half an hour or so I saw a man walk to the water's edge, look at the boat, examine the sand, and return to the

* 'Green, how much I want you, green. Green winds, Green boughs.
Quoted from *The Penguin Book of Spanish Verse* translated and edited by J.M. Cohen and reproduced by kind permission of Penguin Books.

woods. Five minutes later he returned with a companion, they both looked at the boat, examined the sand (presumably Johnny's flipper-foot marks), and returned to the woods. Another five minutes later, three men returned, looked at the boat, examined the sand and returned to the woods. I wondered what kind of monster they visualised.

John was gone a little over two hours. The first I knew of his return was a crowd of jolly children skipping along the beach with two adults, one of which was Johnny, the other the Island's schoolteacher. It was now about mid-day and extremely hot, making the inviting freshness of the island almost overwhelming, but John returned with a very long face, saying 'Bad news, darling'.

From John's Log

7th October, Thursday   165th day
'Swam ashore and eventually, wading along the beach, found a little boy who took me to the settlement, about half a mile distant. Washington Island is privately owned, together with Fanning, by Fanning Island Plantations Ltd., a subsidiary company of Burns, Philp & Co. Ltd., and, with the aid of Gilbertese labour, they harvest copra. The Manager of the plantation, William Frew, J.P. was inspecting the roads. I was told by the chap who took charge of me — turned out to be Eria Tokoa, schoolteacher of the plantation and one of the few who spoke English — that they had no idea when he would return. He took me to the office-cum-First Aid depot and there had coffee with Tetaake, the local medic. Settlement very colourful, people charming, but they have no safe anchorage, no pier, and the surf on what was supposed to be their best beach, looked positively horrid for a long way out.

'Returned to *Brit* and gave Sy the news. If this Bill Frew turned out to be a decent fellow we would be all right. If not, we were in for a lot of work, as I could just see myself wading through that surf carrying five gallon jugs. The locals had outrigger canoes so I told Sy that if the Aussie — Bill was Australian — was on the level, he would turn up before night in one of them. If he didn't, he was most likely some kind of unsociable S.O.B. and the sooner we left the better.

'About an hour before sunset a crowd gathered on the beach and among them an unmistakeable looking European. To get into the outrigger, brought by tractor, he had to wade through the water, thigh deep, and I figured that that was as good a sign as any that he was going to be OK. By God he was! Brought some iced beer with him and we had a most pleasant chat for a while, but the sun was setting and they had to go back, as it would not have been possible to negotiate the surf in darkness.'

Here, from Bill's plantation log, is how he viewed our arrival and the events of the following day.

Thursday 7.10.71

'Weather fine and clear, wind light to moderate S.S.E., surf fair to poor. Inspecting block boundary roads and diagonals this day accompanied by Willie and road cleaning men. Took rifle for pigs but saw none. Returning along N.W. coast mid afternoon met young Tabaki who informed us small vessel with European man and woman aboard was anchored close by. Man had swum in over reef, walked into Settlement and later returned to vessel. We doubled back and had walked but a couple of hundred yards when we met Marina and the boys and Sapeta, Taubo, Tokibara and others on the tractor. Sent Rimon with the tractor to pick up Lauina's canoe and a few cans of cold beer. The rest of us strolled out on to the beach where we saw a peculiar looking craft riding at anchor just over the reef. Sat on the sand in the shade to await return of tractor. Kept rifle out of sight to avoid any possible misconception! Kids (Donald and Daniel and their young friends) had the usual fun playing in the water and sailing makeshift boats. Lauina turned up about an hour later with his canoe and he and Willie and I paddled out to the vessel taking with us a plastic bucket containing the beer.

'Met John Fairfax and Sylvia Cook and surprised beyond measure to learn that they were rowing their craft *Britannia II* from San Francisco to Australia. They had arrived off W.I. the previous evening after a non-stop voyage of 105 days from Ensenada in Mexico. They looked extremely fit and were so cheerful, casual and easy-going that we found it rather difficult to comprehend and fully appreciate their remarkable achievement. However, we felt immediately at home in each other's company and downed a few cold cans of ale and yarned for half an hour or so.

'John and Sylvia remarked that they stood in need of some fresh water as their saltwater distiller was not functioning satisfactorily, and that they could use a few provisions if such could be spared. They were also experiencing trouble with the generator which charged the batteries for their radio transceiver. We assured them we would do all we could and with utmost pleasure. This we meant wholeheartedly, for the thrill that their arrival at Washington Island must have occasioned them could scarcely have surpassed our own delight at so unusual a call. Returned ashore a little before dusk after promising to see them again in the morning.

Friday 8.10.71
'Weather as yesterday. At 8 a.m. loaded Ueleses' canoe on tractor and some food prepared by Marina and Willie in portable icebox. Arrived off *Britannia II* 8.30 a.m. and hailed John and Sylvia from beach with electric megaphone. Sent off two canoes (Lauina's and Uelese's) to bring them ashore. They breakfasted on the beach — iced pawpaw with lime, icecream and jelly, biscuits and coffee plus a shot or two of scotch. After breakfast we all boarded tractor for return to Settlement leaving Etene and Uoa as watchman aboard the vessel. Arrived back at Bungalow a few minutes before 10 a.m. radio sked with Fanning and Christmas Islands. J. and S. met Marina and family and later spoke with Phil Palmer and John Fleetwood on Fanning, and Jock Bryden and Dave Carmichael on Christmas. Jock copied message from J. and S. addressed to KMI Radio San Francisco for information Ivan Sharpe advising arrival Washington etc. . .

'Mid afternoon took tractor back along N.W. coast with J. & S. and men. John off to *Britannia II* in Lauina's canoe with Ioram, Baiai and Iebeta. John dived 70 feet to free anchor and moved vessel farther out from reef. Surf building up rapidly by late afternoon. Unable return ashore by canoe. Ioram, Baiai and Iebeta remained aboard as watchmen for the evening while John, Etene and Uoa swam in through heavy surf. Returned to Settlement. After dinner Sylvia attended movies with Marina and girls leaving John and I yarning over a few drinks.'

That morning Johnny and I had risen bright and early so that we would finish our breakfast before the arrival of our visitors, little expecting the exotic feast awaiting us on the beach. The two canoes had come out to us through quite heavy surf and their four men had been very interested in our *Britoo*, but no more so than we in their canoes. They were Ellice canoes, which are dug-out from the breadfruit tree, twenty to twenty-five feet long, about two feet deep and only fifteen inches wide, with an outrigger, supported by three parallel supports, to their left. The wooden strips serving as seats, outriggers, and all other joints, were fixed with string made from coconut fibre and no nails were used. The insides were painted green and the outsides black with coal tar. Lauina, a quiet, wiry Ellice Islander, together with Utah, his Gilbertese friend, had only just finished building the one which took us both ashore.

Even had it been a calm beach, I would have been delighted with the ride, but to sit in the canoe whilst such experts timed the waves and then paddled like mad to ride in with the surf, was a real thrill. It must have been a week after this that Bill told me they would never normally have taken their canoes out under such conditions.

Once ashore Bill introduced us to many of the Islanders as we staggered happily around on our sea-legs. We reached a clearing between the trees on the edge of the beach where palm leaves had been laid out in a circle for seats and all was cool, green and friendly. What a welcome, a dream of paradise! Soon we were sitting on the palm fronds eating jelly, ice-cream and paw-paw, drinking scotch and coffee.

After we had finished our sumptuous island breakfast, we all piled into the big open trailer behind the tractor, which is commonly known as 'the island bus', and set off into the woods, where the green shade was brightly dappled with the brilliant tropical sun. As we drove through the tracks which criss-cross the Island's 2,092 acres of coconut palms, we saw that the Island was not a plantation in the strict sense of the word, but a huge, natural coconut grove of great age from which an abundant supply of copra is produced with very little artificial aid. Behind the tractor straggled a long line of laughing children on their bicycles.

Before long we had arrived at the clearing in which the Island's main Settlement, Arabata, is situated. One of the first buildings we saw was the Company subsidised Government school, which is attended by most of the children. Eria teaches the older ones and the infants are taught by Marina's half-sister, Sapeta, and Tetaake's sister, Benian. The remaining children attend the mission schools run by the Roman Catholic and the Protestant Pastors. A very small percentage receive no formal education through choice.

From the eighty Company employees on Washington Island comes a population of some four hundred and forty, out of which around one third are of school age. There appeared to be children everywhere, beautifully behaved children with apparently very little supervision. They seemed to mature much faster than English or American children and two year olds ran freely around, walking and talking at a far earlier age than our kids ever do. The Islanders seemed to have little regard for age and an eleven year old, when asked to name her best friends, may well name children of six and adults of thirty in her list of nearest and dearest.

The Settlement was well planned and attractive, with the majority of the dwellings being either wood-planked or hardboard straightwalled buildings on a raised concrete platform with a corrugated roof. The others were typical Gilbertese houses, open sided structures with a thatched roof supported by four stout wooden corner posts, sloping almost to the ground, or stopping higher and having pandanus woven shutters to drop for protection or privacy. The kitchens were outside and open, the oven a raised oil drum beneath which coconut husks were burnt. The buildings were widely spaced with grass between and plenty of huge shady trees, but, according to Bill, we were unlucky as this had been an exceptionally dry year so the lush emerald green grass was now rather sandy coloured.

Eventually we reached Bill's long, low wooden house. Built in 1917, it stood raised above a large fenced garden along the sea shore. We walked through the red gate, across the lawn, beneath the terraced bourganvillea and up the central steps through the large, double doors. The house was spacious, cool and comfortable, its walls hung with grass-skirts, shell necklaces and fans, mostly made by Marina. Its doors were never closed, and there was a constant string of children and adults drifting it and out all times throughout our stay. Often they did not seem to be visiting anyone particular, but were just drawn by its warmth and friendliness.

Indoors we met the household, Bill's wife, Marina, from Funafuti (capital of the Ellice Islands), their two sons, Daniel, almost two, and Donald, three and a half. There was also seventeen year old Sapeta, their fourteen year old cousin, Tuli, Taubo the cook, Akineti who helped with the house, Oti who did wonders with the children, Tiari, Bill's thirteen year old Alsatian, and the two cats. Later I noticed one of the cats had enormous feet and Bill told me that, in common with half the cats on the Island, it had six claws. Tetaake later told me that some even have seven and, much further on in the crossing, at Tarawa, we heard these cats referred to as 'Christmas Island Cats' and that their extra claws are generally regarded as a mutation resulting from the atomic tests.

We had arrived at the house just in time for Bill's bi-weekly radio schedule with Fanning and Christmas Islands. This is the Island's only outside contact other than a Bank Line ship which comes twice a year from Australia, bringing the everyday supplies of civilisation (fabrics, tools, bicycles, sugar, rice, toiletries, etc.) and taking the annual harvest of copra to Europe and the UK. Under these circumstances it was hardly surprising when Bill, in reply to his friends' enquiries as to how he was doing, was not believed when he nonchalently replied, 'Oh, fine thanks, just had a couple of jokers row in from Mexico.'

It was really funny because they went on talking as though he had never said it and Bill had difficulty returning to the subject to introduce us! One of the men we spoke to, out there in the middle of nowhere, Dave Carmichael, Agricultural Officer on Christmas Island, had spoken to us at the Earls Court Boat Show in London before we started the trip, which I thought a pretty strange co-incidence.

Other than these two ships and radio contact with the two neighbouring Islands, the only outside contact is the occasional Colony Government Vessel calling from Tarawa, capital of the Gilbert and Ellice Islands of which Washington, Fanning and Christmas Islands form a part. This might happen once a year, or it may be that the odd year sees three such visits. The Colony vessel brings the District Commissioner from the Line Islands, Kitiseni Lopati, an Ellice Islander from Christmas Island, who, together with Washington Island's resident policeman and Bill, administers the Island. An Assistant Medical Officer is usually aboard the vessel as well, otherwise medicine and first aid are looked after by Tetaake and Bill, who can seek advice from the doctor on Christmas Island during radio schedules only.

In the afternoon we set off back to *Britoo* to see how the surf was, as it had appeared to be on the increase when we had left her in the morning. John was worried that our anchor line might be getting cut by the coral. We had only just eight feet of chain, the rest of the line was plaited nylon because we had intended making our crossing non-stop, in which case this problem would never have arisen. As his log describes, it was a fortunate decision:

'We went out in a canoe and very lucky it was, as the line had got itself wrapped around a coral head and was chafing rapidly. The problem became acute when, after repeated tries, we found it impossible to raise anchor. The damned line was so tangled it would not come up. Second mistake, in spite of having experienced same difficulty yesterday morning, I did not tie a buoyed line to the anchor. There was no choice but to dive for it only this time we were anchored in seventy feet and, after half an hour, I had been unable to reach beyond sixty feet. The sun was setting rapidly and I could see people ashore, not to speak of the chaps on *Britt*, getting increasingly nervous as the surf was building up quite alarmingly.

'In the days when I used to spear fish commercially in the Caribbean, I could free dive to a hundred feet without a second thought, but too many years have gone since. In desperation I hyperventilated until I felt dizzy — a very dangerous thing especially if diving alone, as one may black out without warning by anoxia — but I had no choice. The only thing that prevented me from getting to the required depth was the terrible pain caused by pressure on my unaccustomed ears, and to ease it I had to take a long time going down. Also, it looks as if it would take me a while to disentangle the mess, and I knew it was very unlikely that I could dive twice in the short time available. Oh well, I made it in what seemed to be the longest and certainly most painful dive of my career.

'Once up I had to assure my worried Gilbertese friends on *Britt*, none of whom was a diver, that the reason I bled from ears and nose was of no importance, a simple matter of superficial blood vessels which had burst under pressure. By time we moved *Britt* further out and I checked the bottom surrounding the anchor to make sure there were no standing coral heads, the sun was setting and the surf was too high to risk the canoe, so, leaving both canoes lashed alongside *Britt* with three relieved watchmen, the rest of us swam ashore.

'Having read about, but never tried before, the exhilarating experience of body surfing, I tried to see what it was all about and nearly got myself drowned in the process. By what I seemed to remember one has to get behind a wave and attempt to ride it just behind the crest as it starts to break. I thought it would be easy for a chap that could swim properly and proceeded to wait for a big monster, whereupon I placed myself right on top of it at the precise moment it broke.

'Next thing I knew I was being bashed, mashed, twisted around like in the grip of a giant mixer, and the only thing that prevented the breaking of my silly head against the coral bottom less than five feet below was that what little sense I had left I used to concentrate on going limp to let the forces of nature carry on. Next time I will, sure as hell, choose a sandy bottom — if there is a next time which, at the moment, I doubt very much. Forgetting my usual stubborn headed pride, I took my cue from the Gilbertese swimmers and ducked under the breakers in a much safer, if not quite so spectacular, way.

'After a delicious dinner Sy went to the movies — they have a small projector provided by the company — with the children and Bill's wife Marina — while I stayed yarning with Bill until well past midnight, slowly drinking myself to semi-consciousness. What a blissful night!'

Who would have guessed that my first night ashore, mid-Pacific, on an island of only five and a half square miles, would be spent at the pictures? The Company sends a selection of films on each boat and the weekly cinema is a highspot of the week, even though the films are at least twenty-five years old. Marina insisted on lending me some of her clothes for the occasion and I went cleanly and neatly dressed in a pretty floral skirt with a lacy white blouse and, together with Daniel and Donald, with pillows for them and a pandanus mat for us, we went off across the clearing to the Maneaba. This is a large open walled meeting hall with a thatched roof.

We found all the women with their children, most of the youngsters, and some of the men, sitting chatting on their mats waiting for the show to begin. Obviously this was a big social event so I, being the first European woman on the island for five years, aroused considerable interest, especially amongst the younger children, one of whom spent the entire performance trying to touch me without the notice of her parents. The film was in English, which very few of the audience understood, and those that did had difficulty in hearing above the chatter of their countrymen, but after a while all was quiet, the children fell asleep on their pillows or mats and the adults watched the action. It was very corny, all about some nice, reliable little man receiving his gold watch at the end of his forty years service, and the audience laughed

with a heartening honesty at the stiffness of the wifely pecks
on the cheek, and the artificial formality of the parties.

The following morning, in common with all my mornings
on Washington Island, but completely out of character
elsewhere, I was up and about, cold showers and all, before
six o'clock. After an extra radio schedule for our benefit, we
decided to follow the advice of Phil Palmer and John
Fleetwood, by moving *Britannia II* to the more sheltered
south-westerly side of the island, in front of a canoe passage
called Vaarua nearly a mile from Bill's house. It was hoped
this would make it easier for the canoes to reach *Britoo* for
loading and taking equipment ashore for repairs. This single
incident, as related in John's log, should help to explain why
we spent one whole month on Washington Island:

'With two canoes we towed *Britt* — the canoes equipped with
outboard motors — into position in front of Vaarua and had
her securely anchored by mid-day. Bill has given me some
fathoms of steel cable to attach to the anchor chain and now
there is no chance of the nylon line chafing against coral.
While going back ashore the local pilot of my canoe
misjudged the surf, with the result that we broached to and
capsized over flat coral bottom alongside the passage, only
waist deep in that particular place, and it was a sheer miracle
that nobody got hurt. However, the outboard hit coral and
was damaged and momentarily we lost everything that was in
the canoe. Momentarily because later, with the help of three
local divers, we were able to recover almost everything.

'At one time I was terribly upset thinking that the log
books, this one and Sylvia's, were irreparably lost but they
were found in the canoe, where, by another miracle, they had
jammed under a wooden cover at the bow. In the evening
there was a party called "Island Night" and we thoroughly
enjoyed ourselves.'

10.10.71   168th day
'During the morning, diving at Vaarua in spite of surf, we
recovered almost everything except three boxes of Edgar
Sealey Fish Hooks, (which I was taking ashore as a present to

the men that had been helping us), one of my flippers and a few small sundry items of no importance. By the way, yesterday I did not write as the log was being dried over a Coleman lamp quite successfully by the looks of it. Must say that these Pentel pens we are using have indeed proved to be as good as guaranteed, there being no signs of smudges whatsoever. Our intentions upon arrival were to stay only two or at most three days, but Bill's hospitality is so great that we have decided to postpone departure until next week. We can use the rest and sure need a change of scenery. My guess is that we'll spend the next few days loafing, but what the hell? Haven't we earned it?'

Having spent my first night ashore at the cinema, my second was passed at a dance in the same Maneaba. This was called 'Island Night' and was held every couple of weeks, as a fund-raising proposition by the Social Club that Marina runs. Before we left, Marina had fun dressing me up, tying my hair with two orange chiffon bows and finally placing a flower lei over the lot. At last we were ready and I trotted gaily along with Marina.

Once we were there I sat on a chair round the wall with everyone else, mostly teens and younger, whilst Marina said a few opening words — but I fear I attracted more attention than she did! Johnny and Bill had promised to join us after half an hour, but an hour passed with no sign of them. Gilbertese twist music wafted out of a taperecorder, but the dancers seemed too shy to dance and sat giggling and whispering (obviously, I thought, about me). I sat grimly telling myself it was natural for them to be curious under the circumstances, but felt more and more like a dejected fish out of water.

Food appeared, and the guests took plates and began serving themselves, till suddenly I could stand it no longer and, being convinced they were all too engrossed in the fare to notice me, gulping back my tears, fled for the door and the darkness beyond. I strutted out across the field to the house. But I was being followed, no, it wasn't imagined, a torch was flickering on my feet. I decided to play it cool, defied the instinct to run, and kept plodding till I reached the gate when children's voices behind me said, 'Goodnight, goodnight.' They had been lighting my way home for me!

I went in, secretly, and tearfully hid in the bedroom till I talked myself into wanting to go back with Johnny and Bill. I attacked them both for not going sooner and Bill was most concerned. To convince me how upset the kindly Gilbertese would be to know of my distress, he called his right hand man, Willie, to hear the story. Willie had been with Bill for fifteen years and had been his cook until Bill's marriage five years ago. He spoke excellent English, learnt from his Convent educated mother and improved by constant reading, and was very big and jolly.

By the time I had finished my tale of woe for the second time, Willie had us all doubled up with laughter at my stupidity and we all returned to the dance, where we had a really wild time with lots of clowning and twisting, and even a song from Johnny!

The Islanders are extremely sociable and Washington Island had three maneabas, the Company owned one and the other two were run by the Protestant and the Roman Catholic Churches. Besides the Social Club, Marina also runs the Girls' Brigade, whilst Bill and Eria lead the Boy Scouts. There is also the Homemakers' Club, where women learn and compare cooking, handicrafts and hygiene. Every Wednesday the committee of this organisation, wearing smart gingham uniform dresses, tour the settlement, making spot check examinations of the homes.

Initially Bill received complaints that some of the village women would not join. He replied that if they did not want to join he could not make them, but later he discovered that, whereas no-one could be forced to join, according to Gilbertese law, they could not refuse to have their homes inspected and were liable to the various ten cent fines levied, (for a dirty floor, or a dirty pantry, or whatever), whether they liked it or not. I can imagine how this arrangement would be greeted at home in England!

Bill's office, the hospital and his home, were no more exempt from this invasion than anyone else's, but, far from resenting it, everyone looked upon it as another occasion for a good chat. The house would be stripped of all its mats, furniture all moved out, and the whole place turned completely upsidedown on inspection morning. Since the committee began its tour at 9 a.m., the place had to be spotless and tidy by then so as much as possible was done the previous day. Every day new flowers were arranged all over the house but, to the Islanders, this wasn't just a question of sticking a few stems in a vase of water. They removed each bloom from its stem and threaded several on to a fine cane of suitable length, thus avoiding the long bare expanses of stem so often seen in English vases. These flower-covered canes were then stuck into a vase of sand, possibly with a few specially selected leaves. One day I saw all the vases outside the house waiting for the flowers to be changed. I had nothing to do and Akineti was busy so, deciding to be helpful, I sat myself down to thread the canes and refill the vases. Feeling rather pleased with the results, I wandered off.

Later I came back, just in time to watch Akineti chucking the fruits of my labour into the rubbish bin and substituting the lot with plastic flowers. Akineti spoke no English so there was nothing I could say, but the following day I discovered the reason was that the plastic flowers kept their crispness till the Homemakers' Club inspection due that morning. Poor Akineti was absolutely mortified to hear the story. Whenever I met her during the next few days, we would both laugh uproarously.

Despite inspections, housework, like everything else on Washington Island, was an easy-going affair. It wasn't unusual for a card-school to start up in the middle of bedmaking, or a game of Teboiri (Gilbertese ball game in which the ball is kicked with the inside of the foot around a circle of players who clap their hands with each kick) to begin spontaneously once the furniture had been cleared from the lounge.

Although relaxed and fun-loving, the Islanders are certainly industrious and clever. There were several spare-time building projects in full swing during our visit, all of which were purely voluntary efforts continued in the evenings. Sometimes till midnight we could hear the tractor trundling

along with loads of sand or rocks. A new Protestant Church
was under way, its walls then standing about fifteen feet
high, and we watched Pastor Boata and his men making their
own bricks. The Roman Catholics were currently involved in
building a new bathroom for Pastor Toanuea. A third
schoolroom was being constructed by a party of parents, and
the boy scouts were well under way with a new playing field.
Quite a handful for a community of four hundred!

Other handicrafts were many and varied, especially considering the only materials naturally available to the people
were coconut palms, sea-shells, and the pandanus tree.
Embroidery was very popular and the girls took their little
baskets of work with them everywhere. It was very unusual
to see a plain pillowslip, they were usually lavishly embroidered with a message in the centre, such as 'A little gift for
William Frew' or 'Sleep well, Daniel', surrounded by flowers
or scrolls and a crotcheted border, in gay colours.

Most of the women owned a sewing machine and made
clothes for all the family. From the pandanus leaf they made
hats, baskets, mats and grass-skirts. Beautiful necklaces and
bags were made from the sea-shells, and the young coconut
leaf was used to make the many lovely types of fan, often
bordered with feathers. There was no hurry on Washington
Island and infinite time and patience was poured into these
crafts and even the head garlands, or ternae, which only last
two days at most, took nearly an hour to make.

I often used to borrow a bicycle and ride off in search of
the little white flowers used for most of these flower leis.
After half a bucket of flowers had been collected, I would
return to the house and sit where the girls were gathered,
either in the porch or at the top of the steps to the house,
and pass a few lazy hours plaiting garlands. Some were made
with the little white flowers patterned with other coloured
petals and others were mainly frangapani. The coconut leaf
was skinned and split into strands for use as the base. Usually
five strands were plaited for strength, but they were also
made with three strands for lightness. I was very pleased with
myself, firstly for being able to make a passable ternai and
then for learning to plait with five strands. I had aimed to

make one for all those who had been especially helpful to us, but it was a hopeless task, there were so many I should have to have made one for every man, woman and child on the Island!

Although there was not really so very much that needed doing as far as *Britoo* was concerned, it was not possible to do it as required because the surf often prevented anyone reaching her. This meant that Biribo, Bill's brilliant mechanic, would have a piece of equipment all ready for us and be waiting for the next, but no-one would be able to get out to *Britoo* with it, so the days would pass — very pleasantly I might add!

Johnny went spear fishing almost every day, surf or no surf, and I had the strong impression that the Islanders thought him more than a little crazy, especially as they had never seen anyone fish in this way with that type of speargun before. However, there was no doubt that they were most impressed by the huge line of fish he used to drag ashore at the end of the day.

It was not only the Islanders who were impressed with John's fishing prowess. The sharks thought it was pretty good too, and swimming back to the beach with his line of fish in tow, he frequently had to jab them on the nose to discourage any cheeky thievery on their part. One day a large Black Tip shark was more persistent than usual and John was unable to swim ashore in his normal place. Because of this he was caught in a strong current sweeping off in the direction of Fanning Island, seventy miles away, and had considerable difficulty getting ashore at all. Needless to say, when he finally did so, he still had his haul in tow. In spite of his successful catches, John was a little disappointed with the reef, which he said was too flat, without many big holes or coral formations and, consequently, with few fish.

Strangely neither the people of the Gilberts, with the exception of one or two of the Islands, nor the Ellice peoples are very enthusiastic divers. There were only a couple of men who dived at all on Washington. They were keen canoe fishermen and enjoyed splashing about in the water's edge, but that was where their interest in the sea finished. Bill had a passion for turtle meat and, as they were rarely caught ashore, there was seldom turtle steak on Washington Island. Johnny went out turtle diving several times and brought back four forty pounders and one hundred pound whopper. On one occasion, as his log tells, he bit off more than he could chew:

12.10.71   170th day
'I came across a huge turtle and, without a second's thought, went after it. Managed to close up at a depth of about forty feet and, from a distance of some five feet, utterly confident that I could not possibly miss the head, I let go. The spear went clean through the turtle's neck instead and, after a second of shocked surprise, it took off like an express train, diving deeper and deeper towards the two hundred fathoms drop at the end of the reef, towing me like a bit of rubbish in spite of all my efforts to hold it back. I had no choice but to release my grip on the speargun and she disappeared with the gun in tow — my very best one at that. This is the first time I lost a gun in such humiliating circumstances, but I richly deserved it.'

14th October, 1971   172nd day
'An incredible thing happened to-day. Deciding to explore a different section of the reef, I entered the water about a mile further than my usual place, and lo and behold, about thirty yards from the beach, lying on a sandy spot among the coral, what do I find but my lost speargun! The spear itself was nowhere around, but I have plenty of them, so who cares? With luck such as that there is little doubt that we'll make it to Australia.'

Whereas most of Johnny's catches were either stored in Bill's deep freeze or distributed amongst our friends, one was rather a failure. This was on a Saturday when a communal fishing trip with canoes and the surfboat had been planned. At eleven o'clock Island time (in other words, noon by everyone's watches!), we were all ready to go, but no-one could find John. He was eventually spotted climbing laboriously out of the water, all alone, dragging an enormous three hundred pound manta ray, together with one much smaller. It caused a real sensation, bets were taken on its weight and there was great excitement all round. It was then left beside the house with an open invitation for all who wished to help themselves. Unfortunately it wasn't their idea of a tasty dish and when we returned, empty handed, after a miserably cold and wet fishing afternoon, the monster was still lying there untouched.

His huge hundred pound turtle met the opposite fate. She was given to Marina for cooking in the early evening and after Lauina had carefully cleaned her and jointed all the meat, Marina started to cook it in her Gilbertese style oven by the beach. Next morning Johnny casually asked why we weren't having turtle liver for breakfast and learned that Marina's cooking had developed into quite a nice little party during which half the Island had dropped by for a chat. By the time the turtle should have been cooked, there had been none left.

If Johnny's fish and turtles added to our popularity, I should have thought our denying the Island its electricity supply for the duration of our stay would have more than counteracted it.

We had arrived just at the time when Biribo had disconnected all the electricity in preparation for transfer to a more powerful generator, but he had been spending so much time fixing our bits and pieces, that there had been none left for continuing with the electricity supply. He was a real genius, as half the stuff he repaired for us he had never seen before in his life. He made new parts and repaired our generator, torches, sea-bag zip fastener, hydraulic speargun, rubber speargun and spear shafts.

I must say he seemed pleased to do it and we never heard a murmur of a complaint from him or anyone else. Actually, it was only when we had returned to sea that the reason for the lack of electricity occurred to me. Lighting was all by paraffin pressure lanterns and cooking, the deep freeze and refrigerators were all paraffin powered during our stay.

Whilst re-arranging the deck of *Britoo*, Johnny discovered our two canvas drogues to have rotted through completely. It would have been suicidal to continue without them, as they were our only method of keeping head on to the waves should we hit bad weather. Bill's foreman, Tenoa, together with Atitoa, his assistant, spent many sweltering days remaking the drogues completely by hand. They also made a new entrance cover to the galley, because the zip on the original was irreparably broken. The results of their labours served us well and valuably during the final stages of our crossing.

One afternoon Bill took us up the Island's artificial canal, said to have been dug by Tahitian women in about 1860/70. The canal was extremely beautiful, being overhung with palms, grown with papyrus, and having sudden clearings of peat bog on which grew taro, or Babai, a staple food of the residents. Suddenly it opened out into a vast and lovely freshwater lake, measuring almost seven hundred acres and bordered on all sides with coconut palms growing right to the water's edge. Originally this had been the Island's lagoon, but it has long been landlocked and become freshwater. Since the lake is a popular nesting place, we saw many of the sea birds we had encountered whilst at sea. Bill identified them for us, so we need no longer speak of witches (Frigate birds) and duckies (Booby birds).

John swam a little in the hope of spearfishing but, because of the peat, the water was not clear enough to see anything, so we continued across the lake into another canal which wove its way to Manounou. We surprised a family bathing and splashing about at the end of the canal. It was idyllic. The mother was topless but, in deference to us Europeans, she hastily covered herself on our approach. Here we left the boat and took a stroll through the settlement, which housed fourteen families and was picturesquely situated by the sea, but, I must confess, the main activity appeared to be rummy, as, to Bill's disgust, was the current craze all over the Island.

When we left, we were escorted by the children who ran along the canal bank, waving and shouting farewells until we reached the lake. Here they climbed and swung on over-hanging branches, making a charming picture but one we were unable to film as, once again, our casettes let us down badly. A dozen of those we had taken on the trip had been duds.

Music plays a big part in the Island life and there are many tape-recorders in evidence. Music from Hawaii or Radio Tarawa is picked up quite well on a transistor radio and taped. But they are not merely listeners, in fact it often seemed to me that Bill, Johnny and myself were the only folk on the Island unable to play a guitar or ukeleli. Willie was especially talented in this direction. He was the leader of the larger of Washington's string bands, besides being an excellent trumpeter, guitarist and ukelelist. They play plenty of European music, usually translated into Gilbertese and given a very definite flavour of the Pacific, besides their own music, which I could not attempt to describe but found most enjoyable. Many of the children were fine instrumentalists, especially Willie's smashing little ten year old son, John. At the frequent impromptu concerts which broke out around the huge table in Bill's kitchen, or anywhere else at any time, the guitars passed from one to the other as the mood took them, and the voices harmonised effortlessly, in a way which would belittle many of our professional groups.

The twist, Gilbertised, was all the rage during our stay and the way they danced it was really sexy — but they are extremely proper and it was a case of 'anything-goes-but-you-can't-touch'. In fact Marina did not even know who was going out with who amongst her closest friends, and the single girls never danced more than once with any one man in an evening. When they bathed in the sea it was always fully dressed, but cotton dried fast in their heat so this is not as uncomfortable as it might sound. Fully dressed for a girl usually meant a pair of pants, maybe a bra, a loose cotton blouse and a sarong type skirt called a tebe. For a man, a pair of shorts with a tebe on top. For church on Sundays the men wore white shirts with white shorts, or a few wore long trousers, while the women wore pretty dresses, usually waisted with a full knee-length skirt.

The church was a lovely light cane and trellis work building with a corrugated roof and a bright white altar. The service, hymns, reading and lesson were all in Gilbertese and they had their own Bible. The worshippers sat on the mats provided but the Pastor offered chairs to Marina and myself, which would have been extremely embarrassing so, as I often sit on the floor anyway, we declined and sat comfortably on the mats instead. The hymns were sung with great gusto, in spite of having no organ or instrumental backing, which was surprising for a people so shy and reluctant to sing unless rehearsed and accompanied.

Although I never attend church in England, there I thoroughly enjoyed it. This may have been because the people I liked most all seemed to be pillars of the church, whereas at home none of my friends number amongst the churchgoers. I had, and still have, no religious feeling whatsoever, so I felt rather uncomfortable when Pastor Boata translated each sermon solely for my benefit, in spite of being rather shy of speaking English before his own people. He was a marvellous person and a fine example of that rare being, a good practising Christian.

It was Pastor Boata, the Protestant Pastor, jointly with Pastor Toanuea, the Roman Catholic Pastor (in itself a remarkable achievement) that we have to thank for our fabulous Welcome Party on 13th October. The party started with a few introductory words from Bill and the following speech by Pastor Boata:

'On behalf of everyone here tonight, I shall speak a little to open this party, but first we give out thanks to God the Heavenly Father who has taken care of us throughout our daily life from the beginning till to-night. We, the people of this Island, were very glad and interested to see you when you first came on shore, and most happy to see you here to-night. When we heard that you came from America we knew that you have had a very long journey and we thought that you would be exhausted and weary, so we mean to do something to make you happy, and we also give thanks to the Manager, and his wife, Marina, because they are very kind and lovely to all strangers who come to this Island.

'We know that your voyage has been very hard and dangerous and you have a long way yet to go to Australia.

'We know you will endure and we pray to God that His blessings will accompany you all the way.

'The people of this Island give you their greetings gladly and to your friends in Australia, America or wherever you go.'

This moving welcome was immediately followed by an Island style twist, at which the sole performer was an elderly lady in a long, loose dress, with strange eyes who was cavorting about and had the whole Maneaba doubled up with laughter. I thought this was part of the programme, but apparently the poor dear was mentally deficient and just felt like enjoying herself!

The Maneaba was beautifully decorated with palm fronds and greenery and looked coolly exotic. I think the entire population of the Island was present, wearing their Sunday bests, complete with flowers, leis and necklaces, even the babies and children. The youngsters were never put to bed in the early evening, they went out with their parents or alone, and when they got tired they fell asleep. Consequently, the party had a partly dormant population but no grizzling children — they woke up and went back to sleep according to their instincts, not to parental order. All this convinces me that we in England pack the kids off to bed and foster the idea it's good for them to give the parents some peace and quiet, rather that because the children need it.

We were fed like kings and presented with some super pandanus woven sun hats and a beautiful lidded basket. It was a thoroughly delightful evening with a good assortment of Gilbertese ceremonial dancing, intermingled with a few twists, some singing, and ending up with a stick dance. The ceremonial dancing was really amazing, from my viewpoint like a scene from a film, 'King Solomon's Mines' perhaps? The music was weird and varied, and the dancing very skilful. The men wore a ceremonial tebe (or skirt) of a mat with coloured threads woven into the pandanus strands and tied about the waist by a sash made from a woman's hair. (Later Tetaake gave me his to use as a wall ornament, which I shall be most proud to do). The men danced around between one to four little girls of six to ten years old wearing black grass-skirts stamping and chanting toward the little tots, who steadfastly stood their ground wiggling their hips and dancing with their hands and arms, till the men suddenly halted just before they would have been crushed!

In other dances the women stepped with outstretched arms, each arm decorated with four floral bracelets, topped with one large flower, putting great emphasis on their hands which twisted and turned so gracefully, yet never moved the flowers!

In one particularly moving dance, also emphasising the hands, four impressively large women in grass skirts lined up facing us from the opposite end of the Maneaba. The music was out of this world as they gradually advanced and retreated, with tiny little steps and plenty of hip wiggling, each time a little closer to us than the last, till finally the four dancers reached us and placed a beautiful ternae on each of our heads — I had an awful job not to cry! — before dancing back as they had come.

During other dances, some of the men sat round beating a big quarter coloured square drum with their hands whilst other Islanders danced about them. As I write I am playing the tape recording I made of this party and now the whole thing, in fact our visits to the Islands, and even the trip itself, seems like an exotic dream of which I was never a part — or is it our mechanised life in suburbia which is unreal?

I was sure that all these dances must portray legends or be highly symbolic but, regrettably I could find no-one to tell me the stories. The last dance of the evening was the stick dance. In it two rows of dancers wove in and out of each other with a stick in each hand which they tapped together and against each other in passing. It was very rhythmic and looked great fun, but, despite urging from Bill, we dared not join in for fear of ruining the whole pattern.

It was a fabulous party and I have never known Johnny dance so much. I danced rather more than usual myself, mainly with my favourite dancing partner, a really nice boy with the most delicious sloe eyes, called Tabeaua. John and I both lost our tebes whilse twisting, not together or at the same time, I might add. Everyone roared with laughter on both occasions, so any embarrassment on our parts was soon dispelled. We were not completely disgraced though, Johnny thanks to his swim trunks and myself thanks to a petticoat.

The evening was closed with a few words from Bill and Pastor Boata, and hopelessly inadequate thanks from Johnny and me. I had meant to say so much but, with the whole population agog, my nerves got the better of me and sadly little emerged. It was a really wonderful party which we will certainly never forget.

One noteworthy point was that there was no alcohol as, in common with some of the other Islands, Bill prohibits it, apart from a few of his more senior men who are permitted a certain weekly quota. It was interesting to see how little alcohol is really needed for people to loosen up and enjoy themselves, in spite of their inherent shyness.

Although for me most of our stay on Washington Island passed lazing, socialising or twisting, as far as Johnny was concerned, it was rather more productive. Most days he swam out to *Britoo*, or was taken there by canoe, to check that the anchor was holding, if nothing else. Three times he found it in bad shape, once hanging on by a thread, because the line had chafed through on the coral. Then he had to dive in order to cut away the worn part and rejoin the remainder to the cable. Although Bill had two watchmen permanently on *Britoo*, either aboard or from the shore, it is difficult to imagine what they could have done had the anchor gone. Maybe a couple of non-English speaking Gilbertese would have turned up in Australia and we would still be living it up on Washington Island! John would never let me go with him to the boat because I am such a poor swimmer, but I can't say I missed our little home in the least! Other than restowing completely, there was very little he could do either, because all our repairs were so expertly done for us. My only contribution, as far as I can remember, was to spend a day with Taukaban and Uoa packing the hoards of lovely goodies Bill gave us, into polythene bags and suchlike.

As Johnny's log tells, after Biribo had repaired our generator and we had had time to recharge the batteries, we managed to make radio contact with San Francisco.

31.10.71   **189th day**

'Also, we have been able to get in touch with Ivan, last Thursday, after repeated tries until we called at sunset. We had sent two cables to him but apparently he did not receive either and, having last heard from us six weeks before, had again asked the coastguards to put an alert out for us. This really infuriated me as I thought we were absolutely clear on the matter before leaving Ensenada, that, in case of not hearing from us, he would not bother the coastguards again. We have two S.A.R.B.E. emergency transmitting radios and, in case of trouble, we would use them, but I could hardly send a distress call without reason. Therefore no news was good news, meaning only that our Marconi tranceiver had gone on the blink. At this rate the coastguards will end by thinking we are a couple of silly jokers and, if something really happens, they might very well — with all the reason in the world in my opinion — tell him to go to hell.

'Apart from that, I should have thought that, since the last he heard from us was that we were making for either Fanning or Washington Islands, the obvious thing to do, before crying wolf, was to check with them. I suppose that I sound like an ungrateful bastard and things may look different from the shore, but that's the way I see them. After all, nobody asked us to do this caper and I really hate to create more fuss than necessary about it, especially if it involves messing up, and even — at it's worst — risking, other people's lives in a useless search!'

Johnny took Bill out to *Britoo* for quite a number of radio tries but the very time he was successful, he was also alone, so Bill missed the great day. However, Bill, Marina, Willie, several friends and I, all listened to a crackly rendering of Johnny's transmission on the little transistor in the kitchen — the unofficial social centre of Washington Island. Although, the Marconi being single band, we could not hear Ivan's side, it was a great thrill to listen and know it was operating once again. Little did we imagine that would be the last time it would!

Communications were often a problem ashore too. Not

many of the Islanders spoke English and those that did were mostly very shy of doing so, especially in front of each other. Consequently I would often speak to an English speaker and receive a string of Gilbertese in reply. Marina, whose English is excellent — although she hardly said anything unless we were alone — was often reluctant to act interpreter. It wasn't until we had been there three weeks or more that I discovered some of the people I had been asking her to interpret for spoke as much English as she did. And my gorgeous twisting partner, after over two weeks of *Korupa*'s (thank you), suddenly said, 'I am tired' from which it transpired that he also spoke very good English. Otherwise my interpreter was a delightful little girl called Taiana, who I think (think, because no-one seemed very definite about relationships there) was Marina's niece.

Most of the younger ones had standard English sentences, 'What is your name?', 'What is your brother's name?', and 'Where are you going?'.

I hate to think how many times I answered these three questions. A little group of kids would stand asking them over and over again, for an hour or so, lovely kids, but how I sometimes wished they would go away. At times I was almost afraid to leave the house, unless by bicycle, as a host of them would appear from nowhere and follow, giggling, wherever I went.

Bill's household was a masterpiece languagewise. Bill has never learned to speak Gilbertese, his wife is Ellice and they have their own language but, living on Washington Island, predominately Gilbertese, she now speaks Gilbertese. Their two small sons, speak only Gilbertese, not a word of Ellice or English (their parent's tongues), although they do understand English. Bill speaks to Marina in English and she replies, not in Ellice but in Gilbertese. In fact the few Ellice families on the Island all speak Gilbertese, since they are in the minority. Besides the language difference, the Ellice people are Polynesian, whereas the Gilbertese are Nicronesian but, just as there is no religious tension, we saw no signs of racial or origin friction. In fact the Island is a complete Utopia and it is easy to see how Bill has lived there happily for fifteen years and never wants to leave it. Even the weather is perfect, warm nights rising to the mid eighties or nineties in the daytime, with an average annual rainfall of a hundred and twenty inches, coming in short, sharp showers, to keep everything fresh and green.

For me the only thing which marred the Island's perfection was the mosquitos. For the first few days of our stay there might as well not have been any, but after that they found me and I was soon a mass of swollen red blobs, with barely an inch between them. I was the only person on the entire Island that got bitten; in fact Bill said it was the dry season and there *were* no mosquitos.

One day I had a high fluctuating temperature and ached all over. The following day all was well till 6 p.m., when my right foot swelled alarmingly from a mosquito bite. By midnight I was in such agony I was unable to move it, even in bed. Then I got a pain in my shoulder, similar to that I'd had with peritonitis, so I was convinced that I was going to die there on Washington Island! Bill put me on a five day course of Tetracycline tablets and it cleared up well, but we extended our visit by a few more days, just to make sure. A couple of days after the cure, I read that Lord Carnarvon died of an infected mosquito bite following the opening of Tutankhamen's Tomb — glad I hadn't read that before!

Other than mosquitos, Washington Island was agreeably free of unpleasant livestock. There were domestic pigs and chickens, enormous crabs and even more enormous coconut crabs, geckos, and cats, but only two dogs. Apparently there used to be more dogs, but the dogs killed the cats, causing a rat problem, so Bill outlawed dogs, leaving his and one other. When a pig or chicken is going to be eaten, it is tied by its leg to a stump or rock where it is left all day, often in the sun with no refreshment, to be casually kicked by passing children.

I thought this was pretty cruel till Tabeaua asked me if we had pigs and chickens on 'your island'. I answered that we did but we never saw them because they were kept in little cages — and then it occurred to me that this is a darned sight crueller than letting them lead a normal life before finally subjecting them to a single day's hell.

Nevertheless, the Islanders certainly don't have our senti-mental attitude towards animals and I think I was thought pretty crazy when I got myself rather involved with kittens. It began with a very young tabby turning up at the foot of the stairs to the house one evening. It seemed starving and I took it in and it ate a tremendous amount. The following day it had a lovely time playing with me and Johnny, when he returned from *Britoo*, and sleeping. The day after it became tottery and weak, so I started to feed it with a dropper, but about five, it died. Awful, I knew it would die as soon as I saw it was ill, having nursed plenty of sick animals and birds, but never one that has recovered. I couldn't bear to have the little staring corpse in the room with us, so Johnny and I trooped off with spade, kitten and tears, in front of all and sundry. We buried it in a grass-lined grave by the beach half a mile away, putting plenty of rocks on top (to deter the pigs) and laying a garland I had just made over all.

The next day saw the arrival of our kitten's twin brother. It was presented to me by a brigade of little girls led by Taiana and her six year old sister, Asenati. We called the second kitty Crumple because of a bent ear. If our boat had not been so small and open, we would almost certainly have taken Crumple with us, but as it was, the poor little thing was left to be fed, but otherwise ignored, apart from being pulled about by the kids as long as its novelty value endured. Anyway, it was an awfully nice thought of Taiana's to have given her to us and a very touching gesture. Before we left a black and white kitten of about the same age was fostered on me. I christened him Crimple. Initially they fought viciously but by the second day they were playing and sleeping together very happily. It was sad to leave them and separate them, but inevitable.

One day we went off into the woods to film the copra process. The nuts are found where they have fallen into the bus and thrown on to the nearest path. From here they are collected by tractor and driven back to Arabata for weighing, after which all the meat is spread out in the sun on huge racks to dry. As our excursion was solely for filming purposes, it was rather like a big family picnic, with everyone, kids and dog included, piling into the tractor trailer and chugging off in real party spirit, and finishing with us all drinking coconuts on the beach.

On another day we went for a real picnic. With dozens of children, baskets of food, plenty of beer, and several grown ups, off we went to spend a day on the beach near where Johnny and I had first landed. Most of the older children and the adults spent the day playing cards. I went shell collecting with Johnny and Taiana, very successfully.

Near the day of our departure, Marina organised a farewell party for us at the house. The huge table was covered with palm leaves which were hardly visible through the maze of dishes which included a whole pig, glazed and beautifully decorated with flowers. The pig, we learned, was Marina's pet which she had tearfully rescued from an untimely death a couple of weeks before. Now it was the party centrepiece, but I never discovered whether she let it be killed as the highest tribute to a fine pig, or to save herself further agonies of decision regarding its future, or whether in honour of John, the party and myself. In any case it made a sumptuous feast and the party was a riotous success.

Although this was our farewell party, it was several more days before we finally left. The first delay was when Johnny discovered the generator was on the blink again. The second was when he returned it repaired to discover the gimbals had another break in them. After that the surf built up alarmingly so no-one could get to the boat for three or four days. What a sad time it was. Bill and Marina had been exceptionally kind to us and there was nothing we could want or consider without them bending over backwards to help. The children had been unbelievably sweet, often bringing me presents of shells or chicken eggs (a scarcity there, since the hens roamed freely and the eggs were allowed to hatch naturally). Beautiful gifts had been lavishly bestowed on us during our stay. We had been completely spoilt by everyone and I have never met such thoroughly nice people. We were extremely fortunate to have landed on Washington Island and it was an experience neither of us will ever forget.

Whenever we were delayed, yet again, Johnny would be so disappointed and miserable, but I would snap out of my gloom and be deliriously happy. I wanted to finish the trip but I did not want to leave Washington. I felt this was the life for me, ideal climate, kindly people, leisurely atmosphere and beautiful, unreal — it was so pretty. It was a life I doubted I would ever live again and I was reluctant to leave it. But I did.

9. Christmas aboard *Britannia II*

The dream ended at 5 p.m. on Friday, November 12th. It ended with heartbreaking farewells at the house, more farewells to virtually the whole population of the island gathered on the beach, and final farewells to all who escorted us in their boats and canoes.

Sylvia wrote in her log:

'Now it is over, and once more my only reality is the sea, the sky and this little boat with all it contains. How I long for the day when this too will become a dream.'

I know she spoke for us both. Leaving the island was one of the hardest things we had to do on the whole adventure, and yet I knew that the longer we stayed the more difficult it would be. I wrote nothing in the log for over a month, at first because the weather was miserable and then because I couldn't be bothered to. Even Sylvia didn't put pen to paper until we had been at sea ten days.

From Sylvia's Log

21st November, Sunday   210th day

'Haven't written till now as have been too fed up and writing emphasises things. The first three days were the worst. It kept raining and I felt utterly dejected and so miserable that I spent the time convincing J. and myself that I was seasick. Didn't row a stroke during this time, and, thanks to Bill and the Islanders, didn't have to cook either since we had a plentiful supply of fresh cooked pork and bread-fruit. After this started rowing again, hating every stroke, got pretty unfit on Washington, I think, because my back is aching a lot lately, but I think improving.

'Hate this boat more than have ever hated anything, and have never not wanted to do anything more than I didn't want to get back on board — wonder what sort of fool I am to be here? Already everything has been thoroughly wet at least twice and I had the first signs of salt water sores after three days, and now own a good crop of them again. J. is getting some too.

'Another part which doesn't improve my mood is our pretty poor progress; actually we are north of Washington Island right now, presumably because of S.E. winds combined with strong westerly current.

'As yet very little action or signs of life. We had two trigger fish follow us on the second day, but the following two days only one and after that he deserted us too. Didn't really care because they weren't like Porgy and Bess and we never even fed these two. We were also followed by a school of small unidentified fish, ate two for dinner and they were good. Saw one dorado chasing flying fish. Were investigated by a large school of bottle-nosed dolphins. Very few birds about, but suppose they were following our tuna before, not us, and this time as yet we have no tuna.

'One strange happening was on 15th at about 3 p.m. It was not raining and the sea was quiet and calm until we suddenly heard it chattering in the distance. The chattering became a babble, but we saw nothing for about ten minutes or so, then the surface of the water became ruffled and bouncy, in a popply sort of way with little ripples and breaking wavelets in all directions. Soon we were in the centre of the whole thing where the crests were about four or five feet high, but we could see away from us they became smaller. It was very noisy now, also very eerie. We gradually rowed our way out of it and I suppose the whole phenomenon lasted about 45 minutes. It looked vaguely like two strong currents meeting, or maybe fast-flowing water running over a shallow — which this didn't appear to be.'

30th November, Tuesday   219th day
'J. and I are getting on each other's nerves, which everyone expected so I suppose I should say "at last". He drives me

mad by not answering, or mumbling unintelligibly through his pipe. I drive him mad by talking, not that I find much to say, but he's so damn miserable I feel obliged to try to cheer him up — it never seems to sink into my thick head that I always have the reverse effect.

'Sunday was my birthday and one of the worst days since Ensenada (excluding the birth of the tropical depression) and definitely the worst day since Washington Island. It rained almost all day and night, the sea was breaking in every two or three minutes and the wind was cruel. Consequently bed was a wet sog and everything was wet and miserable, including ourselves. Too rough to open hatch containing birthday present, too rough to cook, so it was M. House meals all day and a tin of blackcurrants (my favourite tinned fruit) was my birthday treat.

'No drama or excitement yet. Maybe I am terrified when there is, but it does create something to think about, talk about and write about. This is just one great enormous bore, when not a tired, hot, sore bore, then a tired, wet, sore bore.

'Haven't mentioned the blasted radio yet. That's another pain. Tried every Thursday and Friday night since leaving, bar one, when it was too rough. Called KMI, CQ all ships, and Radio Sydney and P. & O. Line's ships, including a special call when, according to their itinerary, their liner, *Himalaya*, was within five hundred miles of us, never had any reply from anyone. Whilst at Washington J. changed the schedule, at the suggestion of Phil Palmer, to just after sunset for clearer reception, so we now have the added complication of packing the lot up and restowing the galley by torchlight — a jolly caper indeed. The indicator needle shows we are transmitting and we hear things from time to time, so what's going wrong?'

On December 8th my ungraciousness forced Sylvia into making a £5 bet with me — the most she's ever wagered. I said that the Ellice Island canoes were planked and the Gilbertese were dugouts, and Sylvia insisted it was the other way about. We had one helluva row about it and Sylvia made me sign the entry in her log!

She won!

Both of us were getting run down physically as well as mentally by now. Every little scratch or cut festered and swelled and took a long time to heal. We tried taking two vitamin pills a day, but I don't think they made much difference.

To add to our troubles, the aft dagger board, which we had removed and checked while we were on Washington, was now so warped that I could not remove it. I tried several times, but it was jammed so solid that had I forced it, the sides of the hatches would have given way or at least torn badly enough to cause severe leaking.

What was more, we weren't making either good time or direction. The winds were now either south or south-east, and this meant that Sydney (our original goal) was completely out of reach. The nearest we had got to the Equator by mid-December was 2.16° North, before the winds pushed us back again. The best we could hope for by now was Brisbane or farther north, and my big worry was that we might end up in New Guinea. On December 15th, I wrote, at last, in the log:

'After suffering from boils, which are gradually improving, we seem to be getting back to form but feel absolutely fed-up with the whole thing. This caper is taking far too long and God knows how much longer it is going to be. No. 9 hatch — aft, under the generator — sprang a leak but managed to repair it with sea putty. Radio most likely on the blink but cannot see anything wrong with it other than the fact that, in spite of all our efforts, we have been unable to communicate with KMI or for that matter anybody, not even when crossing a couple of shipping lanes and calling CQ. Have not sighted a single ship. If, after three or more tries, we cannot get in touch with somebody we'll have to attempt to reach the Gilberts to pass on the news that all is well, otherwise our parents will be worried stiff.

'Had a school of dorados following us for the last two weeks and bumped the occasional shark. A few tuna and wahoos around as well.

'Guess this is it. Will try to keep the damned log up to date from now on but quite honestly can't really promise to do so at all times. Never been more fed-up with everything — and this includes myself — in my whole life.'

16.12.71   235th day
'Becalmed. Heat torrid. Impossible to row at all during the day from 9 a.m. to 5 p.m. At night it gets better but still very hot and drinking more water than usual, imperative. With no wind to help, the going is very slow. Apparently there is a northern current too which makes things worse.'

It was hellishly hot now, and I spent as much time as possible in the water. Sharks — white tips and the common brown jobs — were our constant companions, and I shot several. I persuaded Sylvia to have a shot at one from the boat, but she missed from about two inches. Sylvia's interests were different:

From Sylvia's Log

13th December, Monday   232nd day
'Southerly wind blowing still and we have been driven north again. The elusive Equator never wants to see us, but one day . . .

'Our dorados are still here, but won't be fed. We've tried two or three times and each time only one will eat. They love *Britoo* and play with her for an hour, or so before sunset and around 9 a.m. They, sometimes half a dozen at a time, weave in and out of her dagger board and rudder very fast, often pushing themselves up the hull out of the water on their sides, as they come out. They spend a lot of time swimming on their sides, like a flatfish, and when doing so glow pale turquoise fluorescent, darkening as they turn to their normal position into their usual dark saxe blue spotted navy with a gold or green tail. Their pectoral fins glow sky blue, or at times shaded from gold to green. Sometimes they are darker blue with big mottled green spots on their backs, and when hunting they become bottle green with wide vertical black stripes.

'Their leaps are spectacular, frequently more than thirty feet long and exceeding ten feet in height, but best of all when, as they seem to enjoy greatly, taken from the crest of a wave into its trough, when the height could well be twenty feet or so. Strangely the school we had before Washington always jumped in threes, that is a fish would jump usually three consecutive leaps, otherwise six. This present school appears to leap in twos, either two or four jumps. Besides the jump they have what can only be described as a flick. To do this they wiggle and swim with great speed, propel themselves just out of the water and twist, slamming their tail down hard on to the sea, thus creating the most colossal bang and splash, when once one has done this plenty more start leaping or flicking and the fun generally continues a good half hour or more.'

14th December, Tuesday   233rd day
'One of those rare, noiseless days with only the faintest swell breaking the still of the sea and only our little *Britoo* lapping, breaking the silence.

'A school of something big, black and snorting passed by but we saw very little.

'I think our beautiful larder has deserted us. Although they have occasionally absented themselves for the odd hour, they have always returned to play with *Britoo* before sundown, but tonight the water stayed still and silent.'

15th December, Wednesday   234th day
'Small black whale surveyed us briefly in the early morning.

'By ten this morning the sky to our north, east and west was deep steel blue, and we watched it gradually engulf us, pouring rain and whipping the sea up from absolute calm to a mass of frothy white caps and three feet waves, all within half an hour. By evening the white has left and there is a big slow swell — much easier for rowing than all that choppiness. The effect of a sudden change in the weather like this, is to make me feel very far from where I was before the change. In spite of watching the weather approach, the resulting change feels so different and looks so different, instead of sweating in the bare minimum, it's now a toss-up whether to don an anorak, and instead of looking down, down into a prism of blue, one looks now on to shimmer of depthless gun-metal grey, and looking up one sees a constantly changing pattern of greys, and no longer the endless, infinite blue, that the impression is of great distance as if no one place can show such acutely contrasting faces, therefore we must be somewhere else . . . if only!'

16th December, Thursday   235th day
'The dorados have definitely gone and all we have in tow now is a cheeky little 2½ foot shark, which keeps whacking itself against *Britoo* and flapping about causing all sorts of noises and plenty of splashes.

'The weather is very hot, sea calm and a northerly breeze comes and goes, at least it's the right way and if it persists, we may see the Equator yet before Christmas.'

Oh, yes, Christmas. Sylvia was determined to have a celebration on Christmas Day, but she drove me crazy with her memories of carols, parties, cards and all that. It has never interested me as a festivity. She was also getting neurotic about dirt — dreaming of cockroaches eating the soles of her feet. She hadn't seen one yet, but she swore she felt one crawling up her leg one night. Then she found a microscopic maggot on her body and said there must be dozens around. She went mad with the insecticide gun. She also pestered the life out of me to have a look at the cooker which was burning badly and was making soot. I'd had a lousy bout trying to fix up the generator which went wrong and told her the cooker would have to wait, soot be damned.

From Sylvia's Log

21st December, Tuesday   240th day
'Horror of horrors! Last night it happened. I awoke and felt something land on my leg, moved and it stayed, so I grabbed it in the dark — it was bigger than a sixpence, hard and spikey. Have a ghastly feeling it could only be a cockroach,

but was unable to find anything by the torchlight.

'J. hoping to make Howland or Baker Island, but I don't fancy them. Both uninhabited and only one has any trees, and that only a fifteen foot clump, and one has hordes of little grey Pacific rats all over it — ugh!

'Swimming J. counted nine dorados.'

22nd December, Wednesday   241st day

'Getting furiouser and furiouser every time I go near the galley — I get smothered in soot, not only do I get smothered, but the deck gets it, the water jerry gets it, the kettle already has it and the messy stuff gets everywhere. All because the flames are burning red on the cooker and we don't know how to fix them. You've no idea how infuriating this is, the more so since it's mixed with cooking fats and therefore difficult to remove. How I hate this filthy little boat.

'As far as I'm concerned, rowing is still the least tormenting part of this joy-ride. This is probably because I don't do that much of it and the weather lately has been generally rowable. I start about 5 to 5.30 usually, row a couple of hours so that, with breaks, I go to bed at eight and J. takes over. Around 12 he wakes me and I row another hour, while he rests, then return to bed and he rows and rests till about 6. About 6 I get up and row a couple of hours and get breakfast for about 9. J. sleeps till breakfast. This is hot weather routine, if routine it can be called, for we are not over strict on our times if the weather is dull and or windy, we try to get as much rowing as possible done during the day. Otherwise the days while themselves away with us cat-napping, endlessly watching the sea, or occasionally reading.

23rd December, Thursday   242nd day

'Took the cooker apart and cleaned both burners so one now burns cleanly, the other I've not to use. J. did it and swore at me for my uninvited assistance, so I let him get on with it! Spent ages cleaning everywhere and everything very thoroughly of every speck of soot. Afterwards had a real complete wash myself, including hair. Intend doing this at least weekly — which sounds terrible, even to me — but it's amazing how uninviting a wash with non-lathering soap in tepid sea water can be. To be horribly honest. I think we both stink to high heaven most of the time, but we are seldom conscious of it. Am certain *Britoo* smells foul too, but only because I can remember the stench from *Britannia I* when she arrived in Florida.

'Felt an itch on my leg mid-afternoon as I was sitting in rat-hole entrance. It was a minute, white maggot. Revolting — especially considering where there's one maggot there's bound to be dozens, and God knows what'll hatch out of them. I loathe this filthy place, and it's the dirt and bugs I hate most. We now have a reappearance of the little flies which were so abundant after Ensenada.'

From John's Log

23.12.71 Thursday   242nd day
'Wind from the north-east, choppy seas not too hot. 'Fixed the damned cooker to have peace, nothing wrong with it other than dirt and salt. One burner works well, the other so so but the lady is happy again — except for cockroaches and maggots, for Chrissake, I have to see one yet!'

24.12.71 Friday   243rd day
'Losing lat. somewhat faster. Lat. 2N at last. Rowed 660 miles since the 1st December. Looks like we might cross the Date Line and the Equator on the same day and New Year at that. Another maggot appeared to-day. God help us!'

From Sylvia's Log

25th December, Saturday   244th day
'Awoke to find the sea had become an army of white-capped soldiers marching; but not marching in nice neat regimental row, instead marching higgledy-piggledy all over the place with every few minutes a little group breaking into a run, charging straight into *Britoo*'s side and cascading all over her deck, a mass of white foaming water.

'I have very fixed and rather sentimental ideas of what

Christmas should be and, whereas this one must obviously be an exception, I had put carefully aside a little pile of goodies which were to have been our 1971 Christmas fare. Our only other festive concession was to have been listening to Christmas carols and parties on the radio. Unfortunately this rude rough weather made taking the radio out a calculated risk in which we only indulged a couple of times (and then with extremely disappointing results), and this preparation of a bumper meal an impossibility.

'Consequently, all we had of our Christmas food was a breakfast of chili and beans (our favourite M.H. meal, now running low and reserved for best), a coconut from Washington Island (I've been keeping three, one for now, one for Equator and the third for New Year), and the last of Ivan's most appreciated gift of a bottle of Napoleon brandy.

'Christmas Day for us was an anti-climax, but for the fish and the birds it was a delight as the rougher the weather the more they seemed to enjoy themselves. The fish — dorados, sharks, tuna, all alike — swimming along the very top of the waves and the dorados leaping through the highest down into the troughs below, whilst the birds glide dipping, soaring and swooping in crazy shapes barely missing the water in their happy play.

'J. got up in a lousy mood, his first words being, "I don't like you. I don't like chili and beans and I don't like this tea." And that was the pattern of Christmas Day. I thought of how jolly it must be on Washington Island and remembered Willie kept saying "You'll be here for Christmas," or "Why not stay till Christmas." Then I thought how sad they must be at home and hope they have some company or have gone away for the holiday. Both thoughts made our own circumstance seem unreal — but alas it is all too real and don't we know it.'

From John's Log

25.12.71, Saturday   244th day
'Ivan's parting gift from Ensenada (a bottle of Napoleon Brandy), after I had told him somewhat rudely that the

brandy he had given us in S.F. was on the cheap side — died to-day. Sy got on my nerves with her memories of past Christmasses and I suppose I got on hers with my don't give a damn attitude.

26.12.71, Sunday   245th day
'N.E. wind same as yesterday. Tempers better.'

Indeed they were better. I cheered up considerably because we're now making good time — nearly three knots while rowing. I was sure we had gone faster than we'd expected and reckoned we must be just about on the Equator. I reckoned I'd been a little unkind to Sylvia on Christmas Day, and let her persuade me to play a game of battleships. While I was sleeping, around mid-day, Sylvia lost her favourite faded blue Levi's shirt in the sea. It was all her fault. She used to play a silly game with the washing. After soaking it with detergent in a bucket, she would rinse out the clothes one by one in the sea, throwing them in, swishing them about, tossing them over, letting them go, squeezing them out and then repeating the process. She nearly lost things time after time, but, as she said, 'That's what makes the game.'

This time, the sea being rougher, a bigger wave came along and carried *Britt* away from the shirt. I woke to a great screaming and yelling and much to her surprise, got dressed in mask, flippers, knife, the lot and went in after it. A pocket of air was keeping it up but it had sunk before I reached it and I had to dive for it. *Britt* was drifting so fast she was 150 yards away by the time I surfaced. The reasons for the elaborate precautions of what seems a simple exercise are obvious if you think about it. The mask was most important — to spot a shark if one happened to be around, the knife was to fight it off if it attacked, and the flippers to enable me to catch up with the drifting *Britt*.

Sylvia was really grateful, and put it all down to some belated Christmas spirit. I didn't let on for a couple of days that the only reason I'd gone to all that bother was that the Levi's shirt was the best — if not the only — cloth we had on board for cleaning my sunglasses.

I finally managed to get an accurate fix on December 29th, and established that we had crossed the Equator the night before, probably around sunset. As if by magic, the weather cleared up, but I was still tense from the worry of the past few days and, as we bickered all day, we postponed our belated celebration until the first day of the New Year.

From Sylvia's Log

1st January, 1972. Saturday   251st day
'Breathlessly hot and still onwards from 7 a.m. The least excursion into the sun and the sweat would be trickling down. J. did plenty of navigation work but was hampered in his noon-day sights by the sextant's telescope constantly steaming up — was that hot! In fact 44° C. in the sun. J. went swimming a couple of times and I washed my hair and threw jugs of water over myself.

'You'll never believe this, but in the afternoon we had our celebration! Furthermore, J. actually mustered the energy to rig up all the photographic gear and film it. The main course was a tin of Wilson's Ham with tinned asparagus, Mountain House scrambled eggs, Heinz potato salad, raw onion, and we even had mustard and chutney. This was followed by J. opening the bottle of champagne, presented to us in San Francisco from the officers of the Royal Yacht *Britannia*. The bottle had passed the afternoon cooling on a line thirty feet or so below *Britoo* so, in spite of the intense heat, by the time we came to drink it around 4.30, it was passably cool and tasted absolutely delicious. At this point J.'s nerves got a bit rattled because the damned casette didn't work in the movie camera and once the cork was out there was no going back, so another vital moment is missing from our film! Anyway, it is jolly annoying, when he goes to so much trouble to get good film, to be so frequently let down by malfunctioning equipment.

'For our sweet we have decided to have some Vacu-Dry fruit galaxy and I had mixed this in the morning so it was now a very refreshing and tasty fruit salad. Now was the moment to open our Christmas cake, a touch of 'real'

Christmasses at home from our good friends on Washington Island. I unwound all the sticky tape and pulled off the lid, ooh, surprise, surprise! Inside the cake box with the cake were all kinds of lovely Christmas goodies, a metallic green cake-frill, lengths of tinsel, a little fluffy snowman in tinsel and his brother, a little scarlet Father Christmas, a little package for each of us.

Also inside was an envelope, from the Frew family and friends on Washington Island, containing Australian money, for, knowing we are without a cent, us to 'quaff a few chilled Australian ales for us when you hit the Queensland Coast'. There was a Christmas card hoping Christmas Day would favour us with a 'serene sea, a cooling breeze and what have you', well, there was no such luck, but things are all the sweeter for delays. Then we found four little coloured candles for the cake, one for J., one for me, one for *Britoo* and one for Washington Island. So now I dressed the cake, and we lit the candles one by one, and one by one the wind blew them out. It was all so absolutely perfect, such kind people are rare indeed and we are extremely lucky to have found our friends on minute Washington Island.

We opened our packages and found a beautiful pen-knife for each of us, a really nice, neat one with six different pieces in it. Finally, we finished our champagne, cleared up very superficially, watched the pink sun set and a huge orange moon rise. Both far too happy and far too tipsy to row, we decided to give it a break and I crawled into the rat-hole, while J. fell asleep half in and half out. So that was our celebration, a lovely, lovely time Christmas, Equator and New Year in one big, bumper day.

'Mustn't forget, throughout our party the dorados were treating us to their own exclusively beautiful water ballet around *Britoo*, non-stop with constantly changing antics. Of course, we tried to film this too since the water was as clear and still as it ever is — are keeping our fingers crossed for successful results. Last daylight produced the biggest white tip yet, so the day ended with a shooting from the deck — can't say I felt very happy with tipsy Johnny handling the bullets but he knows his business — I shouldn't worry!'

We now had another problem — not insoluble but worrying. Once more the unfavourable winds and currents had taken us slightly (but enough) off course to miss the twin islands of Howland and Baker. I wanted to replenish our water stocks there, as it was still devilishly hot and we were using up water too fast. As I explained before, we didn't want to use up precious time distilling sea water (it took eight hours to make one gallon) so we were counting on finding land. If we missed the Gilberts, having missed Howland and Baker, our next prospect was the Solomons, over a thousand miles away. I had no doubt that we could make it, but it would be a bore.

By January 5th, the wind had veered to the east, it was very light, but if it held we might just make one of the most southerly of the Gilbert Islands. We stepped up the rowing time and cut down the sleeping. The biggest strain was keeping an accurate course.

From John's Log

5.1.72   255th day
'Very light east winds. If they hold we might just make it. We are now on Lat. S.2° 34, E.177° 57. Arorae is about seventy miles almost due west from us and we can only afford to lose ten miles of latitude. With an E. wind this should be feasible. We'll see. There are almost no birds around which shows how misleading it could be if one goes by them to judge his nearness to land. The fact is that unless there is a sizeable school of tuna or other big fishes feeding on the surface, the birds just disappear. We only have the dorados to keep us company but they are only thirty or so. Spent about an hour taking underwater pictures of their antics as we are bound to part once we get within sight of land.'

6.1.72   256th day
'The east breeze still with us but for some reason we did very poorly having covered only twenty odd miles from yesterday noon to noon. Fortunately we didn't lose latitude: in fact we actually gained two miles and are now forty-six miles from

Arorae. During the afternoon it became cloudy until the sky was completely overcast and that is still the situation at the moment, midnight L. time. Been rowing hard as we must reach Arorae before, or at least sight it at, sunset tomorrow, otherwise we will pass by in the night and that will be that. This overcast has me very worried as I must be extremely accurate on my navigation now, the Island being only four miles square, and I'm afraid that if I cannot take sights tomorrow we'll be lucky indeed to get there. Navigating like this is a nightmare for me, what with the heat and the necessity of rowing extra time, as well as the effort of trying to keep my accurate course, gets me so tired that the very last thing I feel like doing is thinking and calculating this and that. Hell, I'll be real glad once we either put to or bypass the bloody island. At least then I'll be able to relax again, for a while anyway.'

7.1.72   257th day
'Squally, total overcast and the wind from the S.E. I have no choice really but to abandon any hope of making Arorae now. The only other alternative is either Tamana or Onotoa. Tamana is nearer but half the size of Arorae, which was small enough. Onotoa on the other hand is 12 miles long but some 90 miles from our present position, assuming my DR to be correct. This means at least two and a half days to get there, providing the wind stays on the S.E. as the island lies north of us and we must recover about 30 miles of Latitude. If the wind changes we'll miss Onotoa and it will be goodbye to the Gilberts. Personally I would much rather forget about them and keep going, but we ought to send a message home to allay their fears, as they have not heard anything from us since leaving Washington, and, if the radio is really on the blink, won't hear any for a long time still. Actually the wind change is not so bad as it will be easier to hit Onotoa than Tamana and the situation, in case of missing either of them, would be the same, so let's hope for luck.'

8.1.72   258th day
'Going fine, weather same but able to take sights. Nearer

Onotoa than I thought and hope to get there some time tomorrow. We are rowing extra time in case the wind changes and are both horribly tired. It is now or never and there is no chance for me to sleep until we get there, as we are rowing during the day as well. Drinking a lot as a result because we are absolutely parched after one hour, and if we miss Onotoa we have water for 25 days only. Wish I had a big scale chart of the Gilberts. Dorados still with us. I suppose we'll part company soon.

Luck seems to be holding, wind changed to N.E. this afternoon, after a brief spell of calm, and cleared the clouds completely. Beautiful starry night and approaching Onotoa from the east, which is bad for landing as it is the weather side, but we have no choice as I don't want another Fanning.'

Why the hell do I write these things: 'Luck seems to be holding?' Well, I suppose it did, in a way, things could have been much worse.

10. Shipwreck

From John's Log

9.1.72-13.1.72   259th-263rd day
'Sighted Onotoa at dawn of the 9th. According to my fix we were then 17 miles east of it. On approach we saw what looked like a gap dividing the island in two and made for it. I have no excuse for what happened next. To approach a coral atoll on the weather side with a ten knot wind behind, in a rowing boat, is nothing less than sheer bad seamanship. To do so without a clue as to the lay of the place, utter lunacy. However, as I said, Onotoa is twelve miles long and, while it would have been easy to round it while we were still ten miles or so off, to do so would have meant an extra ten to twenty miles, depending on which side we rounded.

'After two days without sleep and tired as we were, the idea was anything but appealing, so I took the shortest route — through the middle. By the time we realised we could not get through, we were two miles from land with the ends of the island curving slightly behind us, and a string of continuous, ominous-looking breakers all along it. There wasn't a single gap in the reef, not even for a boat like ours, and the water seemed to go deep right up to it, so there was no hope of anchoring either. For three hours during the worst heat of the day we struggled to clear the breakers at the nearest end, the north-western one, but, tired as we were, it was a losing battle.

'All this time the beach had gradually become crowded with local people and I swore I would not give them the spectacle they were obviously waiting for. What's the use? Relentlessly we got nearer and nearer, until the breakers were looming up about thirty yards from us and we still had a mile at least to go before we could clear the danger.

'As it turned out, what we thought the end of the island was not really, only a jutting prong, and even if we had managed to clear it, beyond it the reef went on for another three miles.

'In spite of that we were still in deep water, although we could see the bottom suddenly rising up about ten yards away, which would give us only about twenty yards of scope before the point where the waves started to break, this supposing the anchor held right away. I knew it would never hold but there was nothing else to try. By then Sy, who had gradually become more and more afraid, was shaking like a leaf and about to start crying, but she didn't panic, thank God, which is a measure of her courage because the sight of those breakers was indeed awe-inspiring when looked at from that distance and from a little boat like *Britt*. They would suddenly rise, seven or eight feet higher than the other waves, and as they curled and broke in a cascade of foam, one could see through them the jutting, brownish heads of coral, some completely awash, others barely submerged, waiting for us. They could afford to wait, all the time in the world was theirs. Add to it the deafening roar of a thousand breakers and you will have a picture of it. There was no hope in heaven for *Britt* to go through that and survive.

'My arms were by then two dead lumps. I had no strength left to grab the oars let alone get her out of it. I let go the anchor. I knew it would not hold for long, if at all, but there was nothing else to do. A few agonizing seconds went by. Suddenly we were in shallow water and the anchor held immediately. I let her have thirty feet of scope. Just beyond us the first breakers rose like a wall. I lashed the oars, then unshipped the rudder and one of the dagger boards. The other one was stuck and I couldn't have moved it even if I had wanted to, which I didn't as that dagger board might take the first bangs and spare *Britt*'s bottom, for a while at least.

'I can't remember what Sy was doing during this time and, other than yelling at her to stay with the boat whatever happened, I completely forgot her. *Britt* was unlikely to capsize but even if she did she would be safer on board, especially since she didn't know how to swim. I had barely finished unshipping the rudder when, with a lurch, the anchor line snapped and *Britt* started drifting again. There remained only one thing for me to do. I had seen a little gap between two upthrusting coral heads, wide enough for *Britt* to squeeze through. Beyond that it was very shallow but the coral was flat all the way to the beach. *Britt* was lying broadside to it but, miraculously, just then there was a lull. However, the next breaker would smash her right against it unless I managed to point her head to the gap and hope for the best.

'There was only one way I could do this in time. Without any thoughts beyond the safety of my boat, I dived into the churning water and, grabbing the eyebolt at the bow, I pushed, attempting with the mad strength of desperation to swing her round. If I failed, it would be curtains for me as I would undoubtedly be squashed against the coral by *Britt*, but this at the time I did not even consider. Somehow I managed to get her round. How far round I shall never know, for suddenly all went dark and with a tremendous lurch *Britt* jumped forward, sweeping me aside and under with such force that I lost my grip on her. It all happened in a second. One moment I was hanging on to her, pushing like a mad horse, the next I was in a swirling maelstrom of foam and felt her go right over me like an express train on one side of my body while the other touched the coral bed.

'When I finally managed to surface, she was through, about ten yards away from me, lying on her beam ends at a 90° angle with Sy in the water, desperately trying to get back on board. The only thing that prevented her from turning turtle was that there simply wasn't enough water under her to do that. I got to her with the next breaker which righted her again and finding Sy frantically trying to unhook the line of her lifesaving harness while attempting to climb back on board. I unhooked it and told her to make for the shore.

'By then the Gilbertese were wading towards us and I knew they would grab her, which they did, lifting her up and carrying her like a baby. The water was then only about waist deep but the waves were still coming hard, although half their strength was already spent. *Britt* was just about floating and keeping her stern to the oncoming surf I managed once more to save her from the worst of it. Soon a crowd of happy Gilbertese surrounded us, men, girls and children, laughing and blabbering away, treating the whole thing as a huge joke and with their help we managed to get *Britt* in ankle deep water.

'I found that the bottom had stoved in in two places but, without a careful inspection, it was impossible to see how bad the damage was. Being low tide, she was all right for the time being but I had to arrange for her to be beached. Fortunately among the crowd was the doctor of the island, Dr Taketiau Beriki, who spoke perfect English. With his help we arranged for *Britt* to be pushed along the island back to where we had tried to pass, there being a very narrow passage. The Doctor invited us to stay at his house and later that night at high tide, with the help of a couple of dozen people and kids, we pushed *Britt* around and into the bay. The whole business was an absolute nightmare as the surf kept breaking over us and *Britt* hit so many rocks that by the time we got her around — five hours later — her bottom was a write-off.'

Sylvia's version of what could have been a watery end to our trip differs slightly from mine; after all, she had a different view of things!

From Sylvia's Log

21st January, 1972, Friday   271st day
'By Sunday the 9th, we were incredibly tired, because each attempted island had meant hours of extra navigation and much extra rowing, since we had been frightened to let *Britoo* drift lest we had a repeat of the Fanning episode. So, by the time John had calculated his dawn sightings and we could actually see Onotoa downwind from us, our relief was considerable.

'The island lay from south-east to north-west and we were

being borne fast down on it by a ten m.p.h. north-west wind.
As we approached it looked like two large islets, with a tiny
islet between in what appeared to be a passage through to the
lee side of Onotoa. We decided to aim for the passage,
intending to save ourselves the twelve or so miles hard rowing
in the mid-day sun necessary if we were to take the only
alternative course and aim for rounding the northern tip of
the island. By the time we could see not one tiny islet
between the two, but three, and that these were linked by an
apparently unbroken line of breakers, we were well south-
west of any position from which it would have been easy to
retreat north, as we were now forced to do. Obviously we
were in for a big fight, which we were by no means sure to
win.

'Now it was close to noon and the heat was beating down
on us relentlessly, but we could not rest, our only hope was
to keep *Britannia II* moving in a desperate bid to get her well
out to sea and clear of the big white lines we could see
extending far beyond Onotoa's northern point. We were in
very deep water (pun?) so anchoring was also ruled out, we
had no choice other than to sweat it out.

'It had been pathetically easy getting where we now were,
but getting away again was a very different prospect. J. took
the oars and I took the rudder, forcing it over as far as
possible, but the wind was catching us broadside, giving us
such a lee that I had to tell J. to row only with his right
(shorewards) arm. By 12.30 I had a pretty shrewd idea we
would pile up on the reef amidst those huge foaming
breakers. Sweat was pouring down Johnny as he rowed flat
out beneath the mid-day sun.

'He couldn't see how we were doing and kept asking me,
and all I could say was, "Not well enough". After an hour of
the hardest rowing of his life, I took the oars for a few
minutes to give him a break. I had never rowed so hard in my
life either, yet, when we changed back again, I could see that
my hardest and best had only served to lose us ground. We
were now further inshore and closer to the edge of the reef.

'Two-thirty came and the fight was still on. We knew we
were losing but something inside doesn't let one give up.

People gathered on the beach and we watched them signal and wave, but we could only do what we were doing and, besides, we were unable to understand them. Desperately, I lashed the rudder and replaced the other oar in the aft rowing position, so now we were both banging away at the water with all our might. Both of us were nearly exhausted, partly by our lack of sleep, but mostly by our three hour struggle in the hottest part of the day, and I was beginning to wish it would hurry up and happen so we wouldn't have to sweat it out any longer.

'The roar of the breakers was deafening as they curled up and crashed on to the edge of the reef a hundred yards away. Five minutes? Ten minutes? Didn't know and didn't care. J. shipped his oar, told me to do the same. Anchor was unready, as we hadn't dared to stop to prepare it, so J. hastily unlashed it, and tied a rope to its chain. Big swells lifted us, and I was counting the seconds, terrified! My fears had been mounting since our decision to change course three hours ago, so by now I was shaking like a leaf and near to tears. I remember that I kept asking J. what I should do, and receiving no answer.

'The anchor was dropped just at the edge of the reef, a matter of yards beyond the breakers. Through the receding breakers two gigantic, round, red coral heads loomed towards us. I shall never forget the sight of them, but the last thought in our heads was photography so they will remain mine alone until, I am sure, my dying day. Now they were closer, I was sure of it. I thought the anchor line must be too long. I looked down over the gunnels and saw the grey bottom with its vivid pattern of blues and greens coming up, up, up.

'To my horror John dived overboard, as I was busy anchoring myself to the dubious safety of *Britoo* with my safety-harness. Almost immediately we were hit by a pretty big breaker and I remember thinking, one more just a little stronger and just a little more broadside would nicely round off the episode.

'Then the two red coral heads were terrifyingly close, but *Britoo* and I were no longer broadside and passed miraculously between them. Unfortunately, by the time of the next huge breaker, at least ten feet of crashing, roaring whiteness, we were well and truly broadside again. I saw it coming, held on with all I could, and a second later we were over.

'At the time I thought we had capsized completely, but what had happened was that on our way over, the warped dagger board, which we had been unable to unship, as we had the rudder and second dagger board, had caught against a coral head and held us on our beam ends. The force of the wave had thrown me over so I was below water, and having great difficulty in emerging as my lifeline was nearly tangled round an item of deck equipment.

'Hardly surprising under the circumstances, at this point John's story and mine vary slightly. As I remember it, I got my head above water, and unhooked my harness so I could reach the uppermost gunnel, to which I held whilst watching the approach of a second seething dragon. I glanced round but saw no sign of John. We were hit a second time, with a mighty judder. Again no glimpse of John, and this time my anxiety was pretty acute, especially as a third monster wall of foam was already beaming down on us. Another great shudder rocked *Britoo*, then she was still. John popped up out of the sea beside me, and there looked as though there was a lull in the waves.

'The successive waves had each pushed *Britoo* a little more shorewards, and there was now quite a sizeable little crowd of Gilbertese wading out to us from the beach. *Britoo* was in chest deep water and Johnny told me to take advantage of the lull to wade ashore. On my way I was met by three girls who kindly helped me ashore after wrapping my bare bathing costumed legs in a tebe. They were led by a most thoughtful and immensely humorous girl called Tabaia. During our all too short stay on Onotoa I was often sorry she spoke no English and even more sorry I spoke no Gilbertese, but despite this slight handicap she was a born comic and cheered me up no end.

'I was taken ashore and introduced to Dr Taketiau Beriki. Patiently he listened to my burbled and confused account of where we had come from, where we had been, what we were doing, and why we were now wrecked on Onotoa. I am sure the poor Doctor made very little sense of that first conversation of mine, I was very shaky indeed and all I was thinking about was when was I going to pass out. However, it apparently takes more than a mere shipwreck to rob me of my consciousness, because I never did.

'Meanwhile John was still at *Britoo*, now surrounded by a crowd of willing helpers. Regrettably there was great difficulty in communication, since John lacks Gilbertese and the volunteers, to a man, lacked English. Finally the very kind Doctor waded out to the boat, had a lengthy discussion on the possibilities with John, and managed to co-ordinate the enthusiastic crowd so that little by little *Britoo* was pushed shorewards until she was well inside the row of breakers.

'Now nothing further could be done for *Britoo* until high tide, which would be around 10 p.m., when our poor little boat would have to be pushed by hand through the shallows over a coral bottom all the way we had rowed along the shore and through the narrow passage we had originally aimed for, into the safety of the lagoon on the other side of the island.

'This being so, and having pushed her beyond any direct threat of smashing to smithereens, we were only too happy to leave her astride two coconut logs aground in the shallows, and be led to the local maneaba where we were welcomed by the island council, pastor, red cross officials and many local people. The Doctor then took us each on the back of his pop-pop bike to his pretty bungalow nestling in the shade of the palm trees and introduced us to his wife, Aotai, and his nurse, Rineti.

'We were instantly made to feel at home and knew we had been extremely lucky to fall into such kind hands. In fact, we have both concluded that, should we ever be shipwrecked again, we would most certainly choose the Gilbert Islands for the event. Also, we counted ourselves very fortunate in being invited to stay with a Gilbertese family, since an English family, no matter how hospitable, is an English family wherever it goes. As it happened, Onotoa has no European residents in any case, but we were so overwhelmed with kindness and generosity that it was quite some time before we noticed this.

'Before 9 p.m., when Johnny and Dr Taketiau went off to move the boat, I had heard Johnny's side of the story and discovered that the reason for his sudden dive into the sea was to grab *Britoo*'s bows in order to turn her from near broadside to head on to the beach, and thus guide her between my two colossal coral heads and avert her total destruction. My dread that he lay squashed and trapped between *Britoo* and coral, was the penalty he would have paid had he failed, so we were indeed doubly fortunate to be sitting chatting in the Doctor's comfortable lounge that evening.

'The next morning we got up to a delicious breakfast of paw-paw, cereal and scrumptious sour-toddy bread, and then began to work. Johnny told me that *Britoo* had bounced her way over the coral to the lagoon and had probably received more damage through that trip than during the actual wrecking, but there had been no alternative, so that was that. Also, the islanders had worked with him till 2.30 in the morning, and here they were again this morning, as keen to help as though they had slept twelve hours and known us ten years.

'First the boat was hauled up on to the beach and then the job of checking all our supplies and equipment began. John and the men stayed on the beach, whilst I stayed at the house, helped by Aotai, Rineti and other girls. It was no joke. By 10 a.m. the heat was blistering. Johnny was unloading the deck and hatches on to a big push-cart which the boys wheeled up to the house where we girls rinsed everything in rain water, in the hope of checking the salt's corrosive action. Our two transistor radios, one tape-recorder, casettes of exposed movie film and casettes of unused movie film, together with one movie camera, were all dipped and swirled in a big tub of rain water before being laid out to dry and sprayed with an anti-corrosive preparation.

'Tuesday was a repeat of the day before. We were helped enormously by the Red Cross as well as many of the same people as the day before. Johnny discovered we had water in every single hatch in the boat, so absolutely everything was wet. All our tins and packets of food were washed and all our cans of gas — every single thing was unshipped and either rinsed or thrown away. We discovered many of our gas cylinders to have leaked and be completely empty through rust and were glad not to have relied on making our own drinking water with our still unproved distilling plant, especially as we had already ruined one gas tap and the current one is in doubtful condition. Besides all this our clothes were moulding and bad smelling. I left them in their polythene bags, but the next thing I knew they had all been washed and were strung up along the line.

'Our rudder and anchor had been lost during the capsize, together with several minor odds and ends which had been loose on deck, so this afternoon J. set aside for diving to retrieve them. Off he went, aided by two Gilbertese men, Abetan, a cousin of Dr Taketiau, and Uruabe, both keen divers, returned very successfully two hours later with both rudder and anchor, as well as many forgotten articles which even included a toothbrush! Everyone seemed happy enough, but after a while the Doctor told John that his two helpers had been very frightened diving amidst the jagged coral right in the middle of the breakers. Poor John, it had never occurred to him this might have been so as these brave men had carried on diving showing no sign of fear whatsoever. I really don't know if I felt more sorry for him or for them.

'That evening a visitor arrived at the house and it was immediately obvious that something serious was afoot. We learned that a cable (Onotoa had no telephone) had been received to say that the Government vessel, *Nareau*, would be diverted to call and see if they could assist us the following morning. For some unaccountable reason, this seemed an extremely grave development. I still had the shakes from our little adventure and this message didn't help at all. The general atmosphere was that usually experienced after a sudden death, a very strange reaction indeed to an offer of help. Slowly people returned to normal as we each reasoned ourselves into acceptance of what could only be an improvement in the situation. The Master of the *Nareau*, Captain Lomi, was due ashore at 5 a.m. the following morning, so we returned early to ensure being on the beach when he arrived.

'Getting up at 4 a.m. constitutes a big sacrifice in my book, yet the entire household was up and about long before first light on this particular day. The Doctor, John and myself trooped down to the beach where we waited for Captain Lomi and his party to come across the lagoon from where the *Nareau* was anchored outside. By the time the two parties met there was a crowd of curious people round *Britoo* which included a biggish lady of middle age who was obviously the village wit.

'Standing slightly back from the others she said to me, "What is your name?" I replied, "My name is Sylvia," whereupon she turned to her colleagues, muttering and screwing up her nose in distaste, before once more fixing her eyes on me in mock puzzlement and repeating, "What is your name?"

'This time I just replied, "Sylvia" and the lady in question made as poor an attempt at pronouncing my name as I would have at hers, turned to her friends in incredulity, looked back at me and said, "Very bad! Very bad!" At which all the bystanders, myself and herself included, collapsed in peels of laughter.

'The Captain examined *Britoo*'s bottom and spent a considerable time weighing the different possibilities until it was eventually decided that he would return the following afternoon and tow us to Tarawa, where there was a big boatyard easily capable of carrying out the necessary repairs. In the meantime we had to make the boat as light as possible, by emptying her of all water and supplies, and carry out some sort of patching job on her holed bottom in the hope that she would remain dry throughout the two days under tow.

'*Nareau* sailed away and we were left to prepare *Britannia II* for her third tow to date. Most of the equipment was out of her now and we emptied the last of the water. It was an insufferably hot day, despite which our same valiant band of helpers were still at our side, so a long lunch break was almost a necessity even though it would probably result in Johnny having to work through the night patching and painting *Britoo*'s poor crippled hull. He had to fill and patch each visible hole and finally paint all below the waterline with fibre glass paint once the patching had dried.

'A Welcome Party had been arranged in our honour for that evening and we had agreed to a starting time of 6 a.m. Unfortunately this had all been fixed before the tow had been arranged, so as things now stood, John would only be able to stay for about an hour, as he needed every available minute in order to have *Britoo* ready in time for the return of the *Nareau* the following day.

'My clothes consisted of swim wear, shorts and shirts and lava lava, none of which were suitable attire for a party. Aotai said continually that she had plenty of material and maybe I could make myself a dress during the day. Well firstly I have never made a dress without the aid of a paper pattern in my life, secondly I was worried about the great mound of unready equipment which kept arriving in a ceaseless chain of barrow loads from the beach, and thirdly the only time I ever made a dress in one day I finished it at 2 a.m. I must have looked utterly bewildered and dismayed, because kind, hardworking Aotai then offered to make it for me, which she did within a couple of hours and very pretty it was too, a mainly pink floral design shift dress with two big patch pockets. I did feel rather guilty about it because Aotai had also been up since 4 a.m. and, besides helping me with all those filthy boat things, had spent a very busy day doing mounds of washing, cleaning, as well as cooking and organising the food for the party.

'We arrived at the Maneaba of the Women's Club just after dark, which we immediately realised had been a great mistake as it was beautifully situated almost on the beach overlooking the sunset. We learned that the women had built and roofed it themselves apart from a little help with positioning the four coral corner pillars and the main wooden supporting beams. The evening began with the women standing in their attractive turquoise uniform dresses (very feminine and un-uniform looking) and singing the club song. After this their chairman made a very eloquent speech welcoming us to Onotoa which Dr Taketiau translated for us. John and I replied rather inadequately and the chairman of the island

council also spoke. Two very pretty young club members
approached John and I and placed a beautiful and lovely
smelling flower lei on each of our heads. Dishes, dozens of
them! were brought in and set out before us, and what a
banquet. There was rice, some sort of savoury sauce which
tasted vaguely currified, babai, breadfruit, bread, roast
chicken, roast chicken basted with a delicious sticky brown
stuff, sliced roast pork, the Gilbertese edible fern, our
favourite pandanus sweet, fruit salad and cream followed by
coffee.

'When everyone had finished eating, to the music of the
Apex Band, one of the leading Gilbertese groups, whose
music may often be heard on Radio Tarawa thanks to
recording sessions arranged by the Doctor, the dancing began,
starting with the ever popular twist. Both John and myself
were invited to twist by members of the Women's Club, but
John was suffering very badly with his feet which had been
rendered almost skinless when sand had got into his shoes
whilst pushing *Britoo* round the island, so had to refuse,
leaving me to dance with the pretty girl who had asked me.

'The girls, Rineti told me later that evening, far outnumber
the young men on Onotoa, not through any mass exodus but
just by an accident of fate, so it is they who generally invite
dancing. I have nowhere seen such a pretty bunch of girls and
in any normal place they would be snatched up like hot
cakes, but there on Onotoa they must wait hopefully for a
new schoolteacher, a new doctor, policeman, radio operator,
any Government servant who circulates under a two year
contract. Yet, in spite of their forlorn circumstances, the girls
seem happy and laughing enough.

'Johnny left the party about 9 together with Dr Taketiau
to return to work on *Britoo*. I stayed to have a thoroughly
enjoyable evening. There was quite a lot of formation and
progressive dancing performed by the ladies of the club, and
a couple of absolutely hilarious burlesque turns, as well as
much twisting, all great fun. I had a go at one of the
formation dances with Rineti but rather felt I ruined it — it
did look easy enough, until one tried it! Also did quite a lot
of twisting, in fact my feet were quite delicate by the end of

the evening and I must confess to being somewhat surprised at myself for getting so tired through dancing the night out ninety per cent with girls!

'Returning from the party around midnight we looked in on *Britoo* where John was working, aided still by the Dr. and Euroba, chairman of Onotoa's Red Cross. Euroba was not a young, or even a middle aged man yet he stayed working with them till they packed up at 4 in the morning, and he was back at the house ready to carry on again at 7 the following morning. What remained for me to do was less than I had thought, so I passed a comparatively relaxed day, since there was nothing I could do at the boat either.

'The *Nareau* returned in the afternoon and somehow, with all our helpers and the push trolley, we got all our supplies (packed in cardboard boxes, polythene bags, or sacks) back to the beach to be taken by dinghy to *Nareau* anchored beyond the reef. *Britannia II* was pushed and lifted back into the water and we were ready, waiting sadly on the beach amidst our new friends and many islanders gathered to wish us well on our way. Eventually our provisions were waded out to *Nareau's*dinghy, and we waded out to board *Britannia*, surrounded by a crowd of well wishers shaking hands and saying Tiabo, to be towed out to the *Nareau*. Another sad goodbye, how I hate goodbyes!

'It must have been after eight before we were under way with *Britannia*, empty and forlorn, dragging along in our lee. We ate our first " normal English meal" since *Chusan* in solitary splendour, having embarked long after dinner time, in the *Nareau*'s pleasant little dining room, then we went to bed with a great sense of relief in the knowledge that we had absolutely nothing to do until we disembarked two days later.

'Friday we lounged around and met Mrs Clark and her daughter Dorothy at breakfast. They were the first English people we had met since *Chusan*, but neither they nor we had much to say of our homeland. Theirs was talk of Betio, Africa and similarly exotic sounding places, whilst we spoke mostly of Washington and Onotoa Islands and the sea thereabouts. I spent a chunk of the morning in bed feeling slightly seasick (different movement) and the rest of the day passed in idleness and chit-chat until after dinner when Captain Lomi and a Gilbertese passenger joined Mrs Clark and myself in playing a popular Gilbertese card game.

'The sound of voices and hurrying feet woke me around 2 a.m. and I got up immediately, half afraid of confirming my suspicions regarding the cause of the commotion. Sure enough, the ship's engineer said, 'Your boat has turned over'. Soon the entire crew were up, ropes were everywhere, a boat was lowered and five men dived into the dark waters of the night to rescue our *Britannia II*. I'd woken John and he too dived and swam out to *Britoo*, floating quite unconcernedly on her beam ends. Of course, the *Nareau* had to stop, lights went on, and the concern of Captain and crew was astounding. I know John is afraid of sharks etc. in dark water, and the engineer was concerned for *Nareau*'s swimmers, so I suppose they were afraid too, yet they were in the water a good half hour, until *Britoo* had been hauled upright and bailed free of all water. Then off we went again, this time with two volunteer members of *Nareau*'s crew aboard *Britoo* with lamps, one flash for all's well, three flashes for danger.

'An hour or two later we were awoken again to find *Britoo* once more floating on her beam ends. This time the two boys aboard her righted her on their own and the delay and commotion were very little. Breakfast was retarded by the third and last tilting of *Britannia II*. This time the boys had not worn their life harnesses, for which I don't blame them a bit as these chafe horribly against bare skin, and by the time the *Nareau* had managed to stop they were two little blobs in the water way, way behind us. They finally caught up and clambered happily back on *Britoo*, righted her, treated the entire episode as a huge joke and we all continued on our way.

'It was now Saturday, 15th January, and our 64th day since leaving Washington Island. We were due to arrive in Betio, the commercial centre islet of Tarawa, in the early afternoon We were most impressed by the efficiency of the place, as the *Nareau* had received word that the money we had cabled London for three days before was already sitting

J.F. diving from *Britannia*.

Sometimes there was time for relaxation—S.C. wearing a Gilbertese hat.

J.F. and S.C. rowing. (*Photo Syndication International*)

Two male dorados speared to complement our diet.

J.F. taking sights to establish *Britannia's* position. Celestial observation was the only means used for navigation.

S.C. cooking Christmas dinner.

Preparing the bait for lassoing a shark.

A shark is caught in the lasso.

Playing the shark.

The shark thrashing in the water.

Britannia on the shore of Onotoa's lagoon.

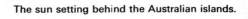

The sun setting behind the Australian islands.

J.F. five minutes after being bitten by a shark.

White-tipped sharks—the same species as the one which bit J.F.—prowling round the boat. Note the spear-gun at the extreme right of the picture.

in the bank waiting for us, it had also been Tarawa officials
who, on receipt of the official cable of our plight from
Onotoa, had asked the *Nareau* to assist, accommodation had
been found for us, as Tarawa's one hotel is not on the same
island as its shipyard, and representatives from the boatyard
came out to the *Nareau* and towed the erring *Britannia II*
ashore to their dock. All as smooth as silk and without urging
on our parts!

11. Tarawa

I suppose you would call it a reception committee which boarded the *Nareau*, complete with customs and immigration forms, to welcome us to Tarawa. Not knowing any of them at the time, and being notoriously bad at names, I won't list them here, suffice to say they were English (which which I include Scots, Welsh and Irish, begging their forgiveness), and unmistakeably so. These were the people we had to thank for the smooth success of Operation *Britannia II*, and I was conscious of John and me having caused them an awful lot of work and trouble before we had even arrived. Nevertheless, we were cordially introduced and it was very pleasant to be amongst our own folk after so long. My nagging feeling for the bother we had caused was soon confirmed by the presentation of a list as long as your arm detailing all the transcontinental telephone calls and cables received on our behalf by the Chief Secretary, Mr John Hunter.

Mr R.E.N. Smith, the District Commissioner, and his charming wife, Elizabeth, were in the party. They were the kind of brave people who offered us, complete unseen strangers — and obviously a trifle mad at that — the freedom of their guest house while *Britoo* was being repaired. However, that night we returned to the *Nareau* to eat and sleep, only going ashore to receive a booked telephone call from the *Sunday People* and do a short interview for Radio Tarawa.

We went ashore at mid-day on the morrow. The little shore-going dinghy piled high with the collection of boxes and plastic bags which were our luggage. All our dribs and drabs were heaped into the back of the mini-bus and Ren drove us to his lovely thatched home by the lagoon. Being Sunday there was no work we could do so we had a heavenly time lounging on the verandah, watching Elizabeth sailing her dinghy round the lagoon with Josh Lewis.

Afterwards we had a fabulous dinner, of steak with our first chips for months and months. It was also the first meal we had eaten with the wife of the house for a long time. Bill and the Doctor both ate Island style, which meant the women and children ate only after having served the man. As a European I had always eaten with the men, but it was very pleasant to have some feminine company at dinner once again. After our meal we went early to bed.

Next day we completed the customs formalities and went to the boatyard to inspect *Britoo*, now on dry land again, and spoke to Alex Robertson, the boatyard manager. After that we went to the offices of the communications department and received telephone calls from ITN, the *Sunday People* — yet again, various Australian journalists and my parents in England. The line to London was not at all good, and long distance social telephone calls are usually rather stilted because everyone's too conscious of the cost. It seemed too expensive for detail and the bare facts made a pretty staccato conversation, so my longed for chat with home was not exactly a roaring success. Nevertheless, it was nice to hear their voices and be assured all was well.

Due to some administrative mix-up, Ren and Liz had no phone at home and, as we were disproportionately popular during our first couple of weeks on Betio, messengers were frequently calling at the house to tell us there was a telephone call coming for us. At this we had to drop everything and either walk or cycle a quarter of a mile down the road to the Post Office, where we were kindly allowed the freedom of an office whose occupant seemed to be seldom at home. Sometimes we waited there two hours or more for the expected call.

One day we left the office during our wait and walked straight back in, talking as we entered. I turned to pick up the telephone to find the desk's Gilbertese owner sitting there, smiling calmly and seemingly not in the least perturbed by our intrusion. It was so rude that I felt ashamed, especially as we had been shown nothing but courtesy and consideration during our stays in the Gilberts.

The bank on Betio is open for only one and a half hours two days a week and, because we had been on the telephone, we had missed it. We decided to go to the neighbouring islet, Beriki, the administrative centre of Tarawa, where they keep normal banking hours. After the forty-five minute ferry ride, we went to the bank, collected our money, then went to the studios of Radio Tarawa. We were interviewed by Alan Robins who afterwards invited us to a most enjoyable lunch with his family. Whilst we had still been at the studios we received another telephone call from Jacky, my lifelong friend back home. It was a lovely surprise but very disappointing as the line was simply atrocious and I only caught occasional squeaks of conversation. Eventually the Fiji operator, who could hear us both, was passing brief messages back and forth and, apart from a short talk with her husband, who had been easier to hear, it was in this manner that our 'chat' was conducted!

It was about three o'clock by the time we were back on Betio, so after doing a little local shopping, we wrote and read until it was time to dress for the party to which we had been invited by Mrs Christine Sharp. The party was a farewell to Alex Robertson, leaving for Australia after six years. It was very nice and very English, with everyone standing around chatting and drinking. The delicious cold buffet, which could have been at home, apart from the first course, (a Gilbertese dish of strips of raw fish marinated in vinegar and coconut juice, served in half coconuts — extremely more-ish!), was followed by dancing and a wickedly hilarious performance by Willie Schulz, slightly risqué and therefore indescribable.

At the party we met Captain Taylor, Marine Operations Manager, who told us that some of our gear had been offloaded from the *Nareau* and was likely to be buried under tons of cargo from a record number of incoming ships unless promptly rescued. Accordingly we shot off to the customs sheds the very next morning where we found and removed the offending items. Whilst there, we met our friend, Captain Lomi, who said our cargo could remain aboard until the

Nareau was due to sail. Another problem solved. It was a few more days before we heard that the *Nareau* had sailed, complete with all our gear! After an hour's panic, during which we tried to discover where she had gone and when she would return, all was well as it became obvious she would be back long before we were ready to leave.

The repairs to *Britoo*, as usual, took considerably longer than expected. Then four more huge worm holes were discovered when she was tested for leaks. Altogether she had about ten holes from the reef and eight or nine from teredo worms.* Consequently we spent nearly a month on Tarawa, leaving just one day before Liz and Ren departed on a tour of the Gilbert Islands — in other words just in the nick of time!

I had really begun to think that offering accommodation for 'a few days' was quite a different proposition from having guests for a few weeks. Not that Liz or Ren ever showed the slightest sign that we had overstayed our welcome. On the contrary, the longer we stayed, the more at home we felt. Once again we were very fortunate indeed. Liz and Ren had made us comfortable in every possible way and Liz was an extremely good cook whose meals we greatly enjoyed. They were both such jolly good company that, had we not been getting so impatient to finish our journey, we might even have been sorry to leave Tarawa too.

The Gilbert Islands are composed of tiny little islets, often not much more than a hundred yards wide in parts, and with no streams or rivers running through them. Add that to the fact that they are entirely coral with no natural soil whatsoever, and it is really incredible that the original Gilbertese settlers, after crossing thousands of miles of sea by canoe, thought they could possibly scratch a living from them and decided to stay. When you stand in the middle of an absolutely flat island, watching the sea to either side of

* These are tropical marine worms which burrow into the wood of boats by the tiniest little hole and once inside eat invisible tunnels through the wood in much the same way as our woodworm. Anti-fouling paint is supposed to be impenetrable to them, but ours probably got in where the paint had been cleaned away during Johnny's frequent underwater scrapings of the hull to remove the barnacles growing there.

you, it seems amazing that even now, with regular shiploads
of commodities, people can live comfortably in such a place.

Tarawa itself, by which I suppose I mean Betio, we found
rather depressing. Apart from the huge Japanese bunkers,
wrecked tanks, and other relics lying around as witness to
one of the most mortal battles of World War II, the
overcrowding under which the local people mostly live,
contrasted oppressively with the European mode of life.
They, possibly, were enjoying slightly higher standards than
they would in England, and even ate the same food, bought
at high prices (seventy pence for a pound of jam) in
the local stores. The bread was yeast baked and bought from
a Chinese bakery, so we never again tasted the lovely toddy*
bread that Aotai used to make. The supermarkets sold
imported sweets and chewing gum, so we never had any more
of that delicious pandanus sweet, or the lovely coconut
sweets that Willie's sister made. Neither did we have any
drinking coconuts (the world's best soft drink), although
there were loaded palms everywhere. Even the breadfruit
which weighed down huge branches of these lovely trees,
were never eaten. In short, the Island's natural foods were
left to the Islanders and never came within our reach.

About every six weeks a ship arrived from Australia,
causing great excitement amongst the English residents since
it brought their only fresh fruit and vegetables. One arrived
during our visit and I went with Liz and her French-
Madagascan friend, Guillemette, to buy peaches, cherries,
melon, rhubarb, carrots, etcetera. Both shops had long
queues, each member of which had a seemingly endless list. It
was quite strange to see people getting so excited about
rhubarb, especially at seventy-five cents a pound!

The Gilbertese and Ellice Islanders flock to Tarawa in
much the same way as provincial Britishers crowd into
London, and it was obvious they were coming in greater
numbers than could be usefully employed. It was very sad

---

* Toddy is the liquid extracted daily from the cut coconut shoots. If
allowed to ferment it is used as the raising agent in bread-making and as
an intoxicating liquor — for which reason it was outlawed on Washington Island. It is also very valuable as a baby food on the islands.

because it is the only city in the Colony and for the outer
islanders to hear of its two cinemas, three stores, half a dozen
small shops and bars, plus a shipyard, docks and a power
station, must indeed sound as though its streets are paved
with gold. In reality the streets are paved, pitted and dusty,
throwing up heat with unimaginable intensity and mostly
bordered by houses so close together that there is no room
for the usual outbuildings for cooking and eating. The
Government is obviously doing its best and many islanders
are now housed in small square bungalows, adequate if not
aesthetic delights. But what can be done when the Gilbertese
invite more and more of their families to come and join
them?

Even the Gilbertese and Ellice peoples, who we had found
to be so helpful and such great fun both on Washington,
Onotoa and the *Nareau*, seemed to be shadows of themselves
in Tarawa, quiet and almost surly. Shopping was a nightmare.
Many of the assistants wouldn't or couldn't understand and
it wasn't until we were nearly leaving that I had sorted out
which were helpful and which invariably said '*agia*' — none —
and walked away with a careless shrug. There were none of
the usual games in evidence at sunset, and all the fun seemed
to be dead. Whereas on the other islands we were seldom
conscious of being anything other than human, here we were
conscious of being different. It is a difficult thing to explain,
and probably I misunderstood much in our short stay. Even
more probably, if I were to remain there long I would
overlook the melancholy and start living (like everyone else)
in sublime acceptance.

The dogs too were sad on Betio. No bitches were allowed,
in an effort to keep their numbers down. Liz's dog, Rommel,
a big boxer crossbreed, used to take himself off, all alone, on
the ferry over to Beiriki periodically. He was quite notorious
and very intelligent. Once Liz and Ren had gone away and
left Rommel in charge of our good friend Ron Summers who
lived next door. On the day when Ron had been due to catch
the 9 a.m. ferry to Beiriki, he had been unable to find
Rommel before leaving. Ron took the ferry anyway and
stepped off the other side to be met by Rommel, patiently

sitting by the ferry awaiting his arrival!

Our own second visit to Beiriki was when we were honoured by an invitation to drinks at Government House. We both had to buy shoes for the occasion and I wore my one and only dress, the one Aotai had made me at Onotoa. We caught the 11 a.m. ferry and were amazed to see small boys sleeping away the forty-five minute ride sitting on the bulwarks, holding the lifeline above it. We were met by Mr John Hunter and his wife, Elizabeth, who took us to Government House where we passed a very pleasant hour talking with Sir John and Lady Field. Lady Field showed me her beautiful garden overlooking the sea. It is very difficult to grow anything at all on these islands as they are coral atolls with no soil, but Tarawa, because of the endeavours of the Europeans, has considerably more variety than I had seen before.

Afterwards we went to lunch at Mr and Mrs Hunter's, where we met their two youngest children, were introduced to Mr and Mrs Dick Turpin, and had a delicious curried lunch. Whilst there I remember complaining that instead of speaking to David Farr at the *Sunday People*, who we knew well, we had been passed on to Lee Lester who, I said 'could be the nicest chap under the sun, but we don't know him'. John Hunter, who had been accepting all the telephone calls and messages prior to our arrival, replied very humorously, 'Oh, don't you? I know him *very* well!'

The weather during our stay on Betio was very unsettled and I was often glad we were not at sea, especially as Hurricane Wendy was 180 miles off the Ellice Islands, which is not a hurricane zone. There was plenty of rain and some pretty heavy seas. Sometimes the lagoon looked dark and brooding, more like the Lizard in a gale than a reefed lagoon. A couple of times the sea, helped by an exceptionally high spring tide, was blown right across the garden almost to the steps of the verandah, stopping only just short of the guest house. The neat crazy-paving laid down along the top of the sea wall was seriously dented and the ornamental wall by the verandah mostly swept away. Sand and floating debris were strewn all over the garden. As the walls were composed of huge blocks of coral rock, which a single man had difficulty in lifting, and as the Ocean within the lagoon was comparatively calm, it was rather an awesome demonstration of the power of the sea. We were told they had never had it so bad and couldn't help but feel vaguely responsible as, wherever we went, it seemed freak weather accompanied us. It had even rained in Ensenada — and in June at that!

Besides our countless telephone calls, we received a lovely package containing letters from our families and many of our friends in San Francisco and England. This had been arranged by Ron Mathiesen with the co-operation of Quantas Airlines, who had been holding them since before Christmas to forward to us if and when we turned up anywhere. I was concerned to read how worried they all were that I had had malaria and it was some time before I realised this rumour must have grown from the news that I had had a slight fever and infected mosquito bites whilst on Washington Island. In fact malaria, along with most gruesome tropical diseases, is unknown amongst the Gilbert and Ellice Islands. Fortunately apart from a little leprosy, they are generally relatively disease free.

There was an outbreak of denghi fever during our visit. Poor Liz seemed to be going down with it just as we were leaving but, luckily, we escaped. This is a mosquito carried disease, commonly know as breakbone fever. From the mosquitos themselves, there was no escape. Despite sleeping beneath nets (as did everyone in the Colony), spraying the room with insecticide, and spraying myself with insect repellent, I was unable to avoid another huge crop of bites. The residents said that after two or three months the mosquitos no longer bite you, but we never stayed long enough to find out. I did take Liz's advice and took regular antihystamin tablets, which reduced the irritation, but by that time I was smothered in scratched bites and it took all my time and patience to keep them free of hungry flies. As a result I now have more scars from mosquito bites than from salt water sores.

Once more I acquired a horribly swollen foot and, although not as painful as the last, had to visit the local

hospital and be put on a course of Tetracyclyn tablets again.
Johnny was given the same treatment as not only was the
crook of his elbow a mass of lumps, but behind his knee he
had a colossal swelling, feeling like a collection of cysts.
No-one seemed to identify his troubles so it was assumed to
be vitamin deficiency, and he was given vitamin pills as well.
Once more we had been fit during all our time at sea but
once ashore had had to seek medical advice. Thank heavens
for the modern wonder drugs.

Quite irrationally, the mosquitos were the least of my
worries on Tarawa. In common with all coral atolls, there was
an abundance of cockroaches of up to three inches long and,
whereas they had never bothered me before, once I had
learned that they could fly, I was terrified of the things. I
have almost a mania about moths and there were some pretty
big beasties of those besides some rather large geckos, and
hermit crabs galore. Then sometimes we would find a huge
furry spider walking along the ceiling when we returned to
sleep in the guest house at night — of course I couldn't sleep
till Johnny had knocked that offender down and killed it. All
quite ridiculous, and didn't I know it!

We had plenty of shopping to do and the supermarkets
were very well stocked with sauces, jams, flavourings and so
on. Although the prices were high, we splashed out quite a
bit for variety at sea. We had intended leaving on the
Saturday and to buy our bread, fresh fruit and perishables
then. We also had to buy a couple of transistor radios and a
new twelve volt battery. Our big expensive transistor, which we
had never even used, was a complete write-off, through
exposure to salt water, and the smaller one had been
rendered unreliable. However the generator and the Marconi
transceiver had been successfully overhauled and tested by
Peter MacQuarry, which should have ended *those* troubles.

All Saturday morning I was pedalling backwards and
forwards to the greengrocers and store, making at least six
heavily laden trips, collecting our supplies. Meanwhile
Johnny, with the help of Josh, together with Rodney
Montgomery, a visiting American yachtsman, was frantically
trying to stow all our gear. When the sun wasn't beating

down unmercifully, it was pouring with rain, so the stowing had to stop. Then I returned to the shops to find they all closed at mid-day on Saturdays and we were still short of plenty. Johnny never finished loading because of the rain, so that was Saturday gone and another day's delay to our credit.

We had been invited to a wedding reception that afternoon. It was Peter MacQuarry's wedding, and that morning I had met him in the greengrocer's as calm as if it were any old day. In fact I had been in trouble trying to ask for breadfruit and he had told me I could not buy it but that if he could find any, he would bring it up to the house. An hour later he had come bearing four magnificent breadfruit for our trip. Having only met him once before I was then certain this could not possibly be the bridegroom, coolly collecting and delivering breadfruit for a comparative stranger on his wedding morning! Regrettably, because of our rush for departure, we were unable to go to the reception.

That night, Liz, having been convinced all along that we would never leave that day, had a lovely dinner party, a delicious meal of roast port with all the trimmings, for us to remember at sea. Margaret and Ian Wotherspoon, with their clowning new puppy, and Ron Summers with his wife, Wynn, were the other guests. All very nice, lot of good food, good wine and good company.

Sunday was another rush. Apart from the enormous amount of stores still being stowed. *Britoo*'s working parts all seemed to have seized up during her holiday. We had neglected our usual maintenance procedure whilst she had been in the harbour and now had to spend some time greasing the rowlocks and oar collars with Vaseline Petroleum Jelly, polishing the seat slides, cleaning the wheels and generally restoring her to good working order. Slogging all day in the glaring sun gave Johnny a rotten headache so I tried to persuade him to stave off leaving until Monday. He refused, but by about four o clock there was still mounds of equipment waiting to be stowed and Ron Summers talked him into tossing a coin, tails we go, heads we stay. It came up heads, and so another reprieve.

Incredibly, even Monday was not the leisurely day it

should have been. Then, at the very last minute when Ron was waiting with Liz and Ren to drive us with out 'hand luggage' down to the boat, I cut my finger cutting a sandwich for Johnny. The blood was spurting out in torrents and I panicked. I held it under the cold tap, bound elastoplast round it, and held it high. Johnny told me to get to the hospital quick (also panicking) so we commandeered Ron into rushing me off to the hospital on the back of his pop-pop bike without letting Liz even look at it. We arrived at the hospital and I told the nurse how bad it was — took off the elastoplast — and there was nothing, absolutely nothing, and the bleeding had stopped completely. She dabbed it with disinfectant and put a new plaster on and packed me off. What a fool I felt!

We arrived at the house, chucked everything in the minibus, and off we went.

12. Ship Ahoy!

From Sylvia's Log

'Now we are quite near (30 miles?) Ocean Island. It's hot, hot, with hardly a ripple or a swell on the water. I have just smothered limbs and body in my lovely Vaseline Intensive Care Lotion — very refreshing and I'm sure it is this which has prevented my skin from getting all dry and flaky on this jaunt.

'Nothing much has been happening but we have a large school of a few hundred small blueish fish which have followed us for the past few days. Apart from a pair of white terns this morning, and a bird we both heard but neither saw, a couple of mornings ago, there's not been much other sign of life, although a couple of times schools of porpoises or dolphins have investigated us closely in the night.

'We left Tarawa about 5.30 on 7th February and Johnny rowed out of the mole whilst I steered. To make a good start, we hit a totally submerged rock by the mole entrance which threw me from my standing position at the tiller, straight on to my knees, but otherwise did no damage other than slightly graze a corner of our daggerboard. Once past the mole we accepted a tow beyond the reef, as otherwise we could never have fought clear with the wind as it was. When they finally left us on our own again, it was pretty near dusk. We heard their little outboard motor chugging into the murky distance, and that was that.

'Tarawa was not a place I was sorry to leave. One reason was that we'd lived in such a thoroughly English fashion, surrounded by such thoroughly English people, that it seemed impossible that we were so far from home. There was so much talk of "last leaves", a few weeks away, or "next leaves" a few weeks later, that it gave the impression England was just round the corner, so we weren't really saying goodbye to anyone, as they'd be dropping in from time to time anyway. In spite of all this, as usual, once we'd left, I remembered so many people we should have said goodbye to and didn't. The trouble was partly that we were rushing around in last minute preparations, and partly that we didn't know who would be coming to see us off — hope all those concerned bear us no grudge!

'I suppose about a dozen people were at the boatyard to say farewell, and there were people lining the mole on either side too. John was stowing a few last minute day to day items, while I stood on the dock getting jittery because there didn't seem anything to say and I wanted to get off. Temaia, Liz's house girl, came with the sister of Bwebwe, Liz's wash girl, and her daughter, and they gave us a lovely fragrant flower lei each — our last for how long? and a pretty woven and shell lei for Johnny and nice shell necklace for me. Finally we all said our goodbyes and off we went.

'No tears this time until, on our way to the ships anchored in the lagoon, we were passed by three boats towing each other ashore, loaded with luggage and passengers, from the *Nareau*. The crew waved and called *"tiabo"*, and then we passed close by the ship itself, our last link with what I think of as the real Islands and they all waved and "tiaboed" from her deck, bringing back memories of the clowning on the boom by their youngest two, and the friendly good humour of all aboard, and of Onotoa and Washington. This time I knew we really were leaving and had a job to stem my tears.

'It was quite calm, or very slightly choppy, but as usual the first four days I was feeling queezy, and would only stay up for half an hour or so before I had to lie down again to recover.

'Quite ridiculous after all my weeks and months at sea in this little boat, but it seems that I always start this way. Fifth day found me fit as a fiddle, so back to the oars and life on *Britannia II* continues as normal.'

So far this part of the trip looked a real milk-run, after the near disaster at Onotoa. I found it difficult to keep up with the log and left most of it to Sylvia. In my book nothing worthwhile had happened, just the usual routine. The weather was superb — really Pacific of the movies — with occasional squalls to cool the temperature and the winds never above force three or four, always from the east or north-east. We were now rowing an average of thirteen hours a day, with me doing eight hours and Sylvia five, and yet going excellently both in direction and speed. Twenty days out of Tarawa we were three hundred miles north of the Solomons and expected to pass them in about eight to ten days. We had plenty of food and water and all that mattered now was to get to Australia and finish with all the caper which had become really boring.

The only real trouble was the radio. We had tested it in the lagoon at Tarawa after the overhaul and it worked perfectly. As soon as we got to sea if failed completely. The generator was working (although that too packed in later), but we just couldn't raise anyone on the transceiver. It was the same old faithful that had seen me all the way across the Atlantic and more than half way across the Pacific, so I suppose it had to go sometime. After the duckings it had undergone at Onotoa, they had dried it out in an oven and changed as many of the valves etc. as they could on Tarawa, but we never got another peep out of it. Although I could fiddle with the generator, the radio was the one thing I dared not touch. We weren't worried for ourselves but, with communications on the blink, we knew our friends and relatives would become worried as the weeks went by. However, there was nothing we could do about it, except curse and pray we'd never really need it.

So, the days went by and we coasted along, a very strong south-westerly current going our way and doing exactly, for once, what the pilot chart said it should.

From Sylvia's Log

19th February   300th day
'Lo and behold — a ship. Slow cargo vessel, black with cream

booms and bridge, not very big. Came very close to us as its course cut across our bows at a small angle. Was close enough to have seen us easily for nearly an hour but they never did. Luckily we didn't need them (although would have liked to send a message for Mum's birthday tomorrow, as still no luck with the radio). Seems a pretty poor do, considering they lose an average of one Gilbertese per month in canoes, you'd think the ships round here would keep a good watch. If they don't even see great big orange *Britannia*, I don't reckon the chances of a tiny canoe. Suppose the ship was from Ocean Island or Nauru – not much else around in its direction.'

22nd February, Tuesday 303rd day

'Johnny got up from breakfast with his mug of tea to be carried, as usual to his perch before the rathole. Sea was calm and just a little popply but he lost his balance on his second step and the tea ended up on deck and he went over the side, arms and legs all over the place, completely off balance. Very funny now, but at the time I was, rightly, sure he would bump his head on the side of the boat, so I leapt up to grab him and got there to see him in the oddest position, completely submerged and apparently still. Very nasty moment, but I managed to grab a wrist and he came up, sun glasses askew, bumped head, ruffled dignity, but otherwise all right.

'Quite a pleasant day, only one shower (but lots in the night) and a refreshing breeze with quite a bit of cloud to stop us frying too fast.'

25th February, Friday 306th day

'Last night we had another unsuccessful session with the radio. Before we transmitted, whilst the set was warming up, we did hear both sides of a conversation through Radio Sydney, this being the most so far we felt rather optimistic, but . . . It was our scheduled time with Sydney but we also called KMI on the off chance. Have decided from now – in fact decided on the last effort mentioned – we'll only try on Thursday, as scheduled, if they don't get us even then don't reckon our chances in between.

'Our three larger dorados are still very young and only about eighteen inches long. Yesterday one met the end of J.'s spear and was sacrificed as shark bait, the remaining two are very sad now and swim always very close together. It's the law of the jungle out here all right, when you consider that these three youngsters probably started off part of a school of hundreds — like the lot we've recently lost — and are now reduced to two, you can hardly blame them for sticking close. With luck they'll meet and join a larger school of their own type or else be joined by the odd lone fish here and there till they are a school in themselves. It's funny how stray single fish join in with a school of completely different type quite happily and seem to think themselves one of them until a school of their own passes by and then they are gone, never to be seen again, as if they knew all the time that they didn't really belong.

'More sunsights to-day, as the sun deigned to show itself at the appropriate times for a change. Still seem to be making good time. Keeping my fingers tightly crossed — this isn't the best time of year to be round here. It's something I avoid mentioning and push to the back of my mind, yet every day I feel we've had another escape. There is now so little to go, yet the threat is still there with this sense of constant reprieve.'

27th February, Sunday   308th day
'Went into the hatches beneath the bunk for tobacco and different (non-dried!) veg. and colour film for stills. The new sleeping platform is a pretty tight fit and quite a nightmare to get out, especially in this heat.

'A far cry from Mexican days, when it was almost a relief to row because it warmed one up a bit, nowadays it's so hot, even at night, that I spend most of my time trying to stop myself looking at my watch (which makes time drag for ever) so that time for a drink seems to come sooner. I have a spell of counting, things like "30 more strokes and I'll look at the time", but I don't, instead I'll say "Well that wasn't long enough, so I'll do another 30". Other times I'll choose an episode from my own life, or a film, or a book, and go through the whole thing again, in the minutest detail — but it's amazing how fast one thinks, for it takes very little time.

'Our fish friends — the long yellowtail and the pair of adolescent dorados — have gone. Maybe they met an untimely death in the night, but I prefer to think our company bored them and they left in search of greener pastures.'

28th February, Monday   309th day
'Saw a ship approaching from two to three miles on course to pass about a mile to our west. As she came nearer I said I reckoned she would see us, just because she looked clean and neat and these are the ones that do — the scruffy ones seem to keep a scruffy watch — and, for the same reasons that she was probably Northern European (which to my mind, includes North American, Canadian, Australian, etc!) if not Japanese. Well, she saw us as she came parallel and made a big slow circle to our side, where she stopped. She was the *Tri-Ellis*, belonging to the British Phosphate Commission, on her way to Ocean Island and Nauru to collect phosphate.

'We had written a short message for KMI, telling them our position and ETA, with an even shorter note for the Captain, and these were ready in a tobacco tin for Johnny to swim to the *Tri-Ellis*. They came very gently alongside and J. rowed *Britoo* right to her and so he just stepped from our boat to their ladder. Soon he was back, by a breathtaking dive from her deck straight into the sea beside *Britoo*, with a crewman who volunteered to stay aboard *Britoo* whilst we went aboard *Tri-Ellis* and showered, etc. They were extremely nice and in no sort of a hurry, but I don't much like heights and ladders and, at the risk of sounding horribly ungrateful, I preferred not to have to face all those people who were lined up along the rail, so I said thanks very much but I couldn't face the ladder, and that was that.

'They asked us if we'd like or needed anything and we said a few apples or oranges would be nice. They asked if we'd like a cold beer, and we said "lovely", and a carton of cigarettes for Johnny. Then someone suggested we might like some magazines, so we said "lovely" to that too. They lowered us a whole crate of apples! Followed by an equally large box of oranges and bananas, two cartons of cigarettes, two *dozen* large cans of beer, and half a dozen bundles of newspapers and magazines — more than we can ever hope to read in the time, but very, very welcome. After that, they passed us a hose and we filled all our jerrycans and so we now have maximum water again and won't need to distil any or catch rain water.

'It was very very nice, unreasonably exciting, and very friendly. I suppose we were with them for about an hour, after which they whistled three times and drew slowly away; very tearful. One last whistle of farewell as they went their way and we were on our own again.'

29th February, Thursday   310th day
'Have discovered the box of oranges and bananas contains all sorts of other lovely things too, like passion fruit, nectarines, grapefruit, pears and lemons. Another nice touch of yesterday's encounter, they saw Johnny mutilating the top of the beer can with our can opener and sent down a lovely drink-can piercer, all alone on a piece of string. Also, someone, at the last minute, suggested we might like some fresh bread, and sent a huge fresh double loaf down to us. All goes to enforce my opinion that one needs to do something like this in order to appreciate people.

'The weather still smiles on us and we're having a jolly good browse through the magazines — lovely. All those gorgeous clothes — I literally dream of clothes, and often, out here — and all those ads for beautiful, expensive little gadgets and trinkets, things I doubt I'd buy, even if I had the money, but I love to look and have missed looking very much. The modern shoes look ghastly, hope I can find something without ankle straps and platform soles, I'm too thick for the first and too tall for the second, and, anyway, they're downright ugly.

'My only regret in our meeting with the *Tri-Ellis* is that she took our school of tuna with her, and, consequently, all our sizeable mixed flock of birds too. Tuna are funny in that, although they follow us, it is always they who are ahead, even when hunting they never appear behind us, only to the sides. Maybe so many boats trawl for them that when they find one slow enough to allow it, they prefer to lead. They are a puzzle to watch because every few hours they start leaping, looking like steel grey bombs as they drop vertically back into the water with a colossal splash, most unlike the graceful cavorting of the dorados even in sound, yet, despite their proximity to us and the fact that they are sometimes on both sides of us, we have never seen what they hunt. The birds obviously see it because, after the first tuna jump, they are circling, squawking and diving dramatically, till the excitement suddenly dies, no more than ten minutes after it began.

'All we are left with is our little school of boat-hugging tiny yellow striped fish — no fun, no company and no interest.

'Later in the afternoon a coconut floated almost to within reach of us. Besides fancying a delicious drink, it seemed to me that, being so near, we were obviously meant to have it, so J. plunged in and got it. After the messy job of husking it on *Britoo*'s cramped little deck, J. offered me first sip — ugh! Never tasted anything so foul, sour and bitter, so after all that Robinson Crusoe stuff, I spat it out and we threw the rest away.'

1st March, Wednesday   311th day
'Had pork chops for dinner and a repeat of our most frequent arguments. Why are there no table knives on *Britannia II*? We eat our meat in our fingers and have the same old row so many times you'd never believe it. In S.F. J. categorically stated "No table knives. We will have a penknife, fish knives and hunting knives, there's no need for table knives". Consequently we are eating with a seven inch blade hunting knife or our fingers, and every now and then he says, "Why don't we have any knives?" Which really gets me going as I wanted them all along. Now he is asking why I didn't buy some in Tarawa — there weren't any and even the forks there were rusting before they left the shop. Then he asks why I didn't ask Liz for a couple and, in my opinion, having managed without as far as Tarawa doesn't make them so

essential that we have to cadge them — so, no table knives on
Britannia II. Ever tried buttering a cracker biscuit with the
seven inch pointed blade of a diving knife?'

Apparently reading all those magazines had made Sylvia
fashion-conscious again — as if it mattered all alone out there
in the tropic sea. She had put on over thirty pounds in
training for the trip, as I had told her to. I didn't want what
happened to me on the Atlantic trip to happen again, and
indeed it didn't. Our stops, and the ships we met, allowed us
to replenish our supplies and we were never short of food.
Anyway, Sylvia decided to go on to a diet of fruit and lemon
tea for a couple of days. I suppose she was thinking of the
Australian shops.

We gave ourselves a couple of days' holiday at the
beginning of March, and even so we were drifting in the right
direction at around twenty miles a day. But on the fifth, my
log says, the wind got up and so did the sea. It was a
reminder that we hadn't finished yet!

From John's Log

7.3.72   317th day
'Sighted a volcano, the Tinakula, part of the Santa Cruz
group. About 60 miles to the east of us, supposed to be
uninhabited according to my Pilot books. We are now
entering the Coral Sea with plenty of sea room either side
and another milestone is gone.

'Whatever happens now at least we have crossed the
Pacific. No way to miss Australia now as there are now big
land masses between us. Lots of reefs later on but I will
worry about that when the time comes. We are now roughly
1100 miles from the Australian coast and should get there in
between 35 to 45 days. This is the worst time of the year in
these parts, hurricane-wise, but so far we have had such
incredibly good luck that I just can't believe it won't hold a
little longer.'

8.3.72   318th day
'Fine weather, dead calm and very hot. Magazines finished.
Rolling on.'

9.3.72   319th day
'Beautiful weather again. *Britt* leaking like a sieve, has been
for some time now, but there is nothing we can do about it.
We do resent the extra work very much, every two days we
have to get into every hatch, remove the stores and bail out,
but the leaks are invisible and we just hope they won't get
worse.'

On March 10th, Sylvia got away without rowing her
midnight stint.

From Sylvia's Log

10th March, Friday   320th day
'Last night happened a thing which I had been dreading
happening, we were in an electric storm. The lightning began
on the horizon as the sun sank and it was midnight before it
reached us, huge sheets of colour flashing through pinks to
blues with the occasional blinding white. The thunder claps
started as a distant murmur and gradually climaxed into a
gigantic crescendo which quite literally, a couple of times,
shook the boat. Fortunately there was no fork lightning,
which accounted for my bravery, not much wind, and just a
steady rain throughout the four hours it lasted. Anyhow, it
got me out of rowing as it started just after J. finished his
first stint, so he came to bed and I stayed there, uncomfortable but glad of a pair of nice strong arms in which to hide
out the squall.'

From John's Log

11.3.72   321st day
'Rain in the morning, after that hot, calm, and boring as
usual. With some delay celebrated our entrance in the Coral
Sea with a bottle of wine. Only another bottle left for when

we sight the Aussie coast. In the last seven days we only covered 160 miles in the right direction due to the vagaries of the wind. If we go on zigzagging all over the place it might take us longer to finish than I hoped for, and in this our last leg, the days and nights seem to stretch for ever, but what can one do? At the moment we are heading for some reefs called the Indispensable Reefs, although I'm sure we can do without them. It should not be too difficult to skirt them, but we'll have to be careful all the same. In any case they are still about 150 miles away.'

12.3.72-14.3.72   322nd-324th days
'The days go on. And the nights. And tomorrow another day and another night to follow. Nothing happens. A lot of blue, empty space, up or down it's all the same. A squall thrown in every few hours amounting to the same thing, up or down, a lot of bloody water. We are fed-up with it. Utterly, thoroughly, nauseatingly fed-up. At least now we have started to do well again with nice N. winds, we are keeping an almost S. course. There must be a fair favourable current as well because to be honest we are no longer rowing with the old discipline. It's been nearly a year now of nothing but this and nowadays an hour stint at the oars tends to become fifty minutes. A ten minute rest a twenty minute one. It all adds up. But we are doing just as well as before, which is not to say we couldn't do better. At this stage however, we don't seem to care any longer.'

Life was getting really unpleasant, particularly when it rained (mostly at night). We lost the ventilator chimney of the rathole at Onotoa and they had made another for us at Tarawa. The bloody thing leaked far worse than the first one did, in spite of stuffing it up with newspaper, and sleeping in heavy rain was impossible. We could sleep on a wet sleeping bag, but not under drips and rivulets of rainwater coming at us from all angles.

Sylvia found another problem.

From Sylvia's Log

14th March, Tuesday   324th day
'Have seen two cockroaches around galley, but they were not
large and actually I'm not sure they were not blister
beetles — which would be worse. Also, the bunk hatches and
boat in general are swarming with the little flies we've had
since Mexico. Nothing we can do about reducing the
livestock as our insecticide spray doesn't work any more, so
let's hope we hurry up and get to Australia while there's still
room for us on board!

'Johnny snapped at me for nothing, so I cried, also for
nothing. He's sorry. I'm sorry. It's all getting a bit much and
we're both edgy and the atmosphere tends to get rather brittle
rather often. In spite of this, we still get along remarkably
well, with no serious rows or tensions building up. He's
incredibly patient and I'm a very lucky girl. As far as
romantic activity is concerned — despite all the jokes and
knowing asides we've encountered since the start of this
caper — there is very little. It's too hot, or too wet, always
uncomfortable too and usually one's too tired, besides one
becomes very self-centred and unsociable under these conditions and it's enough to know there is someone here if an
emergency occurs.'

At last something happened to break the monotony.

From John's Log

15.3.72   325th day
'Some action at long last! It happened shortly after sunset,
last night, unfortunately too dark already to film.

'For some time we have been followed by a school of
sardine-like little fishes — hundreds of them, who usually
gather in a tight bunch around *Britt* at the approach of tuna,
dorado or any other big fish, but never like yesterday; they
were so thick around *Britt* we seemed to be floating over fish
instead of water. Suddenly a large school of tuna of about all
sizes between 20 and 100 lbs attacked them in what soon

developed into a feeding frenzy with a big brown shark thrown in, dashing about for whatever scraps he could grab. The sea boiled around us and as the little fish sought protection under *Britt*'s hull, the boat started to rock and was bumped many times by the frantic tuna. As usual Sy panicked and screamed at me to do something to stop it. Must say that it's really nice to have around a girl with such unlimited confidence in my powers. Oh well, this time I had to disappoint her and she scrambled into the rathole and started to cry. Women! There didn't seem to be anything I could do for her other than show her how harmless the whole thing was, so I got out of the galley a little sieve she has and set to work.

'The water along *Britt*'s hull was teaming with tiny fish and all I had to do to scoop them up was dip the sieve, in-out, in-out. It was easy. I'm afraid I got into a fishing frenzy on my own. In a matter of minutes the deck was alive with wriggling silver and I suppose I could have filled the boat with them, but after a while I decided to go for bigger game. By then Sy had recovered her courage and was watching the operations. Using the little fish as bait, I threw the line. No sooner had I done so, a tuna was hooked, then another and another, as fast as I could bring them in, bash their heads to prevent then from flapping all over the place, and throw the line again.

'The fourth was a really huge dorado that had been around for days and we didn't want to kill him, but these Edgar Sealey hooks are so damned good I couldn't get it out. He was too strong to handle so I had to cut the line and lose the hook. By the time I got a new tackle rigged, the activity had abated considerably. Still, I managed to hook a big fellow — 80 lbs or so — who gave a hell of a fight and got loose at the very last moment and after that landed two more tuna, 20 pounders, after which they were gone as suddenly as they had appeared.

'To-day everything is back to normal, sun and rain, nice steady wind and not a damn thing in sight.'

Sylvia wrote then: 'I've had enough of the sea. It seems to

have the power to bore me stiff or terrify me, and nothing else. Maybe it sounds daft to be afraid of tuna but they are immensely strong. An eighteen inch one on a hand line will easily cut the hand and can pull Johnny off balance equally easily. Their faces are sharp and conical with huge eyes and their bodies have full powerful lines accentuated by tapering to almost nothing before the tail and emphasised by their hard, grey metallic skin.'

She has imagination, that girl! She had already dubbed the swordfish the King of the seas and the sharks the Mafia. Now we were to find out how right she was.

13. Shark-bite and Cyclone Emily

From John's Log

21.3.72-27.3.72   331st-337th days
'The 21st brought me trouble. Bad trouble. Some will say no
more than I've been asking for but be that as it may, it
doesn't change the situation which has suddenly become very
grim, to say the least. In the late morning of the 21st, as nice
a day as there could be, I decided to go over the side as usual
for my daily swim. Also I wanted to catch some of the little
fish that were still swimming around Britt, for an afternoon
snack. They wouldn't bite the hook so I had to spear them,
which was not easy due to their tiny size. Before that I had
noticed a small White Tip, 4 feet or so, hanging around, but
again that was usual. When I went over, the White Tip was
nowhere to be seen, so I settled down to spearing dinner.

'After fifteen minutes I had managed to catch only two
and then the shark reappeared. Had it been any bigger, I
would have asked Sy to pass me the gun with the power head
and promptly done away with it, but being such a small one,
I didn't bother. Familiarity does bring contempt. And
sometimes grief. The little bastard was from the start
extremely cheeky and I had to poke its nose several times
with the point of my spear to keep it at bay. After a few
pokes it seemed to get the message and kept its distance and,
other than keep track of its whereabout with the corner of
my eye, I paid no more attention and went back to my task.

'Finally I managed to spear another little fish but before I
could grab it, that son of a gun White Tip went for it and
snatched it away right in front of my nose. That did it. No
shark, big or small, has ever taken anything away from me
without paying for it and that cheeky beggar wasn't going to

be an exception. As I had been using a spear without barbs, which I thought would be easy to pull off the shark once I got it in, I simply reloaded and let the W.T. have a taste of a few inches of steel through the head. The spear went right through, but it was not a particularly good shot and although stunned, the S.O.B. had plenty of fight left.

'I pulled and he pulled and the bloody spear wouldn't come off and by then I was so angry I completely forgot that the situation was an exact replica of another scrum I had had with a Nurse shark the same size as this one, two years before, off the Bahamas. That time I had been bitten on my right arm after grappling with the Nurse at close quarters, and that should have reminded me, especially considering the vast difference in mouth size between the two species.

'Well, I didn't. I closed in, grabbed the little bastard by the gills with my left hand, the tail with the right and kept him immobilised as I swam back to the boat. Once alongside, I pulled the spear free and passed the gun to Sy. By then the White Tip was struggling very feebly and I should have let it go at that. Problem is, I hate sharks so much I just couldn't resist the temptation of doing a real job on that one. So I asked Sy to pass me a very sharp buck knife we keep for skinning fish, and proceeded to rip its belly all the way from mouth to tail. At that he began to thrash like mad and it was all I could do to hold him. Still fighting we went under and drifted away. I guess this went on for a couple of minutes.

'His entrails were hanging out and I was waiting for him to weaken before I let go, but suddenly he slipped away and before I could blink an eye, had turned on me clamping his mouth at the back of my right upper arm. I felt a searing pain while, with my left hand, I grabbed behind his head, pulling him off and away. Once more he wriggled free, only he decided enough was enough and, without pressing the attack, he slowly sank into the blue.

'I had no idea how bad my wound was, but the amount of blood I was losing was anything but reassuring. Clamping my left hand on it to stem the haemorrhage, I started to swim towards *Britt*, by then about forty yards away.

'Sy will be in a better position to say what happened next,

All I can say is that of all the tight spots I have found myself in a lifetime crammed with them, this is at the moment, one of the worst. The most frustrating thing is that there is absolutely nothing I can do to get out of it.'

From Sylvia's Log

21st to 26th March, Tuesday to Sunday   331st-336th days
'Watching J. returning to *Britoo* I tried to make out what he could be bringing that caused him to swim so oddly, but as he came near to he said, "Prepare a tourniquet" and suddenly I realised it was no fish he had been holding, but his own arm. He clambered back on board, said, "The little bugger got me," and then flopped down with his ruddy and suntanned face the colour of ivory revealing hundreds of hitherto invisible freckles, and his eyes so misted and vacant looking that I was certain he would pass out. However, John Fairfax is made of sterner stuff, and so he proceeded to prove by issuing a series of curt orders of such precision and with such rapidity that it was impossible to carry them all out.

'The wound was ghastly, looked like a joint of veal pulsating and bleeding profusely. It was about six inches long, more than an inch wide and over an inch deep, a great chunk of meat missing from the middle. I tied a handkerchief tightly round the arm above the wound for fifteen minutes and splashed rain water over the injury for superficial cleaning. Johnny was looking really grim and suffering greatly. I had this dreadful feeling of helplessness, which has been with me to a greater or lesser degree ever since, while I gave him a swig of whisky, a couple of Tetracyclin capsules and some hot sweet tea.

'Suddenly he mumbled, "Pictures. Take photographs. Go and get the camera", and when I had done so: "Now my pipe — Right. Now take photos — real close." I could scarcely believe my ears. How cool can one keep?'

'Deciding that our drinking water (algae-ridden rain water) was scarcely more suitable than sea water for cleaning the wound, there was no choice other than to boil a kettle of the stuff and, in the tropical sun, that kettle seemed to take for

ever to cool so that by the time it did, much of the blood had
begun to congeal and I was afraid to disturb it too strongly
lest the bleeding restart. Also, to touch that huge gaping hole
terrified me and even just to look gave me an overwhelming
saltiness in the mouth.

'Besides the uncertainty of the cleaning operation, there
was a triangle of about an inch sticking out half an inch or
more proud from the surrounding arm, but we decided to let
that be. The biggest problem was that we had no liquid or
powder disinfectants or antiseptics, only creams. Finally used
almost a complete tube of Tetracyclin ointment applied to
the dressing, wound a bandage round it and there it has
stayed ever since. This is a hell of a dilemma: if we remove
the dressing, which would need soaking off, we risk admitting
infection. On the other hand it hardly seems healthy to leave
a wound of such magnitude beneath the same gauze for a
week — or what happens next week or the next? It hardly
bears thinking about.

'We are totally unqualified and unequipped for an injury
like this. Then J. is on Tetracyclin, which one takes as a five
day course. When his five days are up, is it better to continue
without anti-biotics, to switch to a different one, or to wait
one day or two? and then start a second course of
Tetracyclin? Lastly there is the fear of the arm seizing up or
healing wrongly if now moved enough, or haemorraging
through too much pressure or movement.

'When a little of his old colour was regained, J. tried to
find our position — which involved holding the sextant high
with his slowly bleeding arm — but, hardly surprisingly, the
results were inconclusive and we could only assumed ourselves to be about 200 north-west of New Caledonia's
northern tip. We rigged up the radio in the vain hope that our
unused International Distress frequency would be working,
even if none of the others were, but finally J. turned to me
and said, "We're on our own, baby". And we still are.

'Ninety miles to the reefs which just might be inhabited
— and a couple of hundred to the mainland, these were our
targets, till the wind changed, becoming easterly and blowing
us further and further away towards only a huge mass of

reefs and unsurveyed hazards. What a mess! The prevailing winds around here are easterly so the situation look grim indeed. Worse is that J. cannot possibly row, and that leaves it up to me and the weather.

'This easterly that's sprung up is stronger than anything since Washington Island. It's difficult to imagine a more futile situation, and now, when we so desperately need civilisation. On top of all this, the wind has churned the sea up horribly and rowing is consequently a damned sight harder. I'm trying to row eight hours daily but haven't managed it once yet, instead I'll stop for a break and fall asleep, absolutely dead beat.

'Our only other hope is to meet a kindly ship or contact a plane with one of our S.A.R.B.E. homing beacons, but I very much doubt if planes pass this way, and J. refuses to start it till we hear or see one, as there maybe nothing within range and we'd then flatten the batteries for nothing. We are ready for a ship or a landfall, but both seem highly elusive, land through the varagies of the weather, for which no blame belongs anywhere, and ships, I regretfully conclude, through downright laziness or negligence by the officers of the watch.

'Just before sunset on Friday we saw a large cargo vessel three parts of the way to the horizon on a more or less parallel course to our own. We lit three orange smoke flames, two parachute rockets which bang, I sat on the blister frantically waving the flag above my head, transferring to flashing S.O.S. with our powerful 6 volt diving torch as dusk deepened, whilst J. switched on the S.A.R.B.E. flotation beacon and the S.A.R.B.E. walkie-talkie, yet they kept straight on and sailed away into the night.

'The anticlimax was indescribable, we need a ship so desperately, we had all the emergency signals, yet they neither heard nor saw.

'The very next morning, about 7 a.m. I spotted another ship on similar course but a third nearer to us, close enough for us to see here water-line, booms and bridgehouse clearly. This time there was no jubilation, no excitement, no frenzy to get everything operating, just an attitude of, "Don't expect they'll see us, but we'd better do our bit in case". So

the beacons went on, the flag was raised, and one more
smoke flare went up — leaving us with only one for land or a
more observant vessel.

'Despite how angry and disappointed both ships left us, a
ship still remains our fastest and most likely method of
rescue. Reaching small islands under our present circumstances is extremely doubtful and leaves the problem of
transport to Australia — possibly only a weekly service,
meaning too many precious days before J.'s arm can receive
the surgery and treatment needed. If we are lucky enough to
meet an Australian bound ship with a benevolent Master and
room to accommodate *Britoo*, then we should be there in a
couple of days. Shark bites are amongst the worst infection
carriers and although at present J. shows no signs of
infection, no discoloration and no fever, the danger remains
strong until he is in the proper hands. This is the main reason
for the frustrating urgency of the situation, this, combined
with the danger of its healing badly. Also he is in considerable pain, which he makes light of, refusing to take even
Codeine let alone morphine, and very worried about the
possibility of gangrene setting in.

'Much of our time has been spent considering ways of
attracting the attention of passing ships, as they seem not to
be tuned in for our line of sight emergency distress radios. We
are keeping a twenty-four hour fifteen minutely watch for
ships now and have concluded our best chance of being
spotted comes at night, when we'll flash S.O.S's with our 6
volt lamps — and if they don't see them . . .! Also, Henti-
Lloyd, maker of our superb foulweather gear, gave us some
nylon scraps, amongst which is a four feet by two feet piece
of really vivid fluorescent orange which I've tied to the radio
aerial to be mounted aloft at the first sign of company.

'We also concluded that, since they usually don't look, a
loud and unusual noise must be made to attract the attention
of those on the bridge, so we tried firing bullets from the
speargun's powerhead at a floating can, but the result was
disappointing and not much louder than dropping a heavy
book, so that idea had to be abandoned as we can't devise
any other noise-maker.'

John: I felt as well as I could in the circumstances. My arms throbbed like hell. I could bear it, but what really worried me was the risk of gangrene. I was terrified of losing an arm, which was damn silly when you come to think of it. If I'd got gangrene out there with very few antiseptics and no medical help. I would have died. But I didn't think of dying, just going round the rest of my life crippled.

Sometimes I slipped away into strange, feverish dreams. I dreamed of that time in the Atlantic, when I hitched a ride on a whale, holding on to its dorsal fin and being pulled several fathoms deep. Then I was dreaming of all the cities I knew — Rome, where I was born, Buenos Aires, where I was brought up, or maybe London — I could not remember where I was. And yet through all my dreams there was never a sign of gangrene.

I want to emphasise that even at this point — the lowest of our whole journey — I never thought of giving up. To have come so far and not to have made it all the way would have negated the whole enterprise. What I wanted to find a ship for was proper medical treatment and possibly a quick tow to New Caledonia, the nearest land, so I could rest up and regain my strength to finish the job. Sylvia was a brick — no that's an understatement, she was bloody marvellous. There was I, the great survival expert, a lump of meat sitting in the boat helpless to anything but take the occasional fix, and holding up the sextant hurt my arm so much I could do it only rarely. My life depended on the strength and will of a girl — but what a girl!

By March 27th, the barometer was dropping fast and the wind was rising strongly from the east-south-east. I wrote, bitterly: 'All we need now is a bleeding storm. That will truly make our cup run over.'

When the barometer drops sharply four millibars below the norm, that usually indicates that you are about 200 miles from the centre of a cyclone, hurricane, typhoon or whatever you like to call it. (They're hurricanes in the Atlantic and North Pacific, cyclones in the South Pacific and typhoons in the China Sea and the Indian Ocean, if you want to be accurate.) Our Barry dropped between eight and nine millibars, and I knew we were in for a bad time. Sylvia, bless her heart, tried to cheer me up by saying Barry hadn't been working properly since I stuck my knee through the glass.

The Brompton Reefs were somewhere to the west of us (I could not say exactly where we were as I couldn't get a fix). I feared that with the wind in the easterly quarter, we would get blown on to them and if that was to be the case, we wouldn't stand a chance of survival. There was nothing we could do about it. The sea was getting too rough for Sylvia to row and in any case she would not have been able to change our course significantly. We lashed everything down tight and double-lashed it. We rigged half-inch nylon safety lines right round the boat, for the first time since we left San Francisco, and dug out the life jackets for both of us, also for the first time. When she helped me into mine, Sylvia knew that I was *really* worried.

We also lashed the rudder at an angle to try to keep *Britannia* from meeting the waves broadside on. Strictly speaking this was not seamanlike — in such a storm *Britannia* was designed to ride like a cork. Even had a wave broken right over us, she wouldn't have sunk, but I didn't want us to be rolled over by a wave and swamped. It would have been uncomfortable, to say the least.

For four days we crouched miserably in the rathole together. At the end of the first day the tiller snapped off in its lashings and we were forced to bring the heavy rudder into the boat. With my arm hurting like hell, we could only just manage it. I stopped testing the wind speed with my anenometer when it reached forty knots, and the waves reached a fully twenty-five feet above us. Time and again we were nearly swamped and Sylvia had the miserable job of leaning right out over the gunwales to help *Britannia* right herself and bail herself free of water.

We lay together in the rathole while *Britannia* weathered out the storm, crashing and bumping her way through the waves, but always rising at the right moment. Time and again we watched a twenty or thirty foot wave break only yards fore or aft, but never over us. My Goddess Venus must have been working overtime.

On the fourth day I knew the worst was over. The wind had dropped and I was able to take a sight. We had travelled like hell, and as far as I could judge, we had missed the Brompton Reef by no more than ten miles, passing by on the north. Now it was a clear run to Australia! During the storm we had averaged forty miles a day, and without touching the oars!

We had abandoned the transmitter as useless weeks before, but we now learned on our transistor receiver that Cyclone Emily, coming from the Coral Sea, had struck the Australian coast at Gladstone, and that six Australian sailors had died. I reckon we must have been at the birth of it, or that the centre passed within two hundred miles of us. Well, it was time we had a break.

Our morale improved with the weather, although we had constant discussions, or arguments, as to whether we should accept a lift from a ship if one were offered to us. Sylvia, who was worried to hell about my arm, was all in favour of it, but she saw the force of my arguments and eventually reluctantly accepted my decision that we should press on. In many ways, I suppose, the issue was decided for us. We did see one ship, on about April 5th.

We'd found a shipping station on the transistor and the day before we heard the announcer broadcast Notice Number 13 to all ships in the Coral Sea to keep a strict lookout for Rowing boat *Britannia II* and to report on her position and the condition of her two occupants, J.F. and S.C. etc. Then we spotted this big cargo ship, so close that we could hear her engines for about fifteen minutes. The sea was pretty quiet, choppy, but no big swells to hide us, and we did nothing to attract her attention other than to raise our orange flag, as we were so certain she couldn't miss us. Even after she'd passed at five hundred yards or so, I was convinced she was turning, but she just faded away over the horizon. So much for Notice Number 13! So much for the strict lookout!

However, that was that. Besides trying to step up her rowing. Sylvia had all the cooking to do as well as all the chores which were my share, including the interminable bailing out of the leaking hatches, and she got very tired. She had to row broadside on to the wind to try to force us south — we didn't want to miss Australia altogether! — and this was even more tiring in the choppy seas.

Now we were getting closer to Great Barrier Reef, I wasn't so sure about 'getting a lift' — I didn't want to drift around the Reef without power.

From John's Log

10.4.72   351st day

'Between yesterday and to-day it's been too rough to row and anyway Sy needed a break so she didn't row at all and we drifted. To find out exactly what our drift consisted of, I took sights and to our amazement, we discovered that in 24 hours from noon to noon we did 36 miles. This goes on a par with what we used to do under favourable conditions when we both rowed and makes me wonder what kind of fair play is this. *Britt* is of course practically empty now with almost all our water and supplies gone, still . . .

'Beginning to get worried about our approach to the Barrier Reef. If we are wrecked, which seems to me to have more than 50% of probabilities with no radio and out of range for our S.A.R.B.E. to work, we'll be in a hell of a jam. At the moment we seem to be going well and looks as if we just might make a spot which, on the chart, looks clear of reefs. A twenty miles gap and we rely on drifting helplessly into it! From a distance of 130 miles approximately!'

14.4.72-15.4.72   355th-356th days

'Don't know how we did it, but we did. Got across one of the foulest stretches of water I have ever seen, pushed by 20-25 mile winds in our sleep and not a scratch! Woke up to find ourselves almost completely surrounded by huge breakers about a mile away, in green water and all around us shoal ground. Steered and rowed through it for a while looking for a place to anchor and, after some hair-raising going, found a patch of sand, four fathoms deep. At anchor there since yesterday, fifty yards from our anchorage at low tide, we could walk away. Can only get out at high tide even if we do only draw only one foot or so.

'A really precarious situation arises now. If we let go the anchor — which, but the way, I hope holds — and try to make our way to the west, which seems possible at high tide and is the only way we can go in any case with this E.S.E. wind, we might run into real trouble later on. If the anchor does not hold we really have had it, as it is blowing half a gale and we are completely surrounded by coral patches, although, luckily, the sea is too shallow to break badly.

'Whit Sunday Island is about 100 miles due west from us and, according to the blessed chart I'm using, it should be clear, but that should also be the case of our present position and here we are. If this part of the Barrier Reef has not been properly surveyed, which seems to be so, and we find ourselves adrift in the middle of the night it is altogether too much to expect the same kind of luck twice. So, I have been tinkering with the radio, generator and batteries, I hope to have another go at it tonight. Our only way out of this as I see it, is to be towed by a motor boat or at least have one standing by, as I doubt that any skipper will bring his boat over here. At least I wouldn't. If we cannot get through to somebody, we have no choice but to get out on our own. That would be a desperate solution, almost certain to bring disaster. However, we can't stay here to rot or waiting for the anchor to go. Hell's bells, what a way to end this caper!'

16.4.72   357th day
'Tried the radio last night, but no luck. By using the transistor, we discovered that we are transmitting, and by activating the S.A.R.B.E., that we are not receiving. However, our transmission must be extremely weak, and we only have one battery serviceable and nobody seems to have picked us up, as we tried for an hour and I asked that, if we were heard, to let us know via Townsville radio. If this reef is uncharted, it means that nobody even comes here, which means it's a hell of a place for us to be. If we are wrecked,we'll rot and nobody will ever find out.

'Cannot leave yet because wind still blowing 20 to 25 miles, and we may never be able to clear the reef barrier that surrounds us in a semicircle from N.E. to S.W. We can see the breakers and rocks very clearly at which I judge to be approximately two miles away.

'Occupied spare time readying *Britt* — everything battened down — in case the worst happens when we attempt to leave. I hope that even holed and half submerged we'll still drift and make it.'

So there we were, just ninety miles away from Australia, nearly out of grub (the sort we enjoyed anyway) and just wanting out.

Sylvia said: 'Have you noticed all our little flies have disappeared? I wonder what killed them?'

'Boredom', I answered.

She didn't think it funny, but then, neither did I.

15. Landfall

To spend a few days lying at anchor at the very edge of the Great Barrier Reef was something I had been looking forward to since leaving San Francisco. The water was crystal clear, the coral patches looked absolutely luxurious, and the sea was teeming with all sorts of fish. A diver's paradise and, because of my wound, I could not dive, to avoid the risk of infection. This, and the fact that I had run out of pipe tobacco, made me feel utterly despondent. As I kept complaining about it, Sylvia thought I was mad.

'Stop behaving like a spoiled brat, will you? Here we are, at the very edge of disaster and all you can think of is smoking and swimming. Have you no sense of proportion whatsoever?'

Well, what else was there to do? We were stuck and, as long as the wind kept blowing at over twenty miles an hour, we dare not leave. Looking back on it, I guess that our predicament was truly desperate, since I was utterly helpless to change the situation, I tried to escape reality with a few childish tantrums, venting my frustration on other things.

Our lives depended on the strength of the anchor cable, quarter of an inch steel, rusted throughout after so many months at sea, and looking as strong and dependable as a silk thread. Every time *Britt* swung we could see it getting caught around various coral heads. It took very little imagination to guess that, eventually, there would be one twist too many. The memory of Onotoa was still very fresh in our minds. We had been unbelievably lucky then, but just how many times can one tempt fate and get away with it? How many times had we got away already?

As far as we could see, the horizon downwind from our position was a white line of foaming spume rising as high as

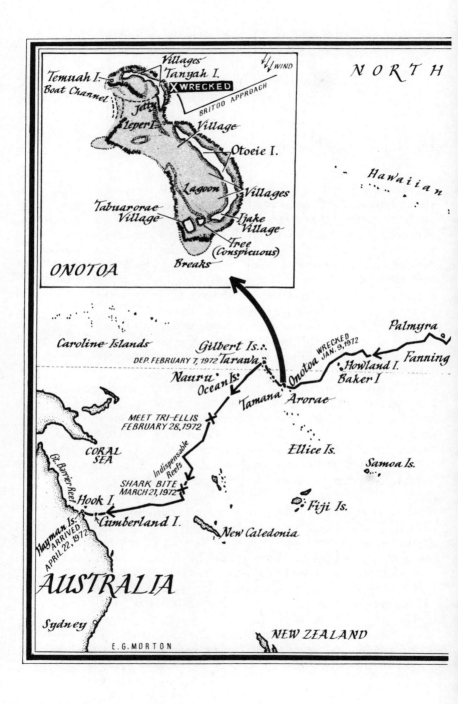

ONOTOA

Temuah I.
Boat Channel

Villages
Tanyah I.
X WRECKED
BRITOO APPROACH

WIND

NORTH

Jetty
Leper I.

Village

Otoeie I.

Lagoon

Villages

Tabuarorae
Village

Ijake
Village

Tree
(Conspicuous)

Breaks

Hawaiian

Palmyra

Caroline Islands

Gilbert Is.
DEP. FEBRUARY 7, 1972 Tarawa

WRECKED
Onotoa JAN. 9, 1972

Fanning

Nauru
Ocean Is.

Howland I.
Baker I.

Tamana

Arorae

MEET TRI-ELLIS
FEBRUARY 28, 1972

CORAL
SEA

Ellice Is.

Samoa Is.

Indispensable
Reefs

Gt. Barrier Reef

SHARK BITE
MARCH 27, 1972

Fiji Is.

Hook I.

Cumberland I.

New Caledonia

Hayman Is.
ARRIVED
APRIL 22, 1972

AUSTRALIA

Sydney

NEW ZEALAND

E. G. MORTON

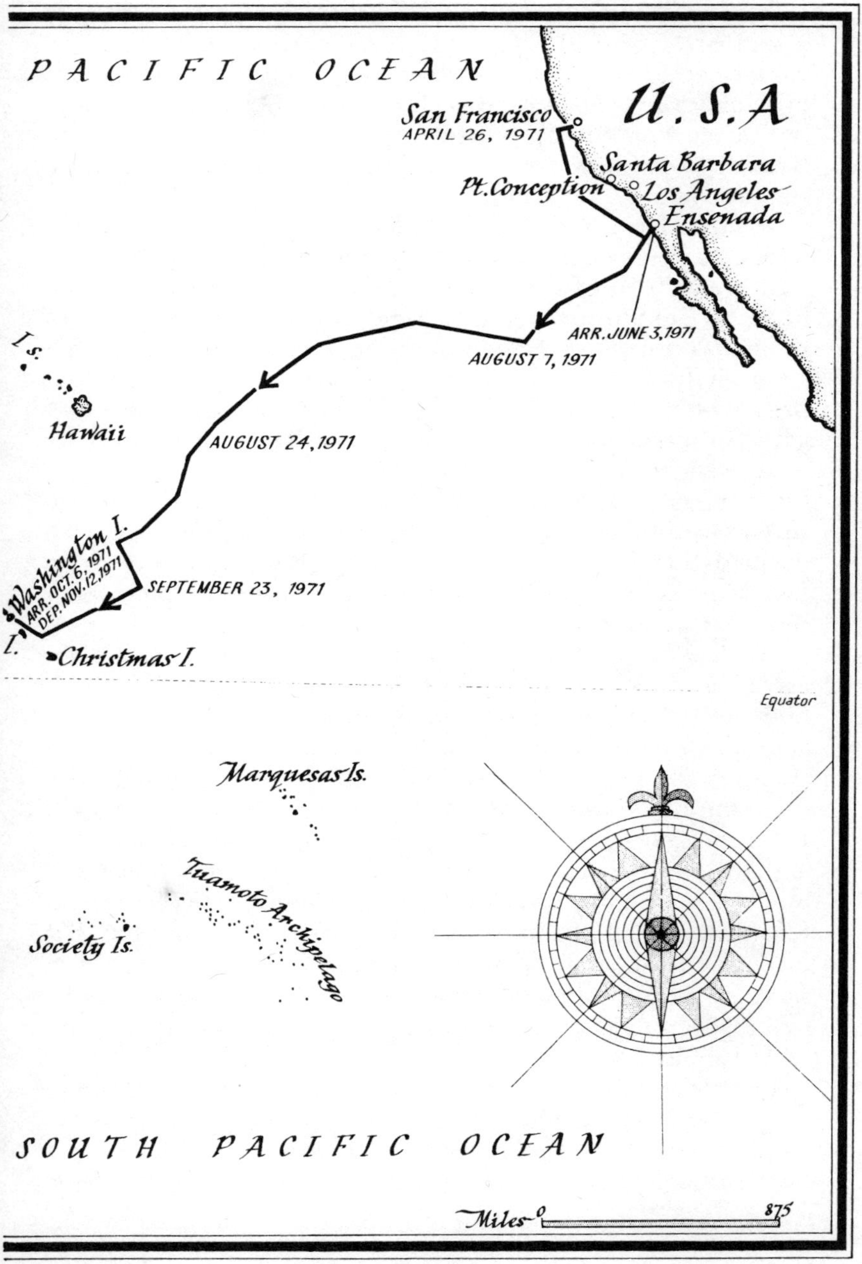

PACIFIC OCEAN
U.S.A
San Francisco
APRIL 26, 1971
Santa Barbara
Pt. Conception
Los Angeles
Ensenada
ARR. JUNE 3, 1971
AUGUST 7, 1971
Is.
Hawaii
AUGUST 24, 1971
Washington I.
ARR. OCT. 6, 1971
DEP. NOV. 12, 1971
SEPTEMBER 23, 1971
I.
Christmas I.
Equator
Marquesas Is.
Tuamoto Archipelago
Society Is.
SOUTH PACIFIC OCEAN
Miles 0 875

twenty or thirty feet at times, almost uninterrupted through a semicircle of 180°. There seemed to be a gap in it and in calm weather I was hopeful about our chances to negotiate it, providing the other side was clear, which we would only find out after committing ourselves to a point of no return. Neither of us, however, was willing to cross that bridge until we got to it.

At low tide the sea all around us would become peppered with coral heads and rocks of incredible shape and colours, so that even a boat of such shallow draft as *Britannia* could only hope to get through at high tide. However, hitting one of them was not likely to do much damage, the sea being rather calm all the way up to the line of breakers. We knew that *Britt* would not sink, regardless of how many holes she might get. The breakers were, of course, a different matter. If we were caught by them, *Britannia* would be smashed to smithereens and, barring a miracle, so would we. Actually, to survive would only have prolonged the agony and we both decided that if it ever came to that, we would prefer to go fast. Morbid thoughts but we had days of nothing to do other than think about it.

We had been at anchor for three days now. It was night again, a dark, moonless, squally night, and as we both huddled under the rathole, we listened to the wind whistling and howling outside. Eventually Sylvia fell into a restless slumber, mumbling unintelligible things, interspersed with shivering fits, like a dreaming puppy. I tried to force myself to sleep as well, but it was no use. My arm ached abominably and for some unaccountable reason I felt that if I did fall asleep, something terrible would happen. There was a tenseness in the air, an eerie tremor of the atmosphere that made my skin tingle with apprehension. I swear I could even smell an all pervading odour of decay, pungent and evil, as if, I thought, a rotting corpse was floating nearby. Premonition? What rubbish! Yet . . .

Like most seamen I'm superstitious. If anyone asks me what of I would be at a loss to say or even deny, emphatically, that I can be swayed by such nonsense. All the same, strange things do happen and I have seen a few. This morning, at sunrise, there had been a beautiful rainbow straddling the gap on the reef, the very one that seemed to offer our only hope of ever getting away from this damned place. If there is such a thing as an omen, that was it, and throughout the day I had been struggling against the urge of weighing anchor and go. Common sense prevailed at last and we stayed. It was the only reasonable thing to do, but it was against my instinct and now I was filled with foreboding. The gods smile but seldom and to defy them when they do . . .

Finally I dozed off. How long I cannot say but it couldn't have been more than an hour. I woke with the feeling that something was amiss although it took me a few minutes to realise what it was. *Britannia* was no longer swinging and swaying as she had been and the wind was coming broadside all the time!

'Hell and damnation! Sylvia! Wake up! I think we are drifting!' I shot out of the rathole and started pulling in the anchor cable in a frenzy of fear. There was no resistance whatsoever and I knew, as Sylvia knew, that the anchor was gone, but I had to go on pulling. I could not give up hope. I could not believe that the inevitable had happened, not until the last, frayed, broken end of the cable was in my hands. For a while we looked at it, without a word, utterly shattered by the realisation that we were helplessly adrift in the middle of the night, perhaps only minutes away from being crushed to pulp in a maelstrom of coral and roaring seas.

Frozen, we stood there, concentrating all our senses in a desperate effort to pierce the darkness, to hear, however, feebly, the rumble of breaking waves. Nothing! Only the wind, whispering now as a gentle breeze and the soft flop-flop of the water lapping at *Britannia.* A fine, cold drizzle permeated the night, like a mist, and everything was so quiet, so peaceful, I had to pinch myself to realise it was not an illusion, that whatever the appearance, we were in a desperate situation and I had better do something about it, quick, before it became too late.

'What are we going to do, darling? Please, tell me what to do!'

'Shut up! I'm thinking!'

Do something! What? We had no idea how long we had
been drifting, in what direction, how fast. Should we attempt
to row? Going where? How could we know if rowing would
take us away from danger or nearer to it? Sylvia was
beginning to cry and for the first time in my life I wished I
could be a woman and do the same. Hell's bells man, take a
grip on yourself!

'Right darling, stop whimpering and help me to ship in the
rudder. Don't worry, we'll get out of it somehow. I'm
indestructible, remember? As long as you stick around me
you will be all right, as usual.'

'I don't seem to have much choice, do I?'

She managed to laugh, between sobs, and all was well
again. There would be a way out, had to be, we had gone
through too much for it to end like that, a step only from
success.

I had decided once more to put my faith in my own
particular belief that when all was lost and I had done all I
could to help myself, the rest was in the hands of the gods,
who could not possibly fail to bail me out of trouble. The
world can be turned upside down but Johnny will survive,
somehow. So we lashed the rudder at what I thought was the
best angle of drift for *Britannia* to head towards the gap we
had seen during the day, put on our lifejackets and lifelines
and cuddled against each other in front of the rathole. Two
hours went by and, although we did not actually make love,
that was perhaps, after a whole year in that lousy, stinking,
lovely little boat, the most tender, romantic time we ever
had. Ah, well, *sic transit gloria mundi . . .*

The water was so shallow in parts that, in spite of the
darkness we could see the bottom rushing past. Sometimes
we would flash the torch at it but soon stopped as what we
glimpsed was most uninspiring. Luckily it was high tide and
with a few lurches here and there we always managed to pull
through. The rudder was no longer in, after scraping bottom
too many times, I had decided to unship it and let her choose
her own way.

It was an unbelievable, fantastic ride. Every so often we
could hear the tumultuous roar of breakers all around us,

sometimes near, sometimes far, and *Britt* would, be in the grip of some vicious current or other, spin around, like a toy boat, while the water around us seemed to boil in a frenzy of bubbles and foam as eddies met counter eddies, but always she would break free and go drifting on, blindly, presumably following the line of least resistance, like a bit of Flotsum.

The wind had died to almost nothing, but the drizzle persisted and we were chilled and soaked to the bones.

At last we could no longer hear the grumble of angry seas and felt sure that the worst was left behind. How we managed to miss the real breakers, I shall never know.

Shortly before dawn we spotted a light, a mile or so ahead of our drifting course. At first we regarded it with incredulity, but there could be no doubt about it. As it did not seem to move, we concluded that it must be a ship riding at anchor. Not knowing what lay ahead, since we were drifting in that direction anyway, we decided to let it go at that, but did try to call their attention by flashing a continuous S.O.S. with our torch.

I could not believe that a Captain would anchor in such dangerous waters without keeping a proper watch, and therefore was absolutely sure that our problems were over as they could not possibly fail to see our signals. Half an hour went by and we received no reply. I was beginning to think that everybody was indeed sleeping when the light suddenly went out. There was no question of us having imagined things. Yet the light was gone as if it had never been.

It reappeared twenty minutes later, and once more we flashed a distress signal. We did not seem to be any nearer than we had been when we first sighted it but, again, there could be no doubt as to its source. Still no reply. Eventually it disappeared again and, at dawn, the sea was empty of life as far as the eye could see. Obviously whoever they were (we were told later that most likely Japanese fishermen, fishing illegally) they had seen our signals and decided to get under way before daylight. If so, I hope that one day, if they ever find themselves in distress, they get the same treatment. With no means to know how badly we needed help such callousness at sea is unforgivable whatever their reasons to preserve the secret of their presence and identity might have been.

Taking our position at mid-day showed that we had drifted twenty miles from our anchorage and, according to the chart, there were no reefs whatsoever between us and the Cumberland Islands, which we had decided would be our best bet as they only lay a few miles off the Australian mainland. Unfortunately the chart was the last thing we could trust as we had skirted reefs and shoal patches throughout the morning. Obviously this part of the Great Barrier Reef had not been surveyed and we were in for a lot of sweating. Without an anchor there was no way of stopping, which meant that unless our luck was really and truly phenomenal, we would never get to Australia in one piece, if at all.

The next two days passed in what seemed a nightmare in slow motion. During the day we could see and pick our way through reefs and shoals which would suddenly rise from the deep, like a wall, then disappear again just as suddenly. At night we could only hear the changing tone of the sea breaking on the shallows as *Britt* would increase her speed, sometimes spinning drunkenly, then mercifully all would be quiet again and we waited, tensely, the approach of the next bad spit. Somehow we got across but that sure is one bit of sea I'll be glad never to see again.

At last at dawn of the 20th April we saw the faint smudge of land rising through the mist over the horizon. By 10 a.m. we knew that they were the Cumberland Islands and — I will leave the last words to Sylvia.

Although the end of our journey was clearly within sight, I felt no sense of relief or joy at the prospect. Remembering how long we had been looking at the cliffs of Mexico before reaching them, I wondered how long we would now spend watching these islands. During the last month of our crossing, I had been so perpetually frightened that now I could only look at the distant island and wonder what further horrors lay between us and them. It seemed that a final irony of fate was bound to strike us down, and the thought gave me a dead sinking feeling in my stomach which made me shiver. But these were secret fears and whenever Johnny mentioned them, intensifying their reality, I tried to shut him up. As long as they were mine alone, I could pretend they were imaginary.

The weather smiled on us that day but we saw four sea snakes. I had spotted the first a week or so before and, without a moment's hesitation or doubt, had said to Johnny, 'Look, there's a snake!' I had never heard of them before, much less seen one, yet it never occurred to me it could have been an eel, or anything else.

He had replied, 'Oh, yes. That's interesting. If one of those gets you you're dead in half an hour and there's nothing anyone can do about it'.

The first ones we had seen, varying in size and markings, had been slithering along the water's surface and I had assumed that was where they lived — until I saw one shooting up from the deep with alarming rapidity. After that I never dared to wash my hair, nor any clothes, and even the dishes were washed with scant attention and utmost speed.

From fear of wrecking on the islands, mostly uninhabited according to the Pilot Books, we streamed the drogue all that day. Had we an anchor we would have carried on and dropped anchor at night had it been necessary. As it was, not having slept more than a few odd hours for days, we took the opportunity of a good rest and lazed away the day and the night as we slowly drifted towards Australia.

We were considerably nearer our goal the following day and by noon could clearly see the rocks and vegetation of the islands. Johnny's arm was still weak and painful but, in spite of this, between us we rowed non-stop throughout the day in an effort to land before nightfall. The sun set when we were still a good five miles from Hayman Island. Even with the drogue we would have drifted more than that, possibly in the wrong direction, so we had no choice other than to continue rowing.

The islands looked black and forbidding in the moonlight and showed no sign of habitation, but little by little we pulled nearer to them until we could distinguish the rocks and bushes on their cliffs. As we rowed slowly passed the light on the south-easterly tip of Hook Island, I began to feel more and more apprehensive. We could now see Hayman Island beyond the point but it looked dark and lifeless. According to the Pilot Book there was a hotel on its south-west coast with a five hundred foot jetty extending beyond the limit of the reef and this was the reason we had chosen Hayman Island as our ideal landfall.

As we slowly approached the south-east of Hayman Island, we could clearly see the passage between the two islands. This would have brought us out right beside the hotel but, according to the Pilot Book, the passage was dangerous and should not be used without local knowledge — and we were in no mood to take that kind of chance. We were far too tired to feel any excitement or satisfaction as Johnny rowed us nearer and nearer to the cliffs. On the contrary, it looked so dark and ominous that I begged him to stay further off-shore lest we ran aground or hit a rock, but he would have none of it, and, swore at me to mind my own business and let the seaman use his own judgment.

We came to within ten yards of the cliffs. They towered colourlessly above us, raw and rugged, strewn with scant shrubbery. And they whispered as weird gurgles and hisses greeted us from their grey faces. It was eerie and I was frightened by their ghostliness. In the shadow of the night, we wearily pulled *Britoo* round Hayman's deserted shores. As I steered I flashed the torch across the rocks looking for some sign of human habitation, but there was none. Suddenly we rounded yet another point and there were ships, at least six of them, ploughing down the Australian coast, the lights of which were now clearly visible sixteen miles away. It was marvellous — now we felt we had made it, nothing could keep us from Australia now.

Bay after bay slid slowly by, all beachless and barren. We began to think that perhaps the hotel had closed down and we were chasing a phantom, after all our Pilot Book was ten years old and it could well have been ruined by a cyclone and gone years ago. Seeing the mainland so easily within our grasp, we decided to continue into just one more bay and, if that too was deserted, to head straight for the Queensland Coast.

A judder went through the boat. We had hit bottom. I started to sweat again, but we unshipped the rudder and there was no repeat. Beyond us a row of huge rocks stood out blackly against the sky. This was definitely as far as we would go. I flashed the torch. Could those be two little boats? We cautiously approached, leading ourselves deeper and deeper into the little cove which sheltered the two pale blobs.

People! They woke us up, half an hour after we had sunk our battery as anchor alongside them. 'Hey, *Britannia II*. Is that really you?' They knew all about us and, in common with the world at large, had given us up for dead after Cyclone Emily.

It was 2 a.m. on Saturday, April 22nd, our 363rd day out from San Francisco, and we had made it. No possible doubt whatever.

We forgot how tired we were and sat enjoying our first taste of Australian hospitality, chatting and laughing until five in the morning. It was marvellous.

The Royal Hayman Hotel was still on the island after all, lying beyond the line of rocks we had seen the night before. The next morning *Sol Tropical* towed us to its jetty. Unbelievably, there was a little open train running from the jetty to the Hotel. We climbed in and chugged back to civilisation.

Epilogue

To the great surprise of all and sundry, we are still speaking to each other. Not only that but we are better friends than ever with a new, hard-earned respect for one another. In spite of this we plan to part. I am having a schooner designed by Uffa Fox in which I intend to hop around the world with a mainly female crew filming documentaries with an emphasis on adventure, and writing magazine articles in the same vein. Sylvia has had her fill of the sea and doesn't feel she is sociable enough to lead the sort of life I will spend on board. Her plans are uncertain at present but, although they may entail some travelling, she swears she will never go to sea in anything smaller than a P. & O. liner in future.

Before we part we do intend having one last fling. The holiday which has been promised us on Hayman Island, followed by a working tour of Australia, the country we worked so hard to find yet were never allowed to see.

If we had dreamed of anything, apart from getting off that damned boat for good, it was of the rest we would have when we got ashore; the comfortable dry beds with clean sheets, the meals of steak, and eggs and bacon, and good Australian beer straight off the ice. And the long, long showers and hot baths to wash the salt out of our very pores.

Had anyone told us how we would spend our first few days ashore we might — just — have turned *Britt* round and headed for the ocean again. One thing our months on the Pacific had not prepared us for was the pace and noise of so-called civilised life and the demands that were to be made on us as (temporary) celebrities.

We had stepped off Hayman Island's little train to be greeted by the manager, Mr Andre Maestracci, with a list of journalists who had telephoned the mainland. As we were unable to speak to any of them before fulfilling our contracts with Independent Television News and the *Sunday People*, he very kindly fended them off for us all morning. We were escorted through the exotic hotel grounds to the luxurious chalet where we intended waiting for I.T.N. and the *Sunday People*, little suspecting that we would not spend even a single night in our millionaire's paradise, nor even eat a proper meal.

The first thing we had to do was to call George Greenfield in London to tell him we had made it, so that we could tell Sylvia's parents and inform our sponsors. Our first call back was from Mr and Mrs Cook. They had been desperately worried by the news reports of cyclones and of our erroneously reported deaths, so, of course, they were overjoyed that we were safe.

After that came a call from Don Horobin of I.T.N. in London, as pleased as Punch, but . . . Where were we? How could we get off the Island? We must get to a television studio in Brisbane in time to be interviewed over the satellite. I hadn't even had time to shower, so I told him to get stuffed. Then we spoke to the *Sunday People* and after that we went to the Island's little surgery for the Doctor to have a look at my arm and get it properly dressed. It was fine, healing properly and there was nothing more to be done. Forget it.

Whilst in the surgery, another call came through from Don Horobin. This time he was on the line for seventy minutes, talking first to me, 'Surely if you can row the Pacific, you can get down to Brisbane?', then to Sylvia, then he wanted to speak to André. All because I told him we couldn't get off the Island as the only way was by a helicopter which was fully booked and due to leave at any moment.

We heard André say, 'Sorry, I can do most things round here, but one thing even I can't do is yank people off a helicopter'. I still don't know how he did it, but we got on that helicopter.

The chopper flew us over to the heliport at McKay on the mainland. We stepped out into a hell of a scene, with the Press and T.V. boys jostling for pictures and interviews and all claiming exclusive rights on behalf of someone or another. We really had no idea what was going on or who had the rights to what, but eventually we were rescued and locked up under guard in a custom's official's office — with the frustrated Press milling around outside.

An Australian television man, Mike Williams, working for I.T.N. hired a Cessna and flew us the two and a half hour flight down to Brisbane. A car met us and drove us straight to the television studios and we ate sandwiches along the way. They did the interview five minutes after our arrival. I was in a filthy temper and hungry, yet they wouldn't even let me have a drink, but somehow we got the interview over. Then, at last, we were taken to The Gateway Hotel in Brisbane and got some peace.

The *Sunday People*'s representative, John Checkley, arrived from Sydney the next morning — to look after us, keep the wolves from the door, and make sure we didn't speak to the wrong people and didn't run away. Problems arose when David Jones opened their main Brisbane store especially for us on a Sunday, offering to outfit us both from top to toe. There was an almighty row because all the television stations and all the press turned up. John Checkley said we couldn't go, it couldn't be done, and they nearly got to fisticuffs again. Needless to say, we went, had a fabulous shopping spree, and everything in the garden was lovely once more.

The next row was because I.T.N. were flying Mike Nicholson down from Vietnam. He couldn't be there till Monday, and that by travelling all hours God sent, and the *Sunday People* wanted us to fly to England on Monday. Anyway, Mike made it, looking more dead than alive, and we flew back to the heliport, catching the helicopter to Hayman Island with one minute to spare. The Island gave us a marvellous reception, practically all the guests and staff met us, and we were greeted with bands, garlands and all. Unfortunately the film of this got mistakenly exposed, so that the sequence was no good. Anyway, Mike interviewed us at the boat and then we rushed to the helicopter, another plane back to Brisbane and returned to the hotel.

All this time in Australia and all we had had time to eat had been sandwiches and half a breakfast! Not only that, but we both hate flying and seemed to have spent more time in the air than on the ground since our arrival. Besides this, we had not been alone once since landing, and being perpetually surrounded by hoards of people after such a long solitude, was really rather overwhelming. As if this wasn't enough, with the time differences involved in trans-continental calls, our telephone never stopped ringing and I don't think we had more than four hours' sleep during a single night in Australia.

We had our first dinner on our last night in Brisbane and the following day, Tuesday, we flew to Sydney and then straight to London on a lovely B.O.A.C. jumbo jet — another thirty-six hours up there! Sylvia's parents and brother came jubilantly aboard the plane with a beautiful bouquet, then we stepped out to a terrific reception at the airport, a lovely welcoming crowd of friends and strangers, photographers and journalists.

It was fantastic and brought us both near to tears. Sylvia's ninety-four year old grandmother was there, having come down from Birmingham with her aunt and uncle especially for the occasion, but we were hardly allowed to speak to her. How she stood up to the crush I will never know. We were strong-armed through the crowd by the men from the *Sunday People* without hurting my arm more than once. It all passed in a dream, till we were packed into a limousine and were able to breathe again.

It would be nice to say we were home at last, but, alas, by courtesy of the *Sunday People*, we had to stay in an hotel room for a week of continuous interviewing.

Only now, with the last word of this book is our work done.

'Slow Boat to China' indeed. I would like to meet the starry-eyed romantic who wrote that one!

Acknowledgements

We extend our most heartfelt thanks to the following individuals and organizations for their friendship, advice and equipment:

Uffa Fox for *Britannia II*'s splendid design.

Clare Lallow for building *Britannia II*.

Expanded Rubber & Plastics Division of Bakelite Xylonite Limited for the Plastazote from which *Britannia II*'s buoyancy chambers were built.

Ayling and Son of Putney for five pairs of oars.

Sims Racing Boats of Twickenham for four sliding seats.

Edwin H. Phelps, Racing Boat Builder, of Putney, for four seat platforms with slide tracks.

Matt Wood of Putney for five pairs of rowlocks.

George Greenfield for his friendship and capable handling of our affairs.

Reg Payne of *The Sunday People* and Don Horobin of Independent Television News for their faith in us.

David Farr, John du Pre and Doug Eatwell of *The Sunday People* for restoring our confidence in good journalism.

Group Captain Peter Whittingham, O.B.E., M.D., of the Royal Air Force Institute of Aviation Medicine, Aldershot, for advice and equipment for survival at sea.

L.W. Madelaine of The British Red Cross, County of London Branch, for advice and first-aid supplies.

Tom Cave and Angie McKelvie of Publicity Machine, for their promotional endeavours.

Malcolm Davies and Calor Gas Ltd., for water distilling apparatus, primus cooker and Propane Gas.

Rolex of Geneva for our chronometers and watch.

Kelvin Hughes of London for servicing my sextant.

Marlow Ropes of England for all our ropes.

Catilators Ltd., for the catilators which preserved our battery water.

Ron Sexton of Murco Ltd., for technical advice and a heavy duty hydrometer.

Yardley Ltd., for Beauty Magic Moisturising Emollient and Sylvia's cosmetics

Henri-Lloyd of Worsley, Manchester, in conjunction with Yardley, Ltd., for two 'Viking Supreme' foul weather suits and two quilted anoraks with hoods.

Beaufort (Air-Sea) Equipment, Ltd., for three safety harnesses and lifelines and three inflatable lifejackets.

Burndept Electronics (E.R.) Ltd., for one Flotation Beacon and one S.A.R.B.E.

W.E. Conyers, Ltd., of Trawden, for our generator.

Sony for our transistor radios.

Nelbarden Manufacturing Co. Ltd., for six bikinis and two one-piece swimsuits for Sylvia.

The Gladding Corporation of U.S.A. for our fishing line.

Edgar Sealey and Son for our fish hooks.

Val Austin for devoting so much of her spare time to trying to make Sylvia a swimmer.

St. George's Ladies' Rowing Club for our table ware, club scarf and a lovely farewell party — besides teaching Sylvia how to row!

In Transit

P. & O. Lines, for taking us so luxuriously to San Francisco aboard *Chusan*, and conveying our mail during the Post Strike.

Holland America Line for safely transporting *Britannia II* to San Francisco in the capable hands of Captain L.F. Dobbinga and his crew aboard m.v. *Kamperdyk*.

Mrs. Hilda Bishop, Mr. and Mrs. Walter Abbott and Chief Officer Terry McCarthy for their delightful company at our table aboard *Chusan*.

In New York

Peter Learmont for being our friend in New York and for kind hospitality at the Royal Manhattan Hotel.

Oliver Swan of Paul R. Reynolds, Inc., for his kind help.

David Llewellyn for his patient endeavours on our behalf.

The Ronson Corporation, both in New Jersey and in London, for lighters, Sea Chef and Table Chef cookers, Camp'n Glow Lantern and butane gas.

Great Northern (U.S.A.), for two Dacron filled sleeping Bags.

John Thomas of Great American Industries, Inc., for our three rubber wet-suits, spear guns, flippers and all our very excellent skin diving equipment.

In California

The Olympic Hotel of San Francisco for putting their fabulous Director's Suite at our disposal during our first visit.

Mrs. Vivian Dahl for being such a tolerant hostess towards us and all our junk during our prolonged stay in her flat.

Barry Brose for a mooring alongside the cutter *Alert* and every convenience and aid while we were there.

British Motor Car Distributors, Ltd., for the loan of a car during our stay.

Anderson's Boat yard in Sausalito for a good job in repairing the damage to *Britannia II* and making her a new rudder.

Ivan and Ann Sharpe for their friendship and invaluable assistance with our many problems in San Francisco and Ensenada and for valiantly maintaining our radio schedule.

Mr. L. van der Vegt of Holland America Line for his kind concern and assistance.

Alex de Renzy and his crew on *The Euphrates* for towing us around San Francisco.

Ernie Martin of Kaar Electronics Corporation, Marine Communications Division, of Mountain View for adapting our Marconi CH 25 transceiver.

Highland Labs of San Francisco for beautifully processing a great deal of our film and giving us the invaluable zippered plastic bags with which we pocketed the rathole.

Dr. John Beale of The Cathedral Hill Medical Centre for various drugs and medicines and having Sylvia's ankle X-rayed.

The California Raisin Advisory Board for the thirty pounds of California Raisins which kept us healthy throughout the trip.

Leonard Schulz and Mary Conroy of The Oregon Freeze Dry Foods Co., of Albany, for allowing us a very generous discount on the mainstay of our diet.

Peter Noone of The Ski Hut, Berkeley, for one hundred dollars worth of food.

Vacu-Dry of Emeryville, for our soups, bouillon, cheese sauce, beans and some freeze-dried food.

The Rich-Moore Corporation (in collaboration with Roos-Atkins of San Francisco), for one hundred dollars worth of food.

Roos-Atkins of San Francisco for gloves, stop-watch, sunglasses, John's swim-trunks, etcetera.

Pentel of Japan for the felt-tipped ball-point pens with which we kept our logs so easily.

Davis Instruments Corporation of San Leandro, for our spare sextant, the Master Marine Davis Mark 12, and a Range Range Finder, a five inch Clear View parallel rule, a B.P.C. Plotter, The Davis Radar Reflector, and a Davis Solar Cooker.

Mallory of Burlingame for the batteries for our torches and transistor radios.

Levi Strauss of San Francisco for six pairs of shorts, four pairs of jeans and six shirts.

Chuck Podesta of Coast Marine & Industrial Supply, Inc., San Francisco, for advice and sundry survival equipment.

Abbey Rents of San Francisco for two Flotation Wheelchair Pads especially adapted to row on — very comfortable but regrettably lost in a storm.

The anonymous gentleman who made a twenty dollar donation to the 'cause' at the *Alert*.

Ken Crutchlow for helping to stow *Britannia II* and many other things besides.

Fenton Fisher for making John's Shark Hooks and helping to prepare *Britannia II* for sea.

Ron Mathiasen for his concerned encouragement to our parents during absence and for much help on the *Alert*.

Eileen and Art Thomas for kindly offering us the use of their empty house during our stay.

Joe Scoma of Scoma's restaurant, on Fisherman's Wharf, for a fabulous farewell dinner.

Walt and Marcie Stack, Bill and Lee Walden, Dino and Anne Landucci, Terry Zabala, Chipper, Ernie, Marilyn Clark, all our friends on the *Alert*, the Dolphin Club and all our friends in San Francisco for their kind patience and assistance.

In Ensenada

Captain Manuel Aguirre and his co-Captain and crew on the *Santa Isabel* for our first tow into Ensenada.

Captain Francisco A. Valero Salas and the crew of the *Mazatlan* for our second tow into Ensenada.

Sr. Albino Huerta of Cementos California, S.A., for his great kindness and assistance in Ensenada.

Captain M. Riveros Rotge of The Port of Ensenada for arranging our mooring and documentation so smoothly.

Don Fernando Kelenberger for his generous hospitality at The Cortez Motel.

Astilleros Rodriguez, S.A., for not charging us for repairs to *Britannia II* , for making two new rudders, and for allowing us their storage facilities to work on our equipment.

Butch Mason for getting our transceiver operating successfully.

Mrs. Mason for her help in preparing our new supplies for stowage.

Ken and Lupita Gundersen, Antonio Rosales Green, Ira Block and Sparky Green for all their friendly assistance in Ensenada.

At Washington Island

Fanning Island Plantations, Ltd., of Burns-Philp, for their every facility during our stay.

Bill and Marina Frew for their boundless generosity and hospitality.

Pastor Boata, Pastor Toanuea, Eria, Willie, Biribo, Taukaban, Tenoa, Atitoa, Lauina, Tetaake, Uoa, Oti, Taubo, Tabeaua, Tuli, Sapeta, Akineti, Taiana and all our wonderful friends on Washington Island for making our stay so thoroughly enjoyable and for repairing and restoring much of our equipment.

At Onotoa

Dr. Taketiau and Aotai Beriki for accepting us wholeheartedly into their household and looking after us so well whilst we were there.

Euroba and The Red Cross Society members, Abetan, Uruabe, Rineti, Tebaia and those who so gladly worked all hours of the day and night to help us through our troubles.

At Tarawa

Captain Lomi and his crew on the *Nareau* for taking such trouble in towing us to Betio.

Mr. R.E.N. Smith and his wife, Elizabeth, for their friendly hospitality in accommodating us during our prolonged visit.

The Wholesale Society for repairing *Britannia II*, so soundly.

Mr. Ron Summers for painstakingly solving many of our technical problems for us.

Josh Lewis and Rodney Montgomery for helping to stow *Britannia II* prior to her departure.

Sir John and Lady Field, Mr. and Mrs. John Hunter, Mr. and Mrs. Sharp, Mr. and Mrs. Wotherspoon, Mr. and Mrs. Robins, Les and Tetake, Peter MacQuarry, Guillemette, Temaia, Bwebwe and all who were friendly and helpful towards us at Tarawa.

In Australia

Christine and John Spackman and Trevor Draper for tying us safely alongside them at the end of our journey, for our first delicious taste of Australian hospitality and for towing us to The Royal Hayman Hotel.

Andre Maestracci, his wife and staff at The Royal Hayman Hotel on Hayman Island for kindly welcoming us so enthusiastically, having such a beautiful landfall awaiting us, unloading and storing *Britannia II*'s equipment in our absence and for their great hospitality and efficiency on our behalf.

Olaf and Elspeth Jansen for friendship and endless hospitality at the lovely Gateway Hotel in Brisbane.

David Jones Stores, Brisbane, for fitting us both out in beautiful clothes once we reached civilization.

The Customs Officials at Mackay Airport for their extraordinary efficiency and courtesy.

Mike Williams of I.T.N. and John Checkley of *The Sunday People* for coping with the trappings of civilized life on our behalf and looking after us so kindly in Australia.

At Sea

The Captain and crew of *The Canadian Star* for stopping and reporting our position.

The Captain and crew of the *Tri-Ellis* for their exceedingly welcome provisions and company.

All those ships which keep a good watch and saw us, offering both help and encouragement.

In London

B.O.A.C. for such excellent service on our flight home aboard their 'Jumbo Jet'.

Mr. K. Swiggs, Manager of Terminal 3 at Heathrow Airport, for his proficient expertise and kindly consideration, especially towards Sylvia's parents, brother and grandmother.

In Addition

Our sincere thanks to all who had confidence in us before and during the venture for, without such minds as theirs, such journeys would be impossible.

We owe so much to so many that should anyone have been overlooked in the above list, we hope they will forgive us and rest assured that their contribution will be remembered and well appreciated.

Our special gratitude, last but not least, to John Parker of I.T.N., for the beastly job of editing our logs for inclusion in this book, and to Sylvia's mother for typing the whole book out.

Equipment and Supplies
carried on Pacific Row

Boat and Fittings: Britannia II, built of double-planked honduras mahogany with self-righting blisters made of Plastazote. 2 sliding seats and 2 spares, 2 seat platforms with slide tracks and 2 spares, 2 pairs of rowlocks and 3 spares, 5 pairs of oars.

English, American and Australian flags.

Ropes: 400 ft 1¾" terylene, 200 ft. 1¾" Nelson, 200 ft. ¾" terylene, 50 ft. 1" Shockcord, an assortment of finer ropes. 1 4 ft. iron framed sea anchor, (complete), 4 fenders.

Tools and Repairs Rubber solution, canvas repair kit for drogues, fibre-glass repair kit, general purpose oil, anti-rust spray, rust cleaner, 2 1lb jars Vaseline Petroleum Jelly, insulation tape, tape measure, 3 screwdrivers, 2 pairs pinchers, 2 pairs pliers, paint scraper for removing barnacles, 2 paintbrushes, varnish, assorted nails, screws, washers, wire, screw eyes, screw hooks, shackles and swivels.

Navigation 2 sextants, 2 Nautical Almanacs, 3 books of computed tables, 12 plotting sheets, 12 Admiralty charts, Star Globe, 2 hand compasses, 1 deck compass, 2 stop watches, 2 parallel rules, 2 pairs dividers, protractor, set square, 12 pencils, Range Finder, Plotter, yachting Speedometer, Radar reflector, binoculars, 2 chronometers, 2 transistor radios, 3 or 4 books.

Communication Marconi CH 25 transceiver with aerial, 2 heavy duty 12 volt batteries, 5 gallons of petrol, 1 generator, heavy duty hydrometer, catilators, spare parts and spark plugs for generator, 2 Nikonos 11 cameras, 2 Bell and Howell filming cameras (one with underwater housing), 2 light metres, interchangeable lenses and filters. 90 50 ft. film casettes. 90 100 ft. rolls of film, 50 rolls 16 mm. film.

Stationery 2 dozen Pentel ball-point pens, 5 large notebooks for logs, 3 notebooks for navigation, 200 polythene bags.

Fishing and Diving 3 rubber wet suits, 5 pairs rubber booties, 4 pairs flippers, 5 diving masks, 5 snorkels, 1 diving belt with 2 4 lb lead weights, 4 diving knives, 2 axes, 2 rubber arbalette spearguns, 1 hydraulic Jaguar speargun, 15 stainless arbalette shafts, 5 Jaguar shafts, 4 metric spearhead adapters, 15 detachable speargun heads, 3 Fireball 22.3 powerheads plus 200 bullets, 5 speargun loaders, 2 speargun pumps, 1 depth metre, 6 feather lures, 6 coloured spoons, 250 assorted

fish hooks, 30 reels assorted fishing line, 1 Intrepid fishing reel with handle.
  Survival 3 inflatable lifejackets, 5 safety harnesses with lines, 1 S.A.R.B.E. beacon and one flotation beacon, 6 orange smoke flares, 10 star parachute flares, R.A.F. Survival Kits, British Red Cross First Aid Kit, Vitamin Pills and medicines, large bottle Solarcaine Lotion, large jar Vaseline Petroleum Jelly, rubbing alcohol, 5 pairs sunglasses.
  Clothes 2 anoraks with hood, 2 foul weather suits, 4 sweaters, 6 shirts, 4 pairs jeans, 6 pairs shorts, 6 bikinis, 2 one-piece swim-suits, 5 pairs swim-trunks, 7 pairs shoes, 14 pairs socks, 8 pairs leather gloves, 4 hats, 2 towels, 12 handkerchiefs, 2 air mattresses, with inflators, 2 sleeping bags, 2 cushions, spare pieces of nylon cloth.
  Personal Hygiene 6 tubes toothpaste, 8 toothbrushes, 6 combs, 2 pairs nail scissors, 2 hair brushes, 1 nail file, 100 rubber bands, 2 pairs tweezers, 3 mirrors, 15 bars salt-water soap, 2 large bottles Vaseline Intensive Care Lotion, 1 lb talcum powder, 2 bottles foam shave, 6 tubes concentrated shampoo, 6 bottles shampoo, 6 jars Yardley Beauty Magic Moisturising Emollient.
  Kitchen and Water 1 propane gas primus cooker, 2 butane gas cookers, 1 solar cooker, 2 spare primus burners, 2 sets copper condensor coils, 3 lengths plastic hose with spare clamps, and clips, 2 umbrellas to catch rain water, 1 pump, 3 plastic funnels, 2 1½ gallon plastic buckets, 4 5 gallon plastic jerrycans, 3 2½ gallon plastic jerrycans, 2 1-gallon plastic jerrycans, 20 10 litre plastic water bags, 3 6″ synthetic sponges, 2 pressure cookers (adapted for water distilling), 1 14 piece campers' kit, 2 can openers, measuring jug, whisk, strainer, 2 large vacuum flasks, 2 pint vacuum flasks, 2 plates, 2 bowls, 2 mugs, 4 spoons, 4 forks, and 5 teaspoons, 15 waterproof plastic storage jars.
  Lights 6 pocket lighters, spare flints and servicing kit, 3 2 battery torches, 3 3 battery diving torches, 1 butane lantern, 200 matches (sealed for emergencies), 4 dozen torch and radio batteries.
  For Pleasure 5 paper-backed novels, 2 bottles whisky, 1 bottle brandy, 4 bottles wine, 4 pipes, 61 ozs. tobacco, 55 cigars, 10 cartons cigarettes, plus pipe cleaners.
  Luck and Morale Little Johnny (John's Atlantic mascot), a stuffed musical rabbit, a St. Christopher medallion's chain, a pair of silver miniature oars, half a dozen photographs of friends and family and the Rosary an air hostess friend flew with safely for years.
  From Ensenada 2 canvas framed sea anchors, 6′, tube soldering paste, 2 wooden framed sea anchors, 18″, 4 5 qrt. buckets, 2 1 gallon and 4 5 gallon plastic jerrycans, 12 large plastic storage jars, 2 large mugs, 1 lb rosin core solder, 10 oz. caulking, sundry shackles, 1 gaff, 1 coil wire, 1 qrt. contact cement, corrugated rubber matting for sleeping platform (anti-slip), non-slip rubber for galley entrance, 200 ft 13 lb rope, barometer, 2 fleecy track suits, 1 Nikonos 11 camera, 2 Bell and Howell film cameras (one in waterproof housing), film for both.
  From Washington Island 2 flag poles, 2 cushions, pillow, 3

pillowcases, 3 eye shades, 6 pairs shoes, mirror, scoop net, 5 lbs. tobacco, 3 can openers, aluminium cooking bowl, knife, 6 torch bulbs, 3 torches, 2 bottles washing-up liquid, 2 cans anti-rust aerosole, 1 can machine oil, mouth-organ and lessons, and a marline, Pacific Islands Year Book and a few paper-backed novels.

Repairs 2 large drogues remade, 1 small drogue remade, 2 torches, New galley entrance cover made, zip on old one repaired, hydraulic speargun repaired, rubber speargun repaired, spear shafts straightened, generator, gimbals, condensor coils and rudder repaired, Sea Chef cooker cleaned and restored, anoraks and sleeping bags washed.

From Tarawa 4 toothbrushes, 2 tins talcum powder, 6 tubes lip ointment, 4 tins Tiger Balm, 2½ gallons petrol for generator, 12 volt heavy duty battery, diving torch, torch batteries, 2 transistor radios, new sleeping platform, 24 ozs. tobacco, 2 cartons cigarettes.

Repairs Reef and worm holes in Britannia 11, transceiver, and generator.

FOOD CARRIED ABOARD BRITANNIA 11

90 gallons of drinking water, 2 lb tea, 2 lb instant coffee, 5 lb drinking chocolate, 1 gallon apple juice, 4 lb powdered milk, 10 lb instant rice, 5 lb instant potato, 3 lb lentils, 4 lb flour, 3 lb polenta, 4 lb peanut butter, 4 lb jam, 6 lb honey, 3 lb sunflower seeds, 3 lb chocolate bars, 3 lb soya flour, 3 lb pine nuts, 3 lb muesli, 4 lb peanuts, 3 lb powdered yeast, black pepper, cayenne pepper, mixed herbs, dried lemon, 1 lb dried onion, oregon, tarragon, parsley, chives, garlic, thyme, sage, mustard, tomato ketchup, worcester sauce, soy sauce, tabasco sauce, lemon extract, 2 pints vegetable oil, 5 packets dried tomatoes, 20 tubes boiled fruit sweets. 30 lb California Raisins.

Mountain House Foods 60 beef stews, 60 beef and onion with rice, 60 pork au gratin with potato, 84 chili with beans, 20 lbs beef patties, 20 lb diced cooked beef, 6 lbs beef steak, 8 lbs pork chops, 8 lb peas, 8 lb corn, 8 lb diced beet, 336 eggs.

Vacu-Dry Foods 3 lb apple sauce, 3 lb fruit galaxy, 1 lb apricots, 2 lbs oranges, 2 lb green beans, 8 lb cheese sauce, 2 lb beef bouillon, 2 lb onion soup, 4 lb tomato and vegetable soup, 3 lb green pea soup.

Rich-Moore Foods 150 pork chops with barbecue sauce, 150 beef patties with barbecue sauce, 5 packets ham and beans, 6 packets oatmeal, 50 chocolate bars, 10 lb biscuit mix, 2 chicken dinners. 30 packets orange drink and 20 packets tomato drink powder.

Wilson's Certified Foods 200 pork patties, 200 beef patties, 48 cans of meat balls.

Fresh Food Taken 2 large buckets of Colonel Sanders Kentucky Fried Chicken.

From Ensenada 90 gallons of drinking water, 4 lb oranges, 4 lb apples, 2 lb tomatoes, 4 lb onions, 2 lb green peppers, 2 sticks celery, 2 cucumbers, 4 large cabbages, jar sandwich spread, 6 lbs jam, 3 lbs honey, mayonnaise, 6 cheeses, 12 tins sardines, 3 whole salamis, dozen raw eggs, dozen hardboiled eggs, dozen preserved eggs, 200 tortillas, 3 lb tortilla mix, 6 large loaves, 2 cooked chickens, 6 lb cracker biscuits, 2 lb margarine, 2 gallons cooking oil, gallon vinegar, 8 ozs curry powder, 8 ozs. chili powder, 2 gallons fruit juices, 20 lb instant rice, 19 lb instant potato, 6 tins corned beef, 6 tins luncheon meat, 3 tins ham, 6 tins zucchini, 2 tins roast beef, 6 tins bean salad, 6 tins peaches, 4 tins blackcurrants, 12 small tins pineapple, bottle of brandy.

From Washington Island 90 gallons of drinking water, 3 breadfruit, 15 lb onions, 15 lb bananas, 6 paw paw, 20 coconuts, 7 lb cooked pork, 40 lb cabin biscuits, 1 lb instant coffee, 3 lb tea, 10 lb sugar, 5 lb jam, 5 lb honey, 6 jars cheese spread, 6 jars lemon spread, 1 jar paw paw chutney, 6 lb tinned cheese, 6 lb tinned margarine, 2 jars peanut butter, 4 lb toffees, 6 lb homemade pandanus and coconut based sweets, 12 pints orange juice, 12 pints apple juice, 2 bottles fruit cordial, 3 packets dried spaghetti bolognaise, 12 cans pineapple, 6 cans blackcurrants, 12 cans baked beans, 12 cans spaghetti, 12 cans macaroni cheese, 12 cans potato salad, 12 cans tomatoes, 2 bottles tomato ketchup, 2 bottles Worcester sauce, 2 tins cherries, 2 bottles whisky, 1 bottle cognac, 6 bottles beer, 3 lb dried onion.

From Tarawa 90 gallons of drinking water, 2 gallon fruit juices, 2 bottles whisky, 2 bottles wine, ½ gallon cooking oil, ½ gallon vinegar, 2 dozen plastic lemons, 3 jars gherkins, bottle mushroom ketchup, bottle anchovie essence, jar horseradish sauce, 3 jars tartar sauce, jar mixed herbs, 2 packets Bisto, 2 bottles cordial, 2 lb tea, 4 lb sugar, 3 lb sweet biscuits, 3 lb dry biscuits, 6 lbs jam, 6 lbs honey, 2 tins butter, 4 jars fish or meat paste, 8 tins sardines, 11 tins tomato paste, 3 tins sweet and sour sauce, 20 chocolate bars, 3 jars of sweets, plus the following tins: 3 pork sausages, 6 beefburgers, 5 corned beef, 5 corned mutton, 2 braised steak, 6 cooked cold meats, 3 herrings in tomato sauce, 2 vegetable and chicken dinner, 2 mushroom beef casserole, 2 spaghetti, sausage and meatball dinner, 3 asparagus, 3 carrots, 6 mixed vegetable, 3 blackcurrants. The following fresh food: 1 marrow, 1 pumpkin, 4½ lb carrots, 1 lb passion fruit, 6 lb apples, 1 lb radishes, 10 lb onions, 4 breadfruit, 20 oranges, 4 large cabbages, 2 packets of bacon and 2 dozen fresh eggs.

Thanks to restocking along our way, we arrived in Australia with enough food and water for another six weeks on board — and that without eating any more fish than we wanted.